SUNLIGHT NORTH

The *Wisdom of the Arctic Wilderness*

Forty-five Seasons in the Arctic National Wildlife Refuge

Second Edition

Clarence A. Crawford

ISBN 978-1-59433-888-5
ebook ISBN 978-1-59433-889-2
Library of Congress Catalog Card Number 2019910739

©2019 Clarence A. Crawford

visit sunlightnorth.com for more essays

Printed In China.

Dedication

America loves its heroes, and likes to see them in uniform. However, another group of patriots does work that is equally, or more, essential; they love America, the real America, its land, water, air, life, and people, in detail rather than in the abstract; they are rarely visible; they often work without government support, though many work for the government; many are volunteers; they help protect us from those people who, though American, want to harm the substance of America; they do work that is among the most essential to our national survival. They build as well as protect, but their monuments are frequently unobtrusive, in the form of trails, or a quiet park, or a restored mine site, or a species returned to its natural habitat. This book is dedicated to the many heroes, named and unnamed, known and unknown, who have worked to protect the natural world upon which we sustain ourselves, and by protecting that world have protected and improved our civilization.

CONTENTS

Introduction: The Call to Explore	*1*

EXCURSIONS

1. Across the Refuge	11
2. An Arctic Quest	33
3. An Arctic Day	55
4. The Quality of the Light	65
5. Fear of Bears	75
6. At Home as a Nomad	99
7. The Refuge in Winter	111
8. The Most Miserable Trip	135
9. The Old People	143
10. Time Past	165

UNAVOIDABLE CONSIDERATIONS

11. The Curse of Materialism	175
12. How the Curse of Materialism Killed the Old Alaska	201
13. Toward an Ethical Advance in Conservation	219
14. Value is Inherent in Nature	239

FOUNDATIONS

15. Reading	265
16. Homo quaestus: The Search for Identity	279
17. Three Foundational Myths	293

AND TWO MORE

18. Spring Canoe Trip	313
19. The Arctic in Autumn	325

INTRODUCTION

The Call to Explore

If one is lucky, or perhaps a bit of an adventurer, one eventually faces some situation in life that is transformative in the most fundamental way. Ever after, that event is a reference point; it defines your life, it tells you who you are. It may be love; travel; formal education; war; perhaps several of these; but in any case, the effect on one's personality is permanent.

For me, the most profound formative experiences of my life have occurred in the Arctic and sub-Arctic regions of Alaska.

The word "profound" seems presumptuous. Let it take a subjective meaning: that the experiences of worth that I have undergone in the wilderness have affected me deeply and penetrated my entire life, and that they may be common to all people. I think I have discovered a few things about innocence and corruption, death, pain, endurance, and patience that may be of value.

As THOREAU well knew, one must leave the common track.

Walking a groomed trail from Point A to Point B, for an afternoon or for a week, can be interesting and rewarding—I do it often, and like it—but it is essentially an artificial experience.

Buy the correct gear; work hard to make the miles; connect as best as one can, however transiently, with the passing environment. Near the end of the trip, one thinks about washing clothes, taking a shower, eating in a restaurant. One sees the car in the lot; as soon as one enters the car, the entire world is altered. One feels stale now, in a way that has not happened during the excursion regardless of how tired or sweaty one was. We re-enter the ordinary. Roads and roadsides feel fast, aggressive, degraded. Go home, play some music, drink a few beers, re-enter the mundane: we've left the sacred for the profane. We people who love the outdoors know this routine intimately, as we chase what we cannot keep, intruders in a place where we cannot stay.

Time, as they say, is of the essence. It is the essence of the human tragedy, and is a consequence of our consciousness, which consciousness is also, paradoxically, what makes us human. An animal in the wild is encapsulated within its environment, knows nothing else, does not seek a change at the end of the trail. It does not pass through time on the way to something else. A moose has all day, every day.

When I was a boy working on a poor farm, I envied my father's hunting dogs. Except when they were being trained or on a hunt, they were inactive. They slept a lot. While I worked and sweated, they sat in the shade with their eyes closed: pure potential. They didn't experience the anxiety of knowing that a whole hour remained until quitting time or that four days remained until the weekend or that you still had to wait two days until the orgy of Christmas or that a month remained until school let out. Ignorance is bliss. Animals don't have bad nerves, unless mishandled by humans.

The timelessness of the Garden of Eden is powerfully attractive, and the idea of a Garden of Innocence is a powerful metaphor. Such ideas lie close to our childhoods, just as they lay at the infancy of Western civilization. But, to obtain maturity,

INTRODUCTION - THE CALL TO EXPLORE

both the person and the culture must abandon them. And though I knew that I could not re-enter Eden via the wilderness—I could not find salvation there—I was nevertheless convinced that the wilderness offered something intensely valuable, life-changing, that ordinary experience lacked. I wanted a transformative experience. To continue with the theological parallel, it is probably fair to say that I wanted redemption, or rebirth. Even in my eighth decade, I find a trace of that impulse in my motives. I suspect that something like this is what motivates people who love the outdoors…except for those who profane the outdoors by using it as a big amusement park or gym.

MY WILDERNESS education was physical, intellectual, and emotional.

I remember Richard Henry Dana discussing hardship aboard the old sailing vessels in *Two Years before the Mast*. (Like Francis Parkman and, later, Theodore Roosevelt, he needed to toughen himself in wild places to correct physical ailments.) He describes the poor food in spare amounts, the inadequate clothing, the lack of medical care. But especially the poor food. And he concluded that the sailors were strong and healthy.

I can understand that. Physical rigor has a salutary effect on the whole person, intellectually and emotionally as well as physically. There are good reasons to decry softness, not the least of which is that a soft life does not allow for full development. One does not know one's capabilities—does not know who one really is—until one has placed stress upon one's self. Many of us have not experienced the joy of knowing, even getting a glimpse of, our full potential.

On my first big trek, all of our party were underfed. As I walked along with my empty stomach I tried to imagine how much energy

I expended each day. How many times did I hoist my pack? How many times step forward or up, or brace myself against gravity? Wobble across tussocks? Fight a river's force? When I thought of these cumulative demands, I couldn't fully understand where this immense internal energy came from. I had trouble understanding how small quantities of food could produce such large results.

I eventually came to visualize myself as a bundle of energy. Energy was my essential quality. I wasn't rational, I wasn't existential, I wasn't spiritual. I was molecular. What marvelous forces could transform a few handfuls of food into enough power to propel 240 pounds of matter, flesh and pack, across ten miles of tundra, tussocks, and mountains each day? After maintaining mental activity and body heat?

But there was more. The energy that provided my propulsion also provided me with the stimulus to feel curiosity, a love of beauty, an appreciation for the details of my environment, a desire to write in my journal each day, and a thirst to read before I slept. Human power and fortitude are impressive. Alexander Solzhenitsyn, for example, did more than just endure and survive the life of the camps; he maintained the ability to be human.

I began to appreciate the narrow margin of life that aboriginals in the North must have inhabited. They needed to extract those necessary calories from their environment, and those calories are often very hard to find. Metabolism is everything. Maybe Dana's sailors were tough because their bodies were trained to extract the last least bit of energy from their sparse rations. The old Gwich'in of Alaska's northeast Arctic must have been similarly trained. They didn't have waterproof boots and synthetic rain gear; no wood stoves to stoke at −70 F; no firearms; they couldn't "start" with food, as we did, and resupply at the "end," since their trip was life-long; indeed, spanned generations; there was no beginning or end, just life.

INTRODUCTION ~ THE CALL TO EXPLORE

THE RAIN FALLS, the wind blows. Wet clothing leaches away heat, cold water lies against the skin of your feet. Yet the internal furnace roars. Begin to walk. Carry, say, a seventy-five pound pack for four miles across tundra, then carry it 1000' up across a pass, then come down off the pass by hopping across slippery rocks, then teeter across two miles of tussocks before making camp. Every time you've stopped during the day the cold rain and wind quickly cools you. Your hands are always stiff. When you stop for the day what you really want to do is just sit and stare into space, but you erect the tent instead. You wonder if the little willows round about will yield enough wood for a cook fire so that you can conserve the fuel you are carrying. You spend a half-hour collecting wood and your stomach complains constantly. After fifteen minutes of effort you finally get the damp wood to burn. Your water boils after another ten minutes and you drop in your jerky, or grayling, or ptarmigan. Cook fifteen minutes or so. After you eat, drink all the broth.

It takes about twenty minutes for your feeling of well-being to return. You're suddenly warm from the food. Look at the sky: the weather may be breaking. Maybe not. Beware unjustified optimism. Study the map, evaluate tomorrow's walk. The sweep of the view up the valley catches your eye; the light has changed; some golden light filters through purple clouds. Maybe you have the energy after all to walk along the stream or to the top of the hill behind camp before turning in.

A CRUCIAL component of a trip is its duration.

Most of us, most of the time, can get into the outdoors for weekends, extended weekends, or a bit more. Our ruthless economy limits most people to a few weeks at most. Most of us are just tourists in the wilderness.

Perhaps we remain tourists even if we spend the month, the summer, the year. The weekend hiker goes from Point A to Point B; isn't the longer duration also point-to-point, with a beginning and an end, ultimately defined by the larger culture that nurtures us?

Perhaps. Nevertheless, duration is important, for subjective, psychological reasons. The longer duration of a trip alters it qualitatively, not just quantitatively. Twenty-eight days in the wilderness is not just four times as long as seven days. It is an entirely different trip at every level, physically, intellectually, emotionally. I have heard many travelers refer to the Biblical forty days and forty nights as talismanic: a length of time sufficient to generate insight, even wisdom. They may be right.

I think that it takes ten days, with the prospect of more to come, to begin to alter one's view of time. Of course, ten days isn't long, but have you noticed that time slows when you deprive yourself of most of your companionships and your daily habits? This slowing of time may for some people result in a feeling of tediousness; a certain kind of person will claim to be "bored." But another transition will occur.

For most of us, if we go out for three, five, or seven days, we're always conscious that we shall soon return, and the end of our trip is the conscious or unconscious goal. But after ten days of a month-long trip we begin to realize that it is senseless to look too far into the future, that the point is to deal with what is immediately before us, that we are alive *now*, that Point B is not a goal towards which we must work but simply the place where we will end our trip. Point B becomes nothing in itself, the immediate moment becomes everything. Time does not present itself as fleeting, to be hung on to desperately, nor as something we are required to kill, as if it were a nuisance. As a surgeon friend of mine said, in reference to the pressures of time: time is your friend. True, true. How absurd that we continually seek ways to kill it.

INTRODUCTION ~ THE CALL TO EXPLORE

WHAT I WANT out of my time in the wilderness is what I want out of all aspects of life: complete immersion. I want what is real. I want authenticity. I want what Thoreau wanted: to find out what life really is, and not to discover, when it comes time for me to die, that I have not lived. This is the core of my wilderness education. All else is based on that.

EXCURSIONS

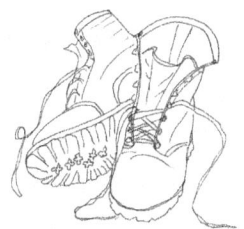

SUNLIGHT NORTH

Diane, on the East Fork Chandalar River

Amy near Spring Creek

Devon and Jeremy, near the Wind River-Junjik River divide.

CHAPTER 1

Across the Refuge

When my wife Diane and I arrived in Alaska in July 1970, from the East, we immediately developed a passion for our new home. I have observed over the years that migrants like us seem to develop unusually deep connections to our adoptive homes. The homebodies who stay deeply rooted to a locale for generations are following a conservative impulse to maintain roots; we migrants are equally conservative. Though we have severed ourselves from our original roots, we have a deep need for new roots. You might say that we make up in passion what we lack in history. In Alaska our local pride is intense, especially as we claim twenty percent of the United States as "ours."

When Alaskans introduce themselves, as in letters to the editor, or at public functions, we tend to use the formula, "My name is so-and-so, and I am an X-year resident of Alaska." A two-year residency indicates a prideful beginning, a resident of five years would like to think of himself as an old-timer, a twenty-year resident is an ancient sage. There is an implicit assumption that the values of one's opinions are calibrated in ratio to the length of one's residency.

However, we soon came to realize that, proud as we were of our new home, we must recognize that there was a group of ancient inhabitants who held true pride-of-place: the several native groups who had been here, not for tens of years, but for tens of thousands of years. I admired the old explorers and sourdoughs who were part of Alaska's tradition, but I came to recognize that the "real" Alaskans (the question of who is a "real Alaskan" is an ongoing metaphysical debate here) were the aboriginals. They were the real Alaskans, and I would never be one.

But I had something in common with them: I wanted to connect to the wilderness, and conversely, I wanted somehow—impossibly—to disconnect from the industrial juggernaut. Native Alaskans, of course, sprang from the wilderness, but were also ensnared in the modern industrial world. They were and are being sucked into the vortex of the more aggressive culture; what they perceptively call The Dominant Culture. I wanted to find my way out of it. I desperately wanted the wilderness: the real thing.

IN THE SUMMER of 1974 I planned an ambitious walking trip in the Alaskan Arctic with a friend and two of his friends: Sam, Dick, Paul. By then I had built up some wilderness experience, but had not put myself to a severe test. I found that I had much to learn.

Our plan was to walk through a portion of what is now the Arctic National Wildlife Refuge, from the village of Kaktovik, on Barter Island in the Beaufort Sea, to Arctic Village, on the south slope of the Brooks Range. Our starting and ending points were determined solely by the fact that there was (sporadic) commercial air service to those points. Otherwise, we knew nothing about the country. Our topographic maps were 1:250,000, a scale which leaves much unrevealed. More detailed maps of that area did not exist at that time, at least not for sale to the public through the United States Geological Survey.

Our route was to cross the Arctic coastal plain, cross the Brooks Range itself, and then traverse part of the more rolling and partly forested ground on the south side. Rather than follow the most direct north-south route, we swung east to catch the higher mountains and passes, which enabled us to see more country and more drainages. It was a difficult route.

We traveled from Anchorage to Fairbanks the old way, via the Alaska Railroad, and flew from old Metro Field in Fairbanks on July 5, on the now-defunct Wien Airlines. I was nervous. We saw, as we flew north of the Arctic Circle, that a summer snowstorm had moved over the entire region north of the Yukon River, and the Brooks Range was a forbidding white and gray, as we could see through occasional gaps in the clouds. The terrain beneath was an ominous mystery. I thought, "We will be walking over all this, foot by slow foot. What am I getting myself into? Are we ready for snow in July?"

It was 33 F and snowing when we landed at Barter Island: gray, wind-swept, bleak under low skies. Snow blew along the gray gravel runway, through the village of Kaktovik, across the flat tundra. The DEW line site, still active at that time, rose a monolith to the west. A small drab building served as a transfer point for air travelers. Sea ice was just visible to the north through the murky light. Our educations were beginning.

On the airstrip, we heard the name "Tommy Gordon" as someone who might be willing to boat us across to the mainland. We walked to his house on the far side of the village and had a talk with him. We learned from him that we didn't need a boat—the ice was still in, the summer was unusually late—but nevertheless we pushed him to show us the way, since travel on sea ice was alien to us. We learned something of his history: that he was originally from Demarcation Point, to the east, near the Canadian border; that he had lived for a while in Canada; that he came to Kaktovik, on Barter Island, in 1953.

Since then I have learned that Kaktovik was not a traditional settlement, but that it formed when coastal Inupiat gravitated to the new DEW Line site (Distant Early Warning, to alert against incoming Soviet missiles) under construction in the 1950s as part of the Cold War nuclear buildup. The pre-contact Inupiat lived scattered along the coast in family groups and were nomadic or semi-nomadic, which makes sense when you consider the difficulty of finding food in the Arctic, and the mobility of the animals, and the seasonal nature of their movements, both whales and caribou. Yet hunting whales and caribou is accomplished most successfully by groups of cooperating individuals, and so they coalesced at times into larger, semi-permanent villages. The establishment of fixed villages is a confirmation of Yupik, Inupiat, and Athabaskan entry into the modern world; for them, the large fixed village is not a natural ancestral aboriginal grouping. (The Aleuts [Unangan] had fixed villages, as did the native groups of Southeast Alaska; only the latter can be described as "large.")

On the USGS map of the eastern coastal plain, a dot on the coast just east of Demarcation Bay is marked "Gordon." On a walk through that area years later I found some old, collapsed sod structures, undoubtedly Inupiat. "Gordon" is named for Tom Gordon, a Scot who came via Canada to the Alaskan Arctic to trade. (The US-Canadian border was a theoretical construct ignored by traders and Inupiat alike.) Had I known this in 1974, I would have quizzed Tommy Gordon, a near descendant of Tom, much more extensively about his past, about life before DEW Line sites and scheduled air traffic. Even as recently as 1974, there was no easy electronic communication in bush Alaska; only expensive, high-powered radios provided communications for commercial and military use. Tommy's story of his youth, though post-contact and not fully aboriginal, would have been a fruitful insight into the old days and the old ways.

That afternoon we crossed the island, then walked across the sea ice (a very short distance) to the mainland. A true Inupiat, Tommy had his gun with him, and he managed to shoot a few ducks while showing us the crossing. July, and the ice was still in, and thick. Willow buds had not yet opened. It was the coldest summer in recent memory, so locals told us.

We followed a north-flowing creek south across the coastal plain a few miles and camped. Cold wind, fog; flat, no clearly defined horizon; no trees; low sky: an utterly alien landscape. Swans and waterfowl beat their way through the narrow band between tundra and low sky. Shorebirds went about their business.

WE CAMPED BESIDE a little tundra creek, a large lake to the south. On its shore we stood and heard absolute silence but for the tinkle of disintegrating ice. An apparently limitless, uncertain horizon expanded beyond us for a full 360 degrees under the low sky. The snow fell into black water.

The foregoing paragraphs are full of negatives. Someone new to the coastal plain falls into this mental pattern: I see what the coastal plain is *not* because I am accustomed to *that*. One must spend time there in order to see what it is rather than what it is not.

More snow fell through the night; I listened to its rustle on the tent fabric; there was a two-inch accumulation on the tents in the morning.

The next day was colder, and the sky began to clear as we hiked. We followed our creek up to its source and camped. During our hike I tried to accustom myself to this new environment. The ground was usually wet under foot, though the creek banks were firm. We could not avoid long stretches of bog. At these points, we simply plunged in and forged ahead, though I found that I could remain much drier if I followed the ridges of the polygons lifted from the surface of the tundra. The Brooks Range, nearly fifty miles to the south, slowly became visible through fog and tattered clouds as the storm broke up and lifted. The spectacle was glorious, mysterious, seductive, frightening. What was behind that mountain wall?

Summer snowstorm

The next day we crossed a long wet flat to the Jago River. We found good footing there, and headed upstream, towards the mountains. The walk along the lower and middle Jago was what I have since come to think of as the coastal plain tundra at its most attractive: broad river valleys; sere, low rolling hills with long, low, barely discernible ridges; the mountains mysterious to the south; to the north, blue sky over the Arctic Ocean.

The great challenge for me was to assimilate an environment that was completely alien to any of my former experiences. The coastal plain was a new world: monotonous, vast, windswept, deceptive. Distances were extremely difficult to judge, as were sizes of objects. A large hill apparently five miles away was in fact a two-foot-high tussock 300 yards away. A radio tower on the horizon was in fact a bare willow stem five feet tall.

Adding to the spookiness of the place was the offshore environment. To the north the ice pack was a shimmering white mirage, apparently a cliff, which it was not. Fog was present almost always somewhere on the northern horizon. It frequently pushed south across the plain, cold and oppressive.

AND THE WIND was constant. It was difficult to find a camp in a lee, and usually the tents were in the wind, but we always tried very hard to find a sheltered spot for a kitchen. The only shelter was behind willows, or in a depression, usually along a stream. The wind stripped your body heat from you, burned your face, tugged at your clothes, made the tents flap all night. (But during the insect season, it preserves your sanity by keeping the insects away. When the mosquitoes are out, you curse a calm day.)

Looking north to the coastal plain

I have since returned to the coastal plain many times, and it remains a weird mystery for me. It stands in stark contrast to the rest of the Arctic National Wildlife Refuge.

The south slope is forested in the lowlands, and has a climate closer to that of the Interior (which has a Continental climate). The Brooks Range itself has its own climate and grandeur, in the summer more benign, calmer and less foggy than the coastal plain. The coastal plain completes the Refuge; without the coastal plain the Refuge would not be whole, neither a complete ecological unit nor a complete human experience. It represents one end of the spectrum of Alaska's Arctic.

Another marvel of the Arctic coast: how did the Inupiat survive here—even perhaps flourish—for thousands of years? I have seen the coastal plain during its most benign seasons, aided by the technology of modern synthetics. I am especially appreciative of my good tents, rain gear, sleeping bags, and boots. The old people had only their wits, their knack for cooperation, their heritage, and their courage, to get them through conditions immeasurably more difficult than I have experienced there. To this day I marvel at how they could extract a livelihood, and develop a culture, in this most difficult of environments. Jean Craighead George has one of her fictional characters say that the three qualities prized by the Inupiat are intelligence, courage, love. I believe it.

Over the years I have located several old houses, sod dugouts, along the coast, and the remnants of tent rings at the edge of the mountains, and a few wooden artifacts, such as sled runners. And a human skull. I have, when examining these things, tried to imagine the Old People, what they looked like, how they interacted with each other, how they spent their days. How could a hunter, or more likely several hunters, find a way to capture a large mammal, either at sea or on land? Including whales! What audacity, intelligence, and courage would be required! How build a shelter, and keep it warm? How prepare food, give birth, raise children? Their ingenuity and intelligence must have been prodigious. How endure months of darkness, weeks of gale? Their emotional toughness and balance must have been equal to their considerable intelligence. Of course, archeologists, anthropologists, and the Inupiat themselves have told us how it was done. We can read about it in the books. But there is a world of difference between the saying and the doing.

I have pondered the skull many times—I revisit her when I can—and wondered how it came there. (The skull has no brow ridge, which, I am told, indicates sex. But for some reason I thought of the skull as "her" before I learned this.) Age? Manner of death? Date of death? And, most interesting to me, why at this spot? Was she here with a group to find caribou in the spring? Did she have some reason to leave the coast, such as illness brought by New England whalers? I let my fanciful side emerge; I always, after cleaning the moss out of her eye sockets and cranial cavity, place "her" where she can see the caribou come from the east. I consider her my friend. I have revisited her and cleaned her many summers for going on forty years.

On the southern edge of the coastal plain, looking north.

The coastal houses stimulate my imagination. Perched right on the edge of the lagoon that lies within the barrier islands, they are like no beach houses anywhere. Indeed, there is no beach as we commonly think of one, no strand of sand, no rocky shore, no tidal estuary. Tundra meets water, with perhaps a narrow band of mud between, on this coast of small tides. The "yard" is damp meadow and marsh. The dwelling, of turf and driftwood, is exposed to the weather from all sides. Fog continually works its way back and forth, inshore and offshore, across the cold water and onto the tundra. The wind blows, and blows.

Was this a winter or summer camp? Did Inupiat whalers hunt from here? How did they bring in their driftwood (and where did that come from? The McKenzie River? Siberia? I have found birch bark on the beach, and spruce and cottonwood). Where did the children play? How did the children play? Judging by the Inupiat temperament that I have observed, they must have been happy.

Coastal plain fog

The poor quality of our clothing and equipment on this first trip illustrates the paucity of excellent outdoor paraphernalia available at the time; but even more, is a testament to our ignorance and lack of foresight (and perhaps our relative poverty). I wore rubber-bottomed, leather-topped boots (with vibram soles, very sophisticated); thick cotton socks; cotton corduroy jeans (probably the last of my bell-bottoms); woolen long-john bottoms; on hot days, a tee shirt (an old pajama top); a cotton work shirt; a woolen underwear top, a heavy Woolrich woolen shirt; down vest; water resistant wind breaker; woolen cap. I can't remember having gloves, or even rain pants. Our tents were pretty good, with coated nylon flies. An Optimus 8R stove with a pint of fuel for stormy days (but we always managed to kindle a wood fire for cooking, saving the stove and fuel for emergencies, which never happened). When I compare my clothing then and now, I think the single greatest advance in summer Arctic travel, where one must travel not only over rocky mountainous terrain but also over extensive bog, is the stout leather boot with Gore-Tex liner.

OUR LIVES WERE dominated by two over-riding considerations: distance and nutrition.

We wanted to complete our trip in exactly four weeks, which we did. That meant that we had to make a minimum distance each day, or the trip would unravel on us, because we needed to consume an amount of energy each day that was equivalent to the effort required to make our miles, and that energy was carried on our backs or in our flesh. We were undernourished; I eventually lost more than fifteen pounds in that month.

The problem of distance was aggravated by the difficulty of the terrain (tussocks, river crossings), the additional energy required to climb, especially over high passes, and the additional energy required to function in the cold.

The solution to the problem of nutrition was simple to understand and hard to execute: ration what we had, and supplement it when we could by hunting (for willow ptarmigan) and fishing (for grayling). We ate perhaps half a dozen of each. The problem here, of course, is that hunting and fishing take time—and we needed to use our time to deal with distance.

In response to the stresses of distance and energy within the context of time, we settled into a routine early in the trip and stayed with it.

To force us to deal with distance, we took but one day of voluntary rest. We also took one day of involuntary rest, while waiting for high water at a creek crossing to subside. We also enforced a rule about starting: up at 5:00 AM regardless of the weather or how we felt, and on the trail quickly; and make camp only after making our miles, regardless of how trail-weary we were.

Of course we became obsessive map-readers and calculators of distance, and we thought much about the weight of our packs, and about foot care. Sam, especially, suffered from foot pain. I had no idea how he was suffering until we were perhaps half way through our trip, and I saw him doctoring his feet with our meager supply of moleskin and tape. Where most people develop blisters, he actually had *holes* in his raw flesh. There was no way that he could avoid incessant, severe pain (the military had rejected him because of his feet). He soldiered on without complain for hundreds of miles, enduring unspeakable pain, without any hope of relief.

Mealtime, especially dinner, was a sacred ritual. We ate no freeze-dried foods. We did have: sugar, tea, hot chocolate, energy bars, peanuts, protein powder, salami, oats and grains, beef jerky, dried fruit. Nuts and jerky were our real sustenance; tea was our treat and comfort. We cooked on wood fires, and a major part of making camp was gathering sufficient dead willow from the meager supplies on hand. Then boil water; tea; boil more water for the jerky; eat our solid food; and drink the broth. Cleanup was easy: rinse the pot. There were no food scraps.

Since that trip I have learned how to plan a menu for a month that provides a balanced diet and sufficient energy, yet does not weigh too much. This first trip was a rigorous apprenticeship. I learned that there is a close relationship between time, distance, pack weight, nutrition, and energy. These factors all intersect, and when one or more are deficient or excessive the outcome of a long trip may become questionable.

Conversation in the evening was limited and predictable: check the maps to gauge the day's progress, our location, and to be sure that we're on schedule; talk about our plans when we get to Arctic Village (we think, but we don't know, that there are scheduled flights in and out of Arctic Village, which has become our mysterious and seductive goal; my wife Diane puts out an alert if we are overdue). We evaluate our food rations; plan tomorrow's meals; and then talk about food. Usually someone (not me, no fan of recreational eating) remembers a favorite restaurant and the specialty of the house. It was remarkable how the narrator could remember the details of a menu, the smell and flavor of a certain dish, even the roads leading to the restaurant, certainly an irrelevant addition, but it allowed him to extend his fantasy. Then our minds would return to the reality of our situation, the rain on the tent, our utter isolation: the excitement, with an edge of fear, of the wilderness.

THE FIRST MAJOR transition of our trip was when we crossed the coastal plain and then the foothills and entered the mountains. Our experience changed drastically here. We learned that the greatest hazard in wilderness travel is crossing rivers, and we eventually had sixteen of those, all time consuming, all uncomfortable, some hazardous. We learned to expect Mother Nature to cross us up: the weather seemed always to become rainy or cold just when it was time to do a river crossing. Or a rare warm day, so comfortable for a change, increased glacier melt, which brought the largest river, the Jago, to flood. We spent several hours trying to cross the Jago under such conditions and had to give it up. The next morning we were up at 5:00 in freezing temperatures to try again. The river had dropped considerably because of the freeze. We chose as our crossing a place where the river split around a gravel island. Stripping to underwear, and wearing boots without socks, Sam and I tested the river without carrying packs and were able to get to the island. We then returned for our packs and our companions. On our next crossing to the island, however, we had trouble. Probably affected by the weight of his pack and his painful feet, Sam went down in the rushing current and was swept through the rapids. He alertly shed his pack and held it downstream of him, and made his way to shore. While he broke into his pack to check on items sensitive to water, the three of us helped each other across. Dick went down but was not swept away. The remaining large channel, and a smaller channel beyond that, came easier, although Sam got wet again, and by the time we were across he was shaking and needed time to recover. Fortunately, the sun had cleared the mountains by now and we could bask in it and recover at out leisure, a fine and comfortable indulgence. So went our most difficult crossing, but others were ahead of us. Each crossing caused mental and physical stress, and consumed time.

We learned that our month of travel time required longer travel days than we had anticipated. At the end of our first week we were already behind our schedule, and we began to monitor our food rations closely. Every impediment to our travel put that much more pressure on us. Not only did river crossings take time; so did navigation and route finding. (After a few years of such travel, I concluded that ten miles of trail walking is equivalent to six miles of wilderness walking.) Anything unexpected, such as a cliff that didn't show on our maps, added hours to our walking day. We weren't getting enough rest, and we weren't eating enough food.

One major marker on the trip was when we passed the point of no return to Barter Island, past the point when going back would be more difficult and time consuming than going on. We had done a number of difficult river crossings, put some high passes behind us, crossed difficult stretches of brush and bog, and gotten deep into our energy reserves. We felt the weight of the daily grind. Our equipment deteriorated. An animal tore up Paul's pack during the night; Dick's boots were developing holes, as were mine; I wore out a pair of pants. (Luckily Paul had a spare pair of jeans.) The food supply was increasingly skimpy, especially when some of our meat spoiled from the dampness of rain or immersion. We felt the pressure of long miles and uncertainty. A little tingle of fear became part of our emotional lives. Fear was connected to distance. When you realize that there is no going back, that the umbilical cord has stretched, then broken, you reach the fearsome, exhilarating point when you know that you have put yourself in the position of being absolutely on your own. Going "back," going "on," going anywhere, are all the same. We had no radio; emergency locator beacons and global positioning systems did not exist. We entered a new and wonderful world of freedom.

WE WERE INCREDIBLY, astonishingly, alone. We saw two contrails a week, polar flights. Otherwise, not a single airplane seen or heard until we were near Arctic Village. Not a sign of modern human use. Just vast, overwhelmingly vast, country; unpredictable and extreme weather; and the pressures of time, miles, and nutrition.

My emotional life was intense. In the background I experienced a general vague anxiety caused no doubt by what I felt to be our perilous and uncertain position. I experienced fear, a more specific emotion, when confronted by some immediate problem, usually a river crossing. Stronger than either of these was a sense of awe that was almost continual, and mixed in with these emotions were excitement, a continual sense of beauty, and a heightened sense of self. I experienced the tedium of fighting pack weight and the nagging tug of the pack straps, especially the last few hours of the day. Finally, perhaps paradoxically, I felt free, in spite of my burden; the untrammeled world was before me, under my feet, encompassing me.

Sharp images of the landscape and its life dominate my memories.

One camp was in a high pass between the Jago and Aichilik rivers in view of two glaciers and ringed by mountains, and in contrast to the big rugged surroundings, I remember best the delicacy of the alpine tundra, red and green mosses in a rill, carpets of avens, butterflies landing on my legs. Or in the Sheenjek valley, after a stormy period and a difficult river crossing, getting up during the night and looking at a lake beside our camp. An eastern mountain is reflected in the calm lake, the western mountains are picking up sun on their northwest sides. To the north the dark clouds are filtering sunlight, which intensifies their lurid appearance; gold filters through the purples, blacks, and grays. (Dear reader, you may be wondering how the sunlight can be filtering from the northwest and north, and at night. Remember, this is July, and the sun will not drop below the horizon, though it does drop below the mountaintops, for some weeks.)

ONE OF THE great satisfactions of that trip was seeing the terrain change as we inched across it. This is intimately connected with a keen sense of one's self. I had the earth under my feet in the truest sense. I could feel the ground: bog, rock, alpine tundra, river gravel, snow. My body adjusted to the slope of the ground: up, down, tilt, flat. Visual sensations—they still make my heart ache—came to me constantly: the big view of crags or valleys, or the intimate view of clear water flowing over rocks and pebbles in a brook. I thought about the pack weight almost all the time. I realized that, though it was burdensome, it was actually the key to my freedom. I marveled—I still do—that I can carry all I need for survival, comfort, and pleasure on my back. Because we weren't eating enough, I became convinced that my body was increasingly efficient at extracting every bit of energy from each least fragment of food I ate. I came to understand myself as a bundle of energy moving slowly across the landscape. Thoughts of the existential burden of freedom and obligation crossed my mind. At times I was Sisyphus, at times Icarus, at times both together. I concluded that pain and joy are inseparable.

I discovered, aside from the pleasures of the pure wilderness, the value of two indispensable cultural gifts. One is tea. The satisfaction of a hot drink under any circumstance, but especially at times of stress, is inexpressible. An old Athabaskan, Sarah Frank, has said that tea is one of the few important things brought to them by the whites. She said that the several other important trade items in the early days were "[firearm] shells, matches, tea, rice, sugar, and flour." Later she adds oatmeal to the list, but adds that it was "mostly tea and sugar" that they wanted. When discussing hard times, she said, "They [the Gwich'in] really had a hard time making a living. There was no tea, so it was a pretty hard time." (From *Neerihiinjik*, English title *We Traveled From Place to Place*, an extremely valuable and interesting reminiscence of Sarah and

Johnny Frank, two survivors from the days before contact. Edited by Craig Mishler.) I too would have a hard time without tea in the wilderness.

My other great pleasure is a good book. Without a book, there is a great void in my life, one I don't know how to fill. (Is this why the Old People told stories? Johnny Frank said that his grandmother, whom his father hauled in a hide blanket in the winter and on his back in the summer, told stories all day long, every day, whether or not someone was around to listen to her.) Peter Mathiessen's *Wildlife in America* enriched my life enormously, though I only had the energy to read for twenty or thirty minutes each evening. The joy of getting in the sleeping bag, warm and dry, letting the body relax, and then entering another world of narrative and ideas, is a great pleasure and a great comfort. Our time to arise was fixed and came early, and when it was time to get out in the morning, one's self-discipline was challenged. But I was sorely tempted to read when I should have been asleep. The joy of the book may have been the most precious part of the day.

The over-riding great satisfaction of our trek was simply that we did it. I can remember thinking, often, "Have I really done this thing to myself? Thrown myself into the wilderness almost willy-nilly, cut myself off from the human race?" At times I felt abandoned in the chaos of nature, overwhelmed by the immensity of my surroundings, humbled by my insignificance in relation to the wilderness. When we finally saw the metal roofs of Arctic Village, I felt that I had done something real.

TWO DAYS BEFORE reaching Arctic Village, we could make out its metal roofs from our camp. By this time we had conditioned ourselves to expect the worst: if Mom Nature could throw up some final obstacle to our progress, she probably would. But in our hearts we knew that our adventure was nearly over. As so often near the end of a long trek, I felt torn. I looked forward to trivial pleasures: doing laundry, showering, eating; and to the most substantial joy: reuniting with my family. But I was strongly pulled the other way as well. I learned then, and I have realized many times since, that I am at my best when on the trail, living the simple and Spartan life, bringing discipline and sensual pleasure to my body and to my emotions, experiencing the joy of discovery, and feeding my intellect through good reading and thought. When all is said and done, I need little else. Later, when my wife and children joined me on my travels, my life was complete.

All I really need to live a good life is love, beauty, intellectual engagement, and physical activity, preferably in the wilderness. The rest—schedules, routines, shopping lists, phone messages, the mire of electronic entanglements, on and on, all the junk that fills our days—is distraction, trivia, anti-life. But I can't escape that stuff until I get out, beyond it, where I can really focus and live. I can't connect until I disconnect. I have re-learned dozens of times: the things that occupy the forefront of my mind when I am entangled in civilized pursuits—materialistic thoughts like re-financing my house, say, or wondering if I should buy a new car, or habits like checking my e-mail—instantly evaporate to nothing when I step into the wilderness.

THIS TRIP CHANGED my life. It was the most revelatory experience I ever had, before or since. Of course I have reflected on it often over the decades, and I have concluded that, though not an essential of life, such an initiation is exceedingly valuable. One should test one's self. Such a test establishes a benchmark; other life experiences can be placed beside it as a reference; our daily lives can be put in better perspective; it is good to be reminded that trivial things are indeed trivial and should be banished from the foreground of our thought. An initiation also establishes our uniqueness, our sense of worth. No one may be aware of what I did, no one may care, I am not famous, or admired for it. But it is my experience, uniquely, and it helps me to know who I am. I can use it to define myself.

MY FEAR HAD walked with me, but my experience of the immensity of the world, and my tiny place in it, placed my fear in perspective. Paradoxically, I found my insignificance in nature to be immensely gratifying. My insignificance was a useful piece of knowledge. My sense of my own obscurity forced me to focus outward to the grandeur of the earth, even, to the small extent of which I was capable, the universe, and it was my knowledge of this grandeur which was fulfilling, and not my knowledge of my petty accomplishment. Yet, though I was humbled, I found satisfaction in being equal to the task. I had conquered nothing, overcome nothing, subdued nothing but myself.

The Arctic National Wildlife Refuge became the repository of my dreams. As a youngster I had dreamed of a mythical North; as an adult I dreamed of a real northern place, one I had begun to learn about in reality. The Refuge became my spiritual home.

I am privileged to have had the opportunity to discover the great world and to discover myself. I am angered that this opportunity may be stolen from the children of the future. What is sacred in America? What does our culture truly hold dear? The Refuge should be preserved intact not because it serves me, but because it is intrinsically valuable. The issue of preservation is not one of "my" narrow self-interest versus "their" narrow self-interest. The real issue is if our nation is capable of recognizing values that are not strictly and narrowly materialistic. Are we petty, or are we great?

An Arctic desert

CHAPTER 2

An Arctic Quest

On one of my trips years ago to the Arctic National Wildlife Refuge, in northeastern Alaska, I happened to encounter a biologist who was studying the Porcupine caribou herd. We exchanged information and shared our experiences, most of which had to do with the mysterious and erratic behavior of the caribou. We also talked of birds, moose, wolves, and other wildlife. I told him of a kill I had nearly witnessed: I had observed a wolf trailing a caribou, the caribou gimping along, the wolf close behind, right on its heels. I left my observation post to alert my partner and when I returned the caribou was down and the wolf was feeding.

When the subject turned to wolves, I learned that there were several packs in the Refuge, and the biologist was kind enough to indicate their general territory during the denning season, without giving away the den locations, and I didn't pry. But a plan began to form in the back of my mind.

To locate and observe a wolf den would be a major challenge for me. I decided from the outset to undertake the task unaided by additional knowledge or technology. The biologists do their work from the air, or at the computer screen, tracking the wolves, caribou, and grizzly bears from helicopters and airplanes, or satellites, usually by following a radio-collared animal. I decided not to seek this information from the experts but to proceed in self-imposed ignorance. I would have my feet on the ground, and I would be alone. My knowledge of the country would have to come slowly, one stride at a time, and from the limited perspective of one small man in an enormous country.

Two years later I was ready to try.

I STARTED THAT trip, as I do all my trips, exhausted. It seems to be a rule of wilderness travel that, no matter how much time I set aside for preparation, I am invariably several hours short; and no matter how early I go to bed the night before the trip starts, I sleep poorly. I seem to start every big trip bone tired.

I flew into the Refuge from the north, from Barter Island, on the Beaufort Sea coast. As the coastal plain rushed past under the low-flying airplane, I recalled previous trips, when the flat tundra seemed barren, forbidding, even frightening. Over the years, however, I had learned to love its peculiar, even exotic, beauty. The Arctic coastal plain is an acquired taste.

THE PLANE FLEW through a gap in the mountain wall where the coastal plain gradually rises to meet the Brooks Range. The transition from coastal plain to mountain range is abrupt and dramatic; suddenly we were in a world dominated by vertical rather than by horizontal lines. The pilot circled to lose altitude and to examine the tundra airstrip. He made his final approach slowly over the tundra hills along the river; then touched down.

He quickly unloaded my gear, taxied, and took off. We parted without ceremony.

One of the loneliest sounds in the North is the diminishing drone of a small plane motor. When that sound finally draws out to nothing, you know that you are alone, about as alone as it is possible to be on this earth. I would turn forty during this trip years ago, and for the first time in my life I was truly, absolutely alone. Not alone as in being home alone, or being alone in the woods for a day, but alone in the sense that I could not *choose* to find someone to associate with. The only choice I had was to rely on my own resources for every detail of my physical, emotional, and intellectual life.

When you are truly alone in this sense, you become acutely aware of time; and, in a paradoxical sense, time disappears. I became startlingly aware of every act. Should I brew some tea? Write in my journal? Take a hike? Move camp now or later? Sleep or eat? Every detail of my life became significant; every act was a real choice, a conscious choice unaffected by habit. You might say that the passage of time ceased to be an abstraction, and instead became embodied in my actions; I was what I did; time was in the deed. In this sense, time disappeared, and my life became regulated by events rather than by a concept. This is frightening and exciting, and changes one's view of the world utterly.

I STAYED IN my base several days, first to rest, then to sit out a snowstorm (on July 10). When the storm broke up, I headed south deeper into the mountains. I wanted to learn to travel alone, to see the country, to observe wildlife, and to look for signs of wolves.

Several miles south of my first camp is an area of cliffs where the river I was following receives a major tributary from the east. I first walked this valley from the south seven years prior to this trip, and I was to visit the area many times in the future, and I was to conclude that this was a special spot.

I have become convinced over the years that there are certain locations in the wilderness that are somehow special; I am tempted to use the word "magical" but that implies an element of deception; "enchanted" suggests something equally unscientific but it is closer to the word I want. It seems that whenever I go to these places, something interesting usually happens, and that is true time after time after time. In this case, I just saw a band of seventeen caribou on the aufies (thick ice formed by water flowing over ice that is bound to the riverbed), including some big bulls. After watching them, I moved a bit farther south and encountered two Dall sheep rams, one full curl, one half curl. They were right on the river gravel at the base of some cliffs. While I watched them my attention was drawn to the higher cliffs, where a pair of hawks were circling and calling. They had a nest; I eventually decided they were rough-legged. I then moved south a short distance and observed a wolverine carcass, perfectly preserved. I assumed it was somehow mummified by the drying cold. Again I moved south a short distance, and now I discovered a gyrfalcon's nest, perhaps fifty feet up a nearly vertical cliff, built under an overhang. There were four chicks in it. And as I watched them a young Dall sheep emerged from somewhere near the base of the cliff and started grazing.

I crossed the river and headed up the east fork a short distance and made camp on a tundra flat near the water. While I made tea and then ate I kept my eye on a grizzly that was slowly grazing his way along the opposite hillside. He was recognizable by an unusual irregular pattern of dark fur on his body contrasting with lighter fur around the shoulders. I wanted to know where he was, at least his line of travel, because, though I am always concerned about bears, I am more concerned when I am alone.

Where something always happens

After eating I walked south on a low ridge dividing the main river from the east fork. A colony of bank swallows occupied a rock outcrop behind camp; this is the farthest north I can recall seeing swallows. They filled the air with life as they circled and swooped incessantly.

As I moved south along the ridge I stopped occasionally to watch the bear as it continued to graze. Moving along the hillside with him were bands of caribou that had been filtering through all afternoon and evening. I was particularly interested in the caribou behavior. They came into the valley as singles, pairs, or small bands. Invariably the caribou that entered the valley in visual range of the bear would immediately show interest in him. Interest, but not fear. Most of the animals approached the bear, trotting up to him at a good pace to about fifty yards, then slowing to a walk and approaching with lowered heads to about twenty-five yards. The bear invariably ignored them, and after a brief look the caribou tossed their heads and were off again.

I found it interesting that a raven also chose to associate with the bear for a time, sitting on the tundra as the bear grazed along.

While watching these activities, I saw in the east fork valley a different kind of movement: unmistakably a wolf, moving along at a steady trot, deviating frequently from his route to sniff or probe at something in the tundra but always quickly assuming his original line of travel. His route paralleled mine, and I continued walking south while watching him, but of course he moved much faster than me, and in twenty minutes he was almost out of view. But he changed his route and headed west, crossing my line of travel, eventually dropping into the valley of the main fork and out of sight.

Observing wolf activity was one motivation for my being here. I had to ask, was his movement indicative of other wolves in the area? Could he be returning to a rendezvous? It was too late in the season for the den in the area to be occupied; yet wolves will continue to meet in the area of a den after the pups are out learning to hunt. It was a bit of information to remember.

THE WEATHER HAD stabilized and become fair. The sun, which does not set in July, hit my tent early, and by 5:00 AM I was hot. I threw off my sleeping bag and opened the tent door for ventilation, determined to rest some more. The Arctic morning was brilliant and flooded with light.

I lay on my back in the narrow tent, eyes closed, half asleep, when I "felt" something at my left elbow. Not literally tactile, but a sense of mass; I don't know what caused the sensation. Then a long and loud intake of air, along the tent fabric at my shoulder; then the ground vibrated; and yesterday's bear ran to where I could see it in front of the tent. I can't remember rising to a sitting position and pivoting, or working a shell into the chamber of my shotgun, but there I was at my tent door, sitting cross-legged, a loaded gun at port arms. The bear rose on his hind legs and weaved his head from side to side, inhaling deeply, then dropped to all fours and galloped upstream, a wonderful sight. Good bear.

I BROKE CAMP and headed upstream also, and made camp in the afternoon at a point where the east fork emerged from the higher mountains. During the evening I climbed the wedge of high mountains that separates the main and east forks.

Many things are memorable about that climb, such as the wandering caribou, the active bird life, (especially the swooping and diving American pipits), and the great sweep of scenery, particularly to the north. But what is imprinted on my memory most vividly is the light. From my journal: "People who wonder why a person would wander around up here must spend an evening on a mountain on a clear day. The views, of course, are fine, but what is really striking is the clarity of the air. Details from six, seven, eight miles away stand out plainly. It's as if the whole world is laid before you for your delectation—you can just reach out and take it." During times like these I come as close to ecstasy as I ever hope to on this green earth.

During my time up high I kept looking for "my" bear, any bear: I would like to spend my time tonight without ursine company. And I don't see any bears until I am almost back to camp, and there he is, my friend, about two hundred yards away from my tent, grazing towards camp. I make a snap decision—this valley is his!—and I break down my camp. For some reason I note the time, and in fourteen minutes camp is bagged, tent, kitchen, everything into the pack and on my back. As I move out of camp he moves in. When he scents me he moves away, and I know intellectually that I could have camped there safely, but emotionally I am still acutely aware of and troubled by my utter solitude, and I walk out of his valley during the night.

A FRIEND ASKED, how do you "put in" your time out there? The phrasing itself raises questions, such as, am I somehow "on the clock," trying to make time pass by the least painful means? Do I "put in" my time as if I was looking forward to checking out at the end of the day? Is the problem of somehow disposing of our time an unfortunate modern pathology? Why is the passage of time a difficult problem? Why do we want to "kill" it?

When you are alone the challenge of understanding the passage of time is always present, and I decided that it takes about a week to make the emotional transition to solitary wilderness living. I tried to answer the question in my journal: "The answer is clear to me emotionally, but hard to articulate. The quality of this experience can't be duplicated elsewhere. There is no place like the ends of the earth. There is no solitude so absolute and indescribable.

"The wilderness throws you back on yourself psychologically. Physically there is little danger. But how does one respond emotionally? I'm pleased to write that I have done pretty well. I'm usually happy; I've never been unhappy. I've found that I'm pretty good company. Time is not my enemy. I'm never bored, and I think good thoughts usually." How do I "put in" my time? By living in the present moment. I am what I do; time is in the event. I may walk; I may watch a semipalmated plover feeding in the gravel; I may read, or write in my journal; I may stare into space, my mind a blank, or my mind freewheeling. I may look for chores to do, or I may do nothing at all. I just live.

A YEAR LATER I was camped just south of the "magical" cliffs, this time on the main fork, again alone, again wondering what the wildlife, and especially the wolves, were doing. I was camped near where the lone wolf, which I had seen a year ago, had crossed from the east fork to the main fork, and I was determined to explore the drainages in that area.

That morning I had watched a dark bear near camp—I don't know if it was my old friend—and also two wolves, or one wolf twice. I saw a dark wolf hunting north to south on the west bank of the main fork, and another near the cliffs, also hunting north to south. I had to wonder if there was a pattern to this movement, a rationale that I should develop.

I moved camp to the south, to the next fork of the river, a smaller fork coming in from the west. It was at this location that I had my first indication that wolves used this area. Eight years previously I trekked for a month, with a friend, from Ambrusvajun Lake (Last Lake), in the Sheenjek valley, to the Beaufort Sea coast. We camped at this spot, and my partner saw here the only wolf we saw all month.

My joy was intense when I peered into the west fork near our old camp, and lo, I immediately saw a wolf. After all my anticipation, this was too good! This one was dark brown, and moved west along the creek, then to a bluff south of the creek, then to a spine of rock where the mountains steepened. By now it was perhaps three quarters of a mile away, and the details of its behavior were hard to observe. It seemed to assume a tense posture for some time—I couldn't figure out what it was doing—then I imagined I could hear howls. But the wind was blowing strongly and I had trouble hearing. Eventually, when the wind stopped momentarily, I could distinctly hear his howls, not the long-drawn howl we expect to hear, but rather howls which were short, sharp, more frequent. He must have kept this up for twenty minutes.

I decided to camp in the area and inspect that spine of rock. Would it make a good place for a den?

It would not: solid rock, no sign of periodic wolf activity. After camping there for a night I decided to walk the valley to the west. Wolf tracks pointed that way. I did a good day's march and was well up in the mountains when I decided to camp.

After dinner I climbed the ridge to the north of camp. It was hot, muggy, and calm, and the mosquitoes were bothersome, but on top the views were spectacular, and I descended to camp in a good mood. I needed to wash, and while doing so, I stood up, and saw that I had company in camp: a gray wolf was studying me. He was very calm. He glanced at me, examined the tent, then back to me; then moved calmly downstream to the east. His glances at me and my camp were evaluative and dismissive. I had the feeling that he knew all about me. He was in view several times as he moved downstream, and at no time did he alter his sedate mode of travel.

During the next few days I explored the west fork until I became discouraged about finding wolves, though I did see caribou, and I saw a fox flush a willow ptarmigan, and another fox traveling the tundra. The latter, upon seeing me, had the audacity to sit down and scratch a bit, then yawn. After resuming his travels, he speeded up for a moment, as if remembering me, but soon slowed down, as if he recalled that I was of little account. I was impressed by his cat-like movements and indifference.

I RESUMED MY journey, selecting a creek flowing to the north as my return route. As I ascended towards the pass leading to this creek, I saw a large light brown female grizzly with two blond "cubs," animals in their second summer, and formidable creatures in their own right. I hastened to gain some high ground, which put me out of their line of travel, but for the next several hours I checked my back trail, wondering if they too chose *this* route.

A FEW DAYS later I met friends and began the second part of my summer sojourn. We walked south up the main stem of the river to my "special place" at the cliffs and camped there. We decided to take a hike in the evening, partly to see the country and partly to evaluate the river, which had risen during a recent rain storm, and which we had to cross. When we got on top, we walked the rolling ridges and the flats, absorbing the grand views that are the reward of every climb. As we topped a ridge, a wolf came into view perhaps twenty-five yards away, medium-sized, dark gray. He wasn't afraid. He took a good long look at us, and then moved along the ridge to the west, looking back at us periodically but without fear.

By now I was ready to make a few observations about the wolves in this area. First, they were abundant. If I was consistently seeing animals from my limited perspective, then there were no doubt many more than I sighted. Second, they seemed to have routes that centered around a certain location, near the junction of the west and main forks. Third, they were not afraid of people. On the contrary, their attitude towards people seemed to be more one of curiosity or indifference than anything else. I hoped, over time, to see enough of the wolves to be able to draw more conclusions.

A MEMORABLE EVENT happened when we completed our river crossing the next day. As we reorganized to resume hiking we noticed to the west a fringe of dark emerge along the skyline ridges. This fringe expanded to become a blanket: caribou, densely packed. They flooded down the hillside, moving east, then north, then west. What was at first a line on the horizon became after twenty minutes a dark mass of animals, steadily expanding. They kept coming, coming, coming, until the size of the mass was overwhelming. A powerful sight.

Male caribou on old overflow ice

Early the next morning we had a different perspective on caribou. At 3:00 AM I heard snorting and movement in camp near my tent, and my first thought was "bear." I put my head out and saw an unreal, ghostly scene. Fog had developed during the night, and it formed a low ceiling about twenty feet above the ground, throwing a dim grayness over the landscape. The noises I had heard were the sounds of caribou. They were everywhere within view, densely packed, in camp, at the cook site, near the tents, and spread across the creek bottom and tundra. They grunted steadily; the calves bleated, sounding to me somehow like waterfowl; and, forming a steady, persistent background noise, their ankles clicked continually like castanets. Their sheer numbers, their proximity, and the fact that they were visible in a narrow band between the fog and the ground, intensified their presence, imprinting a powerful and lasting impression on my senses.

The next morning we had another visitation of caribou which lasted several hours, and we saw caribou throughout the day. It became clear to us that our walking route paralleled the movements of a large segment of the Porcupine caribou herd as they migrated south and east towards their wintering grounds.

We walked with caribou for several days. The tundra was rutted with recently made trails; whole sections of hillsides were churned into mud and smelled powerfully of urine, a strange barnyard smell in the wilderness. Near the end of one day's walk a very large herd was massed in the valley below us, and as we walked towards them another band flowed in from the west to join them, cutting diagonally in front of us. I decided to try to form some estimate of the number of animals around us, so I sat in a comfortable spot and counted caribou for half an hour. I counted only the animals that filed immediately in front of us, about forty yards away. My method was to count all the animals that passed in a certain period of time, and extrapolating from that number I estimated that 1500 animals passed us in that half hour. Since that number represented only one file of animals in one segment of time, and that there were many files passing continuously, I quickly realized that I could not possibly estimate the magnitude of the spectacle we were witnessing. We had been traveling with caribou for four days. We must have seen many tens of thousands of creatures.

From my journal the next morning: "The caribou made another morning visitation, at 5:00 AM. It wasn't as dramatic as the previous mornings, but it was interesting. However, there have been so many caribou around us that we have become casual about them. I have never seen trails as heavily used as those we traveled yesterday and today. The only trails comparable are *human* trails in *heavily used* parks." But, unlike human trails, these caribou trails laced the entire valley, the slopes and the creek bottom both.

Humans on caribou trails

I spent the next two summer seasons in another, equally wonderful, part of the Refuge, but I wanted to return to the area I had previously explored. I did so in mid-June, earlier in the summer than my previous trips. I thought this would be to my advantage, because it would be more likely that the wolf pack would be associated with the den site at this time. True, the puppies would be large and mobile, but I still might be able to view the pack in the area of the den, wherever that was.

On this trip I approached the area of the den, at the junction of the west and main forks, from the south. I was traveling with two companions. On our trek we saw many animals, particularly caribou, and my anticipation on approaching the junction of the west fork and the main fork was particularly keen. Sure enough, as we approached the west fork we did see a wolf high on a western cliff. He was traveling and we watched him as long as he was in view, then we continued north to the creek and camped. During the early evening we saw and heard a wolf on the south side of the creek. He remained fairly stationary, and his howling was persistent. After making camp and eating, we decided to ascend the hill north of camp to spend the evening watching him and whatever wildlife came into view.

THAT EVENING WAS one of the most memorable of my life.

We were on top a short while when we heard wolves, these to the east, and close. We moved that way and peered over the edge, and we saw an entire pack, ten animals. They were playing, chasing and romping. At first they looked uniform in size, but in hindsight we realized that probably half, possibly more, of the animals were puppies. Their large size was astonishing to me; surely they were barely eight weeks old, perhaps ten weeks at the oldest.

After the animals romped for a few minutes, they moved off a short distance to the north, perhaps one hundred yards, and organized themselves in a line stretching up the mountainside, the animals spaced fifty to one hundred yards apart, singly or in pairs. Most of them lay down, but the animal at the top of the line stood, and she barked and howled, howled and barked, regularly for perhaps twenty minutes.

I had no idea why this was occurring until I saw that the single wolf, which we had first noticed on the south side of the creek, and had subsequently forgotten in the excitement, began to move. He left his station where we had first seen him and walked and trotted across the creek and up the mountainside to the barking wolf at the top of the line.

At that point the pack reassembled as a group. They gathered around the "top" wolf, romped a bit, and disappeared as a pack up and over the mountain.

I had some questions about this behavior. First, what status had the lone wolf that the pack waited a fairly long time for him to join them? My conclusion was that he was a pup who separated himself from the group, and one of the alphas talked him back to the pack before they headed out to hunt. This hunt would be important for the pups, because they were learning about life's essential activity: how to stay alive. The pack was off to obtain food. School was in session, and truancy could be fatal.

Why did they form the "picket line"? Perhaps it occurred randomly; perhaps the pack had some organizational plan that I could not perceive.

Why did I identify the alpha as female? My judgment was purely subjective and semi-conscious; perhaps I linked the unity of the pack with maternal care.

The next morning as we ate breakfast, we heard the howling of wolves. They were on a mountainside to the east of us, across the main fork, and as we watched they disbanded and formed a column and moved single file diagonally across the face of the mountain, over the top, gone.

We broke camp and headed west. As we departed, I looked back. A single wolf, black, had come to our camp and was watching us hike away, single file, up the valley.

Two years later I again had the chance to hike this valley, this time with a man and his daughter. I told them we would probably see wolves, and I was so bold as to tell them that I was pretty sure of the den location. This too was an early summer trip, mid-June, and I felt sure that the wolves would be at or near the den.

When we got to the west fork-main fork junction, where I had previously seen the pack of eleven, I used a different camp, at the edge of a large willow flat at the base of the mountain where the wolves had played and waited.

During our first morning at that camp, we climbed the ridge to the west, where the wolves had formed their picket line, and went on to climb the mountain. I could not see a den at the base of our climb, nor could I see one when we returned by a slightly different route, although I wrote in my journal that there were many "interesting nooks" where a den might be hidden. I was determined to see the den on this trip—it had been eight years since I had made my first effort to explore this area—and I was frustrated. I knew that the den was very near; I had been in the area many times now; why couldn't I find it?

After dinner we followed a heavily used wolf trail north through the willow flats. This was the main trail, running north-south, and at the southern end of the willow flats it forked, branching roughly east-west. The trails were of uniform width, about ten inches, firmly embedded in the earth, like a shallow ditch, (though not cut in, as with hoofed animals), completely vegetated, and studded regularly with scat. The trails were purposeful: they led in a clear direction, no meandering or wandering, the highways of traveling beasts.

I wanted to explore the cliffs and bluffs along the west side of the river, because I visualized the den as being excavated into a hill, like a fox den, forming a sort of cave. But we saw nothing like that, and we turned back up the trail in frustration. On our return along the wolf trail I stopped scanning the cliffs for excavations and instead attended more carefully to the trail itself, looking for some indication of wolf activity.

We followed the trail south for nearly a mile. Just where the trail is nearest the ridge where I had seen the pack, I noticed a fork in the trail, very faint. I hadn't seen it before because it was less used than the main trail and was obscured by overhanging plants; almost a tunnel. We followed this trail until it entered willows at the base of the ridge. We ducked and crouched; came to a small stream; and I saw—and my heart lifted—a bank of bare earth just across the creek. We stepped across the stream, scrambled up the bank out of the willows, and we were in the open, on the den site.

I was astonished at what we saw, and delighted with the ingenuity and cleverness of the wolves. The den occupied a horizontal bit of ground of perhaps five hundred square feet. Several tunnels had been excavated into this loose, well-drained soil, dropping down at a steep slope several feet, then running horizontally, I assume into larger chambers. I could not see if the tunnels were connected, but when I put my upper body as far into the largest of the openings as I could, I could smell wolf, and I retrieved a clump of wolf hair from overhanging roots where the backs of wolves must have scraped many times.

I had to admire the genius of the wolves. They had picked a site that was horizontal, therefore not readily visible; it was surrounded by either tall grass or willows, which shielded it from view; the soil was easy to dig and dry; and it was at the intersection of a number of good travel routes. It was also on a likely caribou migration route, or near where caribou travel and spend time in early summer. I had previously been within fifty yards of the site and had seen no indication of its presence. I was very pleased.

By now it was June 22, and the wolves had moved out, though there was one set of wolf tracks in one tunnel.

In addition to the tunnels, there were also several deep depressions dug into the site, where the wolves obviously lounged: the grass was matted there and elsewhere in the area. The wolves had left bone fragments at the den and around it. Trails led away from the den up the mountain and to the cardinal points of the compass.

In addition to the bone fragments, the wolves had also left a half-chewed sneaker in the grass. I tried to imagine what some camper had thought when he discovered that he was missing a shoe. I pictured a wolf padding through someone's camp in the night, sniffing through a party's belongings as they slept, selecting the smelliest object, perhaps extracting it from the vestibule of a tent. A wolf may have carried it scores of miles back to the den. Why? Well, why do canines like to play? A fine chew-bone to work on, good for a puppy's teeth.

THE NEXT MORNING, as I lay in my tent, a wolf began to howl, from the west, in the area of the den. It continued to howl as we got out and did our morning chores and ate, but it was not visible. The howling stopped for some time, but then I noticed a black wolf followed by a gray wolf just northwest of us, traveling south. They eventually crossed the area above the den. The dark one looked like an adult, the gray one a pup. I tried to visualize their future movements, their travel routes, their hunting tactics, their associations with the rest of the pack; but I could only surmise; and I was grateful for this much of a glimpse into their lives.

IN HINDSIGHT, I am glad that I only saw the den fairly late in the season, when it was vacated. Though it would have been a pleasure to see the den occupied by pups, my presence would have been obtrusive, possibly even harmful to the pack. Also, I know very well that some biologists and pilots were aware of the den; it could be seen from the air if one knew where to look. I did not "discover" the den, except that I located it by my own means. The real discovery was the process of discovering myself.

I HAVE HAD many other encounters with wolves: the time my daughter and I watched an adult "training" some pups; the wolf who came to my fire and rolled in my jacket while I watched (did it smell like that sneaker?); the large golden-gray wolf who approached me on the coastal plain, saw me, and moved slowly away with magnificent indifference; the white female with swollen teats who looked down on me from a hilltop at the southern edge of the coastal plain; the wolf who approached my wife and me across a high alpine plateau and lay down before us to study us.

These encounters include some of my most memorable wildlife experiences. Do they rank with others I have had? The grizzly I watched while he was watching my family eat dinner? Or the time I was surrounded by a flock of thousands of sandhill cranes? Or the time my daughter and I sat among a band of Dall sheep? Or the wolverines? Or the caribou? Or the songbirds?

As I write these words, I experience a sense of privilege and gratitude for being able to experience the creatures of the wild, the lesser and the greater. And I am reminded that some of my finest moments have occurred in my back yard, when a red breasted nuthatch lands on the book I am reading, or a hawk lands beside my son as he sits in a tree. A coyote bounds in front of me on an urban ski trail; geese fly over my house and talk of distant places. My heart is filled when I am presented with each of these gifts.

The wolves of the Arctic National Wildlife Refuge represent a special form of encounter for me, because they represent the goal of my quest. Over the course of my life I have been drawn deeper and deeper into the wilderness, farther and farther from civilization's fringes. As I have followed the impulse to penetrate the wilderness of the north, I have also been compelled to penetrate my own interior wilderness. By following my quest, I have had to penetrate the thickets of my own fears, recognize my own shortcomings, face the ugly tangle of my own conflicts and doubts, and place a true valuation on my abilities and worth. What I have learned during this quest is that there is one emotional posture I must assume: humility.

The wilderness has filled me with fear and trembling. I have watched flooded rivers pound the earth, rolling rocks the size of cars, and have felt the earth shudder beneath my feet; winds have made a palpable wall against my passage; fogs and storms have eliminated my vision. I have groped and stumbled and hoped for luck. I have stepped at night from the shelter of the forest at -34 F into a north wind and wondered how it is that life goes on.

Of course it goes on, and the miracle is that it does not require a miracle to continue. Night descends on the north and stays unbroken for months. The cold deepens and deepens and the earth is stricken immobile. While we humans have withdrawn to our towns, our villages, our hearths, the creatures of the wild carry their fierce vitality through the dark and the unimaginable cold. The summer visitors are fled, the sun has withdrawn, and the vole, the hare, the caribou, the wolverine, carry on in their utter indifference to nature's hostility.

Somewhere in the vast dark, on some unimaginable hilltop in a place unutterably far away, a group of wolves stir, sniff each other, inhale the cold air. A wind ruffles their guard hairs. The blue snow squeaks when they turn and shift. They mill about uncertainly. One wolf stiffens and peers into the darkness, then moves down towards a line of black spiky spruce. The rest drop into line and follow.

CHAPTER 3

An Arctic Day

I was traveling with two companions in early June in the extreme northeastern part of Alaska, in the Arctic National Wildlife Refuge, where the mountains meet the coastal plain only a few miles south of the Beaufort Sea. A few miles to the east, the Yukon border and Ivvavik National Park of Canada. Our camp was at the base of the most northern extension of the Brooks Range. We looked north across the coastal plain.

Early June in this part of Alaska is Arctic spring. It was hot summer when we left Fairbanks, green and fragrant, but as we made our way north we flew back in time, and where we left our bush plane the willows had yet to bud and the tundra was brown. Here at our camp, north of our drop-off point, much of the river was still ice and we could feel the cold of the Beaufort Sea ice pack in the northeast breeze. But the weather was fair and we were comfortable.

However austere the landscape, the animal world at this time was active and on the move. This is the time immediately following the great bird migrations: waterfowl, raptors, shore birds, and songbirds. All of these birds, with the exception of a few local residents, had just completed migrations of thousands of miles, from the south Pacific, Argentina, Pakistan, Venezuela, North Africa, Costa Rica, Nebraska, India, the Pacific Northwest, and dozens of other locales.

After their long voyages they plunged into their mating and nesting activities, for they have just a few weeks, barely two months, to complete the mating cycle and begin their southern journeys.

The Porcupine caribou herd is the major mammalian presence in this area. These creatures undertake the monumental task of moving annually north (in the spring, trending to the northwest) and then south (after the period of calving, trending to the southeast) across the entire width of the eastern Refuge and western Yukon Territory, with east-west excursions along the Arctic coastal plain, and apparently random movements in the mountains. They winter in the area north of the Yukon River in eastern Alaska and central and western Yukon. At the time of this trip the herd numbered fewer than about 130,000 animals. (The herd was in an apparent short-term decline. As I write, in 2018, the herd is increasing in size.) Though the entire herd does not move as a unit, large sections of the herd, perhaps tens of thousands of animals, may pass through an area in a few hours or a few days.

Other mammals are also on the move at this time. Grizzly bears have already given birth in their dens, and have emerged and are foraging. Foxes and wolves are tending their young and maintaining a new generation of animals. Musk oxen are browsing across the tundra, their new calves part of the herds. Dall sheep occupy the realm of alpine heights at an Arctic latitude.

WE WERE CAMPED on the west bank of a north flowing river where it leaves the mountains to cross the coastal plain to the sea. George and Martin and I had backpacked for two days from where the bush plane had dropped us off, hiking to the north over the mountains and then east along the tundra foothills. To the south of our camp, the mountain wall; to the north, brown plains backed by cold fog over the Beaufort Sea.

Soon after making camp we spotted two musk oxen bulls several hundred yards away. We had never approached musk oxen before and did a careful stalk so as not to spook them, but when we got to about seventy-five yards we found that they would not flee but would stand their ground, so we simply stood and watched them. Their behavior was interesting: when they became aware of our presence they squared off with each other, staring and snorting and occasionally pawing the ground, then butting heads, engaging in a shoving match. They repeated this behavior often over the course of thirty or forty minutes, until we moved off and left them to themselves. I don't know the purpose of this activity. Were they engaged in displacement activity, directing hostility away from us? Were they displaying their strength in order to awe and cow us? Or were they simply two males determined to test each other?

THE NEXT MORNING was cold and foggy. As so often happens on the coastal plain, the prevailing northeast wind had pushed the persistent Beaufort Sea fog miles inland, and it so happened that the southern limit of the fog bank was at our camp. As we ate breakfast the fog began to sift away from camp and the sun hit us: the air was cold, sub-freezing, but the direct light had warmth in it, and the Arctic light warms the soul as well as the body. We were ready for our day's excursion, a long walk north towards the ocean. Our route lay along the miles of gravel laid down by the river. Away from the river gravel the coastal plain is often a morass of wet tussocks and bog because the soil is poorly drained; the sedge tussocks which grow in these conditions are clumps of vegetation that grow in columns, narrow at the bottom, wide at the top. They vary in height from six inches to twenty-four inches approximately, and usually grow close together, so that the hiker can neither place his feet between them without jamming his foot, nor walk on top of them without teetering and twisting his legs and ankles. The boggy ground adds to the hiker's torment. Sedge tussocks are truly the hiker's nightmare in the Arctic.

On the other hand, the rivers create ideal hiking conditions. Most Arctic rivers carry little water but have wide gravel beds, and the gravel beds that are no longer subject to river erosion sustain a thin growth of smooth tundra, with willow growth in sheltered areas. These tundra flats are where to camp and walk.

The tundra flats are rich in flowers later in June and through July, but in early June what catches my eye is the rich bird life. The hardy northern birds, such as the hoary redpoll, are busy in the willows, which is the primary source of their food as well as their nesting site. The northern shrike occupies areas where the willows are largest; they nest high. Other migrants also use the willows for nesting, the most colorful being the yellow warbler, recently arrived from Central America, and the American robin, that glorious robust singer.

On the tundra itself, the two species which stand out most strikingly are the Lapland longspur, with his stylish black headset contrasting with his rich chestnut body, and the American golden plover.

The golden plover is one of those creatures that, like the common loon, embody the wild spirit of its habitat. When he stands erect the curving silver band on his neck contrasts with his black-and-gold-flecked plumage. His erect posture is the essence of alertness. In flight he is grace itself: deep crisp wing beats, trim body and backswept wings, quick in the turns and fast in the straightaway. But his highest appeal, to me, is his voice: high, piping, wild. It expresses, to this human ear, what is wild, lonely, forlorn, hopeful in the wilderness. He tells me that he endures the winds, snows, and fogs of the tundra, the thousands of miles of migration north, east, and south, across the entire Western Hemisphere, the buffeting winds of high elevations, long ocean crossings. His few ounces of carefully organized and vibrant animal matter produce the song that is plaintive, reedy, delicate, and undaunted. He makes my heart sing. I think of Whitman's lines:

> *From the memories of the bird that chanted to me,*
> *From your memories sad brother, from the fitful risings*
> *and fallings I heard,*

I have many times had my soul nourished.

His cousins the shorebirds nest nearby, just below the tundra benches, on the river gravel itself. Their comings and goings are quick and graceful, and are perhaps best exemplified by the semipalmated plover, who does not fear to show herself to the hiker. She wears a distinctive black bib, and does a convincing imitation of a wounded bird before she is suddenly made whole when you are a sufficient distance from her nest. A northern, or red-necked, phalarope works shallow ponds for minute insect life, alert, erect, and graceful. Teal are tucked into river backwaters, mergansers cruise the river purposefully. Gulls float, living on I know not what. The raptors, prominent among them the rough-legged hawk and the golden eagle, soar. And the graceful, quick-winged jaeger seems to be everywhere, his presence a constant menace. One remembers that death is an unrelenting attendant upon this renewal of life.

We were surrounded all morning by this burst of avian activity. We traveled in the brilliant Arctic sun, in the wonderfully clarified Arctic air. The sun was warm on our skin but the ambient air temperature was low, and a brisk northeast wind blew off the ice pack onto our right shoulders. Gray curtains of fog continually formed along the coast to the north. It drifted, blew in strands, billowed high, shifted in various directions on the edge of the coastal plain, but it never dissipated entirely. However, the sky remained clear where we walked and to the south.

The caribou were on the move. For all the time we were on the coastal plain caribou filtered through the mountains from the east, out of the foothills, through the passes, down the river valley, in bands of five, thirty, fifty, two hundred, moving along in skeins of animals rather than in herds. We walked through a vast pasture, animals scattered for many square miles around us, animals crossing close to us along our line of advance or coming to us and veering off slightly as they approached. Some groups were females and calves; there were a number of barren cows and yearlings; occasionally a band of bulls carried their forest of antlers by. We heard their continual grunts, and their ankles clicked like castanets. They left a rich, almost a barnyard, smell where they passed in great numbers. The pageant continued around the clock during the seamless Arctic days and nights. We were immersed in caribou.

WE TRAVELED SOUTH towards camp during the afternoon of our long day. Now we walked towards the shining mountains.

The sun in the far north circles the sky, swinging, at this latitude, to within a few degrees of the northern horizon at midnight, and higher above the southern horizon at noon. But "high noon" does not exist in the Arctic. The sun's light always approaches the earth at an angle, always more or less acute, and this imparts a soft and subtle appearance to the landscape. The Arctic light is rarely harsh. Most typically, on a clear day the long rays create a series of highlights and contrasts. It strokes the undulating mountains, creating the most sensual landscape I have ever experienced. This effect is intensified as evening approaches. One's sense of distance changes with the light; mountains that seemed distant at noon approach you in the evening; details of the landscape—undulations in the tundra, any irregularity, such as creek banks or cliffs—become highlighted and intensified.

AN ARCTIC DAY

So it was as we walked across the level coastal plain towards our camp at the base of the mountains.

LATE IN THE afternoon, we saw dark forms to our east perhaps half a mile away. They were unlike the moving skeins of caribou—the caribou have a distinctive, head-high gait, and they don't cluster densely together. The forms we now saw were blocky, and stationary, and densely packed. As we approached, we were thrilled to confirm our suspicion: musk oxen!

Musk oxen were common in the Arctic until some time in the early or mid-nineteenth century; by 1850 or 1860 they had disappeared entirely from Alaska, and Canadian herds were greatly reduced. A common theory to explain their disappearance is that they were easy prey for the rifleman, because their mode of defense is to cluster together in a stationary group, which is an effective defense against wolves or bears, but serves only to provide easy targets for armed humans. Other evidence, however, suggests that their numbers were reduced before the advent of the rifle in Arctic Alaska, which suggests that some environmental factor, such as deep snow, was responsible for their decline. Because of their physical conformation, they do very poorly in deep snow years; the Arctic generally is dry, with little snowfall and large expanses of windswept tundra and wind-hardened snow, and the musk oxen do best in these conditions.

Healthy populations remained in Greenland, and in 1930 the federal Bureau of Sport Fisheries and Wildlife transported a group of young animals from Greenland to Fairbanks, where they were allowed to mature. By 1936 these animals were moved to Nunivak Island, where they established themselves successfully, and in 1969 the Alaska Department and Fish and Game and the United States

Fish and Wildlife Service transplanted Nunivak animals to what is now the Arctic National Wildlife Refuge. In recent years there were as many as 800 animals on the coastal plain, 350 of which are in the Refuge. (These numbers may represent the peak of their repopulation. Since these words were written, a very steep decline in their numbers has occurred. Have the animals declined because of increased snow depth in recent years? Have the grizzly bears become more effective predators? Or have the animals simply dispersed?)

The herd we approached included about twenty animals, consisting of females of various age groups, calves, and a few males, at least two. We positioned ourselves on a tundra mound about 200 yards from the herd, and as we did so they spotted us. Their response was fascinating. As a group they ran a short distance, about twenty yards, milled around for a few seconds, and then became stationary, a shoulder-to-shoulder wall of animals facing us. The two bulls stood apart from the herd, each to a side, about ten yards removed from the group. They stood thus for several minutes, then bolted, ran another short distance, milled around, and regrouped. They repeated this cycle several times before finally bolting entirely, stampeding south up the river in a cloud of dust. We felt as if we had just witnessed something primeval, as ancient as the Arctic itself.

AGAIN WE MOVED south towards camp. We hadn't walked far when we saw to the west a large dark shape, apparently burrowing in the ground. It could not be a wolf or wolverine: it was too large. A grizzly, excavating some higher, well drained ground, hoping to turn up a ground squirrel from its maze of burrows. I am always humble and somewhat fearful when near a grizzly bear; they are intelligent, and superlatively fast, quick, and strong. They exude a sense of power that fills me with awe. We were unarmed, the bear was near, and we watched him briefly before moving on.

AN ARCTIC DAY

A camp in early summer

We ate late that night, after a long day of walking. The sky remained clear, and the rays of the sun came to us at a low angle from the northwest across the tundra plains. While we prepared dinner, we noticed two wolves on the opposite, or east, bank trotting south to north along the base of the foothills. Of course they were hunting, and we could tell by their posture that they had spotted something, a small band of caribou. One wolf crouched behind a small clump of willows, the other lay flat on the tundra facing away from the oncoming caribou. I could see through my binoculars that the second wolf peeked carefully back over his shoulder towards the oncoming animals. The two wolves remained motionless.

Somehow, I am not sure why, I developed the idea that the second wolf was the leader of the pair. In any case, he triggered the attack on the approaching caribou. He continued to peek over his shoulder as they approached, and when they were perhaps twenty-five yards away he attacked, his companion right behind. The caribou bolted east and scattered slightly, the wolves in vigorous pursuit. All the animals disappeared over a rise and into a draw in the foothills, and we never saw them again.

When I look back over this one day in the Arctic, my heart is warmed by the memory of what we saw. In a mere twenty-four hours we witnessed the great stream of life in many of its manifestations, condensed, close, and vivid. In a person's lifetime, a handful of days offer such variety and intensity of experience. This single day in the Arctic has imprinted itself on my mind, and on my spirit, indelibly.

My companions and I were able to have this incomparable experience because a previous generation of activists, bureaucrats, presidents, and legislators had the foresight, first, to establish what eventually became the Arctic National Wildlife Refuge, and, second, to include this part of the coastal plain within the designated wilderness area. When I hear someone claim that the coastal plain is a wasteland with little surface value, I remember this day particularly, and the many like it I have experienced.

A sensual landscape.

CHAPTER 4

The Quality Of The Light

Windows or walls?

Philosophers have always wondered, are still wondering, if our physiology joins us to the world or separates us from the world. And the scientists and psychologists have explored the subsidiary but equally important question, To what degree do our brains and nervous systems transform, screen, or interpret what our sensory organs convey or communicate? Do we live in a world of objectivity or subjectivity? These questions are among the most fundamental, the most fascinating, the most troubling, and the most insoluble of all those posed by *Homo sapiens*. In fact, if we weren't "sapiens" we couldn't pose the question at all, suggesting that the questions are in fact not only fundamental to, *but identical with*, human existence.

For most of us, most of the time, our senses are tools for living. The countryman uses them, in combination with the interpretive and judgmental mind, to read the weather, build a barn, run a chain saw, fix a tractor. His urban kin similarly finds his way along the freeway, establishes business relationships, masters electronic communications. In these pragmatic ways we function very well, and can pragmatically and justly claim to live in the objective world.

However, most of us at some time, and some of us most of the time, live for seconds or hours in a more direct and intuitive relationship to the world. The artist, whether graphic or poetic, has learned to inhabit and navigate this latter world. (I exclude the musical artist here, whether composer or musician, because that world, though emotional, is also abstract and closer to the joys of mathematics.) The world of the painter and the poet is filled with the intuitive grasp of sensation; or strives, sometimes with intense yearning, or in frustration, for such a grasp.

THE SEARCH FOR meaning in sensation, or behind sensation, is also evident in our "nature writers." This unsatisfactory designation includes writers who, at one end of the spectrum, narrate their wilderness adventures, or their "return" to nature, or their year in the woods, or their home in the wilderness. At the other end of the spectrum, their writing approaches or achieves philosophical significance. Along that spectrum are writers who are solidly scientific, and writers who pursue self-discovery and aesthetic gratification, and writers, the best, such as Aldo Leopold and Annie Dillard, who are interested in all these concerns. Leopold's well known *A Sand County Almanac* explores, among other things, the right relationship between the individual and the natural world, and society and the natural world. Annie Dillard, in her *Pilgrim at Tinker Creek*, explores more personally, and perhaps more intensely and completely, the epistemological relationship between the human mind and the natural world. But of all our nature writers, Henry David Thoreau remains the most complete, probably because he devoted his entire life to this endeavor.

As with most definitive writers, I suspect that he is more referred to than read, and that an appreciation of the quality of his prose, and his thought, is overshadowed by common assumptions and misconceptions: that he fled civilization for the wilderness (though his famous hut was near Concord); that he "escaped" to the woods (though in truth he sought engagement); that he was a hermit (though he both entertained visitors and was entertained); that he was a cranky misanthrope (though, in my view, he was merely thoroughly analytical, and critical in the best sense of the word). Very likely he did lack empathy for the normal realities of work and domestic obligations, probably because of the ethical standards to which he held himself and the practical circumstance of his bachelorhood. I don't think he was a social revolutionary. The revolution he advocated was strictly personal. He was a conservative, a liberal, and a libertarian.

Thoreau wanted to experience the intensity and reality of the sensual world, and to penetrate, if possible, to a trans-sensual reality—and he was well aware that the latter may be impossible.

If I am right that the painter and poet seek an intuitive grasp of the significance of our sensory experience, then Thoreau is like them in his goal, but unlike them in his method, in that he wanted his entire existence to be the vehicle for this effort. His life itself was the canvas, the poem. He was what he did.

"I went to the woods because I wished to live deliberately, to front only the essential facts of life, and see if I could not learn what it had to teach, and not, when I came to die, discover that I had not lived."

This deceptively simple statement expresses an apparently common sentiment. People wear the phrase "carpe diem" on their tee shirts. But Thoreau is saying much more than this. I am struck by two interesting conjunctions of ideas here.

The first is the linkage between deliberateness and urgency, an apparent paradox. Though it doesn't seem likely that he could foretell his early death, he knew that life was for the living, that time was short, that he must get on with it. Yet he also knew that careful deliberation was more important than sheer quantity. Frantic activity, haste, the simple volume of experience could never convince him, when he came to die, that he had lived. The only way to do that was to insure, first, that the experiences that he chose were in themselves potentially valuable; and then to attend to those experiences with sufficient care that he could extract their total value. Deliberateness here implies intensity, and these qualities would help him answer his life-and-death question, "Have I lived?"

The second conjunction is between "deliberately" and "essential." The task of selecting those potentially valuable experiences, the "essential facts of life," is in itself a difficult challenge. Finding your subject, in Thoreau's case himself in relationship to the natural world, may be fairly easy; but excluding the inessential, the peripheral, the seductively distracting, is far more difficult. Developing the intellectual and emotional discipline, focus, and peace to accomplish this may be either the cause or the result of deliberateness.

In the same section of *Walden*, Chapter II, Thoreau allows that he wanted "to live deep and suck out all the marrow of life…", and later, to work his way down through the detritus of civilization until "we come to a hard bottom and rocks in place, which we can call *reality*, and say, This is, and no mistake; and then begin….I cannot count one…. I have always been regretting that I was not as wise as the day I was born."

This may be the voice of someone who desires to transcend experience, but I think rather that it is the voice of a man who, unlike Descartes, wants to grasp his immediate sensual experience and find his starting point and his meaning and his significance in that. The world is good enough for Thoreau; the world is all the heaven he would ever want. Rather than yearn for something better than this world, he instead wants to make himself worthy of this world. He does not need to transcend the world, he needs to transcend his old self, by refining his character and mind to make them worthy of his sensual experience.

I AM TOO old and too much of a realist, I hope, to expect life to yield much in the way of ecstasy. Yet I have had my moments. The kind of joy I strive for, and hope to relate, is a connection between the physical world, my senses, and my emotions. My intellect serves here, not as a critical and analytical tool, but as an intuitive mediator that makes these connections conscious.

My deepest sensations, my longest-lived and most emotionally evocative—I am tempted to use the word "ancient"—are olfactory. Powerful, and usually powerfully nostalgic, emotions are evoked in me by what I smell. Some of these emotions are half a century old; some occurred today.

I don't consciously remember these odors; they simply ambush me at certain times, and I am surprised and delighted all over again. I can't describe them, though the latent memories they trigger, perhaps decades old, re-emerge with the intensity of the present moment. If I name some of my mine, perhaps the reader will in turn recall some of his or her own.

September in Alaska. The birch leaves are golden, their existence reduced to a few remaining days. Walk a forest path and smell the leaves on the forest duff, the soil itself. A better writer than I am could, perhaps, find a word for this odor. At first I wrote "smell" for "odor," but changed it, supposing that the odor is in the forest, but the smell is within my nerve endings and brain. And what does my brain do? Transport me to a place in Pennsylvania, the hardwood forest in October five decades past; to portage trails in canoe country; to a grove of ancient trees along a hill-country stream. Nostalgia is dangerous; it is the enemy of the present moment, and in that sense is a denial of life. But it also provides a powerful impulse: cling to this, savor it, suck the marrow from it. I lived in the past, I live now. Know it.

A short catalogue of odors: a breeze drawn across a lake; a marsh; warm wind on a mud flat; a river at dawn; the ocean near shore; the ocean off shore; hot air in a spruce forest. You've been there.

OF ALL SOUNDS, that of moving water fills my soul. The metaphors come easier here. The ocean before our cabin variously pounds, crashes, drags; laps, slops, tinkles. It is always up to something. Sometimes, rarely, it is still, which is something too. Its sounds, or its stillness, fill us in varying ways: threat, monotony, peace. It is always there, engaging us. Flowing water has a different effect. Flowing water calls to me, an invitation. I want to follow it up with waders and fly rod, or follow it down in a raft or canoe. The sound of a stream is various, as it runs over shallows, drops over a ledge, rushes through a logjam, parts around a boulder. Spend a week or a month on a stream and the sound is with you, waking and sleeping, a constant companion. A river lives—it could well be viewed as an organism. Not for nothing are our rivers referred to as arteries—an excellent metaphor, approaching the literal.

LIGHT FOLLOWS a direct path to the soul. The quality of the light has a direct and instantaneous effect on thought and feeling.

The two gloamings are the most precious times of the day. In early hours the coming of the light is a revelation, and it is a blessing that the day dawns upon us. But not of a sudden—part of its beauty is its stealth. I savor its slowness. The mystery of the dark is gradually lifted. One relishes the new beginning; life is laid before us once again, another miracle. Anticipation is the watchword; but not to hurry. The rushing earth turns nevertheless by slow degrees, and after the long anticipation, suddenly it is day, and the world becomes ordinary once again.

The drawing on of night is a different anticipation. Now the mystery deepens as the world withdraws from us twig by twig, stem by stem; the far side of the lake loses its definition, withdraws into shadows; then obscurity. The approach of mystery is a calm excitement: one is alert, focused, centered within one's emotional self, quickened.

In the Arctic National Wildlife Refuge, in the mountains. In this desert, when a strong high-pressure system moves in, the sky can remain cloudless, or nearly cloudless, for weeks at a time.

I leave camp in the early evening to climb to a high vantage point. The atmosphere is dry, the sky a rich blue and completely cloudless. The sun is warm on the parts of my body exposed to it, but the air is very cool on my shaded side, because in the Arctic there is in the summer a great difference between radiant heat and ambient heat. A breeze.

I climb to the top of a wedge of the mountains. The narrow part of the wedge faces north. On either side, a north flowing stream, which meet several miles to the north beyond a tundra plain.

I am alone. All around, 360 degrees, endless mountains and valleys, fold after fold, peak after peak. I can infer distant drainages from the ridgelines that flank them, and map the topography of the landscape as if it were laid out like a model. I feel that I could reach out and touch all the world I can see.

SUNLIGHT NORTH

Looking toward the highest peaks in the Refuge

Then it comes home to me: the air contains no distortions that I can detect. No moisture, no haze, no diminution of my view. I can see unimpeded to the curve of the earth. All is laid out before me, the most sensual landscape I know. My eye follows incessantly and without fatigue the endless linked horizontal and vertical lines, flowing seamlessly, around the entire disc of the horizon.

I realize that this is a world of light. It is light that communicates everything in my surroundings to me, that connects me to the world. The northern light: from the world, through my eyes, to my soul. I have no other word for this part of myself than "soul." The world is filled with beauty, the world is beauty, the world is great and good; I reach out and bless it; this is prayer. Something profoundly meaningful has happened to me, but I cannot analyze it or explain it, except that it was the quality of the light.

THE QUALITY OF THE LIGHT

A perfect camp

CHAPTER 5

Fear of Bears

In our nature writing, we read much about nature's serenity, benign aspect, beauty. We also read of her changeable and violent faces: storms, seacoasts, raging rivers. Less often do we encounter, through lyrical or scientific writing, something closer to her reality. Dillard, Eiseley, Thoreau, Leopold, strive, often successfully, to enable us to see something real behind the faces nature presents to us. Sometimes writers conclude that there is nothing there after all, that the serenity and violence are neither a face nor a mask, merely what is, an impenetrable mystery, or no mystery at all.

I suspect that the face of nature that we recognize is the face that we create for her or project on to her. (The selection of a feminine pronoun for "her" is an example.) Certainly, the natural world consists of a vast and perhaps infinite network of events and facts and the interconnections between them. I have faith that there is an objective reality that can be approached in an objective manner; but faith is not knowledge. We *Homo sapiens* have the troubling capacity to project ourselves on to the world. In truth, a major puzzle is, how can we see the world objectively when the tools of our personal thought, and our institutional thought in the forms of the sciences, are themselves human creations? Many of us are disinclined to strive for objectivity—many scorn it—and most of us do not work within the strict rigor of science. Following the human inclination for egotism, we project ourselves onto the world around us, and provide nature with our own faces.

It seems to me that all of us, scientists included, need to struggle against the subjective interpretation of the natural world. Much of our approach to the natural world is made up of old habits and reflexive responses: what a gorgeous sunset (like a flaming furnace), what a striking mountain (like a cathedral), what an inspiring waterfall (like a bridal veil), what a magnificent lion (how regal). Cliched language creates the conditions for cliched thought; we trivialize our experience; nature is viewed as a series of human artifacts, pictures in a gallery, edited for human purposes.

Enough has been written about her inspirational beauty. I intend to explore here the fear which is part of our connection to the natural world and which we project on to her.

Much of my life has had to do with overcoming and using fear.

One of the most important transitions of my life occurred when my parents decided to relocate from the city to the country. We moved to a rural part of western Pennsylvania that had, in 1959, a few large tracts of forest left intact, somehow, after farmers, coal companies, and heavy industry had taken what they wanted. One such tract bordered our acreage on two sides and extended, I think, for some thousands of acres. This forest was largely unbroken, and consisted of mature second growth hardwoods with some hemlock along the creeks. It was a miniature Eastern wilderness.

I was thirteen years old, and I was excited. Here was something like the real thing: the Big Woods.

I knew nothing of the woods. If I possessed a compass, I didn't know how to use it. Other than by noting the course of the sun, I didn't know north from south. I had no access to maps, and if I would have I wouldn't have known how to use them. Methods of navigation were to me vague and remote concepts. I read in the Boy Scout handbook that moss grows on the north side of trees. (I eventually learned that it grows on the south, west, and east sides as well). I learned from the same source that water flows downhill and ends up somewhere, so follow it when lost. My ignorance was complete.

But I plunged into the forest nevertheless, wearing clothing and shoes I wouldn't give to charity today. I didn't even own a raincoat; never heard of hypothermia.

My method of exploration was just to start walking, and trust that everything else would take care of itself. I believed falsely that I had a built-in sense of direction—a particularly good one, like a true woodsman—and no matter how often I got lost, I was extremely reluctant to relinquish that fantasy.

So I would blunder from my starting point into the unknown. The most interesting parts of my journeys always began at the point where I began to feel uneasy: at the edge of my knowledge, out in a great emptiness, where the isolation and silence are keenly felt. I might find a stand of hemlocks, their scent redolent of the North and the Wild. I might encounter a great spreading oak, or a group of lithe and graceful maples, or a tangle of grape vines which harbored a grouse whose sudden thunderous flight made my heart pound. I might locate a ravine where flowed a brook suggestive of far unpolluted places. I always discovered something to tease my imagination and stir my heart.

This joyful sense of discovery was seasoned, though not diminished, by a sense of anxiety. Did I know for sure just where I was, or how to return? How far was too far? I have often, to this day, been tugged two ways: back to safety, and forward to the unknown. My fear stood at the divide between these two impulses when I debated my choices, and when I moved forward, as I always did, fear's finger touched me between the shoulder blades. I have always lived my life at a threshold; I am perpetually moving through that threshold; hence, I have never arrived.

It seems that I am often, while looking for something, getting myself lost, and that this is how I find myself. When I extend myself—lose myself—my fear shows itself at some time, and I need to discipline it. I don't like it, but I doubt if I can conquer it; I cannot let it discourage me. (Re-read Faulkner's great story "The Bear," dear reader, for a fine artistic rendering of this dilemma.)

I TRAVELED WITH my grandfather, father, and friends into wilder country to the north and east to hunt and fish. As we drove into the approaching dark, my interest always quickened intensely. The big rounded hills, mountains to us, rose mysteriously into the dusk; darkness crept into the stream valleys. The darkness and mystery called to me: deep groves of hemlocks, dusky ravines, creek bottoms leading to a place in my imagination. To this day the magic hours to me are the two gloamings, when we anticipate the revelation of a new day, and when the old day relinquishes itself to the night.

That mystery has fueled me all my life. What is at the edge? What lies beyond the edge? If I had no threshold to pass through I would die emotionally, which in truth would be the death of the entire organism: a walking death enclosed in a sham being.

FEAR OF BEARS

ONE OF MY EARLIEST and strongest memories is one of rejection: I intuitively rejected the industrial ravages of my surroundings. I can clearly recall one summer afternoon when I was six or eight years old, in the early 1950s. I was reclining on the steeply sloping lawn of our suburban home in the West Mifflin section of Pittsburgh. I looked across the deep valley of the Monongahela River. Across the river was the steel town of Braddock. Upstream was the steel town of Duquesne. Downstream and out of sight was the steel town of Homestead. Upstream and across the river, also out of sight, was the steel town of McKeesport. And on and on. Along the riverbanks, on both sides as far as I could see, was a dense web of railroad tracks; just beyond the tracks, the steel mills. I couldn't tell where one mill started and another ended. The eye saw one continuous mill. At frequent intervals, piles of coal, piles of slag, piles of scrap, cranes.

The river was uniform to the eye because it was really a lake formed by a series of dams and locks which controlled the river. On the river, barges, most piled with coal. At regular and frequent intervals the river bank below the railroad tracks was pierced by outlet pipes, each of which emitted a steady stream of something dark, or unnaturally bright, such as red or yellow. The river was dark brown. I did not know that these poisons were pumped through the heart of America, to the Gulf of Mexico.

Smoke of various hues, from black to charcoal to gray, boiled from the many smokestacks. Flames of red or yellow shimmered from other pipes. The sky on a sunny day, which I imagine should have been brilliant blue, was just a haze, the sun a blur that poured its intense heat into the humid and smoky atmosphere.

No true forest; but sumacs and lush broad-leafed, stemmy plants, coarse and rank, grew jungle-like in the waste ground on the hillsides. Away from the mills, up the hills and off the river, wound the prosperous suburbs. The houses overlooked the mills where the men worked. They made a good living, in the economic sense, from the factories. These were the factories that made America, so it has been claimed. Here was the industry that built our bridges, provided the girders of which our modern cities were built, gave us the shapes of our cars and trucks, crafted the hulls of ships and aircraft carriers. Here was the wealth of America. This is where our wars were won.

Of course, I didn't know at the time what I was looking at. What I saw had no intellectual significance to me whatsoever. My "understanding" of the scene was strictly emotional and intuitive. In spite of my youth, I "knew" that there was something very wrong with what I saw.

I admit that at a remove of sixty years, it is impossible to be certain what actually constituted my original experience and what has since accreted to it. But of one thing I am certain: something within me, at a young age, said, "This is wrong." I later became convinced that a great sin had been done, to the people and to their place.

What interests me in this recollection is not merely the significance of the ugliness and harm that I saw, but why a child should resist this particular man-made environment. I had been raised since birth in this environment. I had not traveled and knew nothing else. Everyone around me accepted their situation as normal. What would make me, or allow me, to respond as I did? What would make me an emotional outcast in the world to which I was born?

I was too young to apply reason and an ethical judgment to my environment. I simply knew that the ruined streams, air and land were somehow wrong, and in my heart I rejected my surroundings. I was an alien in a world I did not want, and that has remained part of my personality.

Fifty years later I blundered across Frederick Turner's excellent book *Beyond Geography: The Western Spirit against the Wilderness*.

The first chapter is titled "Estrangement," and in part narrates Turner's youthful discovery that his ignorance of America amounted to "estrangement from the land," and that that estrangement was common to Americans generally. A "feeling of American loneliness began to insist upon itself, a crucial, profound estrangement of the inhabitants from their habitat....It was as if those who had inherited the fruits of exploration and conquest had been left a troubled bequest, as if there were some unplacated, unmet spirit of place dividing them from an authentic and comforting possession here." He wonders "how it came to be that neither in proverb nor in history have we been able to come to loving terms with what we must call home." Turner's book spoke powerfully to me. Of course he was neither the only nor the first to comment upon alienation in America, but he was the first in my experience to connect that alienation to our antagonism towards wilderness; and, more generally, to the natural world, wilderness or not. To this day, as I write, a large segment of American life is indifferent to or actively hostile towards our environment. The indifference on the part of individuals is I think the indifference of those who lack connections to the world; the hostility occurs for financial reasons. In either case, we have not come to "loving terms" with our home. Indeed, people who control a large part of our economy attack our home as if they hate it, and simultaneously act as if they hold the moral high ground. To offer one example of many: as I write, the official position of the State of Alaska is that the polar bear should not be protected from extinction, because if it is so protected the State and its corporate patrons, though quite wealthy, might become less wealthy than they currently are. Not that protecting the bear would certainly reduce their chances of gaining more wealth; only that it *might* do so. Even the *possibility* of becoming less wealthy must be defended against—is worth risking the extinction of species.

As I matured, my direct experience and my reason reinforced my early intuitions. My love of the natural world was always shadowed by the opening of new strip mines, the increased size of the coal waste piles, the destruction of more streams by acid mine drainage. Even away from the urban mills and rural mines, the miniaturized landscapes and forests of the East seemed to be disappearing beneath megalopolis. I grew, I obtained a formal education, I did all the conventional things one should do to prepare for life, but always at the back of my mind was a conviction that my real life, if I was to live an authentic existence at all, was elsewhere. My wife Diane and I went west and north.

At the time I could not have said that we were following an old American impulse. West and North were for me a personal dream—literally and figuratively—but I did not recognize then that I was pursuing one aspect of the larger American Dream. For years I dreamed about, tried to visualize, my "real" home (I still am). I first trended west, and then emphatically north.

On our way to Alaska we saw some of the American West as tourists, but it wasn't until we were in the Alberta Rockies that we really put our feet on the ground.

We set out on the first backpack trip of our lives, an overnighter in Jasper National Park in the area of Mount Edith Cavell. Crepe soled work boots; plastic to sleep under; huge Dacron sleeping bags from Sears; flimsy vinyl ponchos; canned food. We didn't know where we were going. It hadn't occurred to us to get maps. We didn't know how the trail system was laid out or how long it would take to get to wherever it was we were going. We just went. Two babes, two fools.

Soon we were in great pain, especially our feet. We hurt mentally, too, because we didn't know our route or destination. The trail was marked, and we knew it had an end point, but the legend on a signboard that said, say, "Half Way Camp 15

Miles" meant nothing to us because we didn't understand what walking-miles meant in terms of time and effort. We experienced hour after hour of pain, drudgery, and mental uncertainty.

And, after fifty years, what I remember most vividly of our excursion is the alpine beauty, the clarity of the northern and western air, and the mystery of the wilderness. It was literally wonder-full. We were two young fools doing something with the tang of adventure in it. Had we not walked through our fear and pain into the unknown, and passed through this threshold to other adventures, our lives would be greatly diminished today.

IN ALASKA WE had careers to make (teaching), a household to establish, children to raise. Professional and domestic life was demanding and satisfying. But I hadn't gone North to live like an Easterner.

In Chapter 1 I described how, in the summer of 1974, I walked north to south across the Arctic National Wildlife Refuge, from Barter Island to Arctic Village, with three friends. I wasn't entirely green when I did that trip, but I had a lot to learn, and I learned it. I came out of that trip emotionally, even spiritually, transformed, and I fell passionately in love with the Refuge. I have since returned there many times, and going there continues to be one of my several annual pilgrimages. One trip in particular placed my fear in sharp and intimidating focus.

In 1979 I walked with my friend Tom from Ambrusvajun Lake (also called Last Lake) in the Sheenjek valley to the Beaufort Sea coast. One night we camped in a high pass near the continental divide. A good camp in a tight notch. We camped there because a late afternoon thunderstorm prompted us to stop for the day.

In the early morning, about 3:00 AM, Tom awakened me:

"Something's out there." He had heard our cook pots rattle.

We slept with our feet to the door of the tent. We sat up, which put our heads about three feet from the door, and Tom unzipped it and pulled it back. Peering at us, head at the opening, was a grizzly.

I remember, first, the rippling of the bear's fur, like a carpet. Then the bear shifted position and its head occupied the center of my visual field just two or three feet away. Of the head, I remember two very large, very wet nostrils, and small, flat, amber eyes.

To this day I have never seen anything as empty as the dull flat eyes of that bear. Empty of meaning, compassion, morality, purpose: anything human that I automatically projected on to it. There was nothing I could recognize in those eyes. They were the eyes of the wild, amoral and opportunistic. I remember thinking, and thinking often afterwards, that this was Death. The deep horror of death was upon me as I looked at those eyes. I saw the absolute indifference of nature personified in that face, and fear was deep in my guts. In two seconds the bear could badly cripple both of us and then gnaw on us, living or dead, at his leisure. Our deaths would have had as much meaning as the deaths of two ground squirrels. My precious intricate body, flesh, intelligence, meaning, history, love, all reduced to bear shit.

I remember watching a large female grizzly with a cub excavate a ground squirrel den in Denali National Park. She must have weighed 700 pounds. To excavate the maze of tunnels, she quickly and easily moved many cubic yards of soil and rock; a tremendous demonstration of strength. Yet when the ground squirrel finally was forced to run for its life between her legs, she swapped ends as quickly as a cat—it was instantaneous—and nailed the little fellow. He had no chance whatsoever. That combination of raw strength, agility, and speed formed an image that often comes to my mind when I am in bear country.

This bear backed off slowly, gave the air a deep sniff, and then ran when we yelled and clapped, depositing a large stool. It too was afraid.

Here was a face of the wilderness I had not yet confronted. Of course by this time I had been traveling in bear country for years, had seen many bears, knew the standard methods of dealing with bears, but I had never had one at my front door that I knew of.

To a bear, a tent is nothing, a filament of fabric with little substance. A firearm (we had one) is useless to a sleeping man, and in any case at very close range it cannot instantly be brought into play. I became aware that early morning of my vulnerability. I learned that, though there are ways of avoiding bear encounters, and of minimizing their dangers, in the end the game is his. One of my great wilderness lessons was that, when all is said and done, the bear is in charge.

I did not sleep again that night, and I did not sleep well for the rest of that trip. For years afterwards, I awakened at 3:00 AM when in the wilderness, thoughts of death in my mind.

What I felt then, and for years, was dread. Fear has an object and prompts action; dread goes deeper: it's when you get a look at the end and it is dark there and you can do nothing to help yourself.

The object of my fear walked abroad, but the dread abided within me. I needed to convert my dread into simple fear, and then learn to deal with the fear. I can't say that I eventually "conquered" my fear, but I did master it, years later, when I took a series of solo trips in the Refuge. Traveling alone gave me an education that I could not have gotten otherwise. I eventually learned to sleep well in the wilderness.

DURING THE YEARS when our children were young we traveled

much in remote areas. Jeremy and Amy both took their inaugural wilderness trips at eighteen months of age, extended trips, by canoe. We continued to travel together until they left for college; we still travel together when possible, though they are now likely to be doing their own trips. Our trips as a family are memorable for their simple pleasure, but I remember too those long nights in the wild, when they were still young. My mind churned. Who brought these kids here? Who is responsible for them? Who is really in control of the situation? Or perhaps "control" is the wrong concept entirely.

Crossing a lake, Amy in Di's arms in the bow, Jeremy between her feet. In the stern I use a kayak paddle because Di often can't get her hands free to paddle, and I can't J-stroke with power adequate to move our load. The load is two adults, two children, one very large pack, and a medium sized pack: enough food and gear for ten days. Plenty of weight.

I usually traveled near shore but open crossings were often necessary. While crossing an arm, a wind comes up, hitting us sideways. A chop builds, and our canoe is in the troughs. I quarter left, quarter right, do my best to maintain a stable boat and make headway.

By objective standards, these conditions are not particularly hazardous. The boat is bouncing but we are in danger only if we do something grossly stupid. But my subjective response is quite different. My jaw clamps down, my mouth dries out, my heart rate accelerates. I brace the canoe with my knees. I yearn for the lee, I push hard for it. I am frustrated that it takes so long to get there. My jaw unclenches only when we slip into shelter.

Who put these children, and this woman, in this situation? Who is solely responsible for their well-being and safety? My intellectual grasp of our objective situation is a reference point for me. I know that we are as safe in the wilderness as anywhere;

I know that the objective hazards are slight. But that knowledge doesn't make my anxiety disappear.

Yet I would never have considered not doing such a trip. Extended canoe trips; sea kayaking; bicycle trips on highways; backpacking in the mountains. Later, extended dog-mushing trips, expedition length treks, wild river floats. I know that wilderness travel is safe given the proper knowledge, equipment, and judgment, but when you have the added responsibility of ensuring the safety of the youngsters, your view of the world changes.

But I—we—passed through each of these thresholds, pushed the borders of our lives back. Fear, however, was mostly my problem. The children, when young, rarely, if ever, felt fear; Di, bless her heart, trusted me.

The burden of fear was worth carrying. That the children did remarkable trips before they were out of their teens had a powerful and salutary effect on their approaches to life.

They learned many things: the practical skills of wilderness travel, such as navigation, providing shelter, cooking; the psychological traits of patience and emotional stability; the intellectual traits of ingenuity, clear-headedness, good judgment; the physical traits of strength, endurance, fortitude. In other words, they learned to be self-sufficient. They learned to live without debilitating fear. I am also sure that, when they began to challenge themselves on their own, that they met fear, faced it, pushed through it to new levels of living.

Scenes from the Noatak River: the kayak rudder jams right, we rotate into a strong clockwise eddy, we can't get out of it. The right side of the kayak sucks down, the rotation is too strong, over goes the double kayak, one of the most sickening sensations I have ever felt. The water was perhaps 50 F. Overcast, strong north wind. When I flounder to the bank I am exhausted, my lungs burn, but I need to be up and chasing our gear, my wet clothes binding me; I feel anchored. Ahead lies the threat of hypothermia, the task of re-grouping, and, most difficult, the challenge of facing my fear of getting back into the boat and on the river again.

On the Noatak, years later, in a raft. Upriver winds force our party to tow the raft *downstream.*

Again on the Noatak, in a raft. It rains upriver for a day, then it rains harder, then the skies just let loose. The river rises seven vertical feet in less than thirty hours. At midnight I move the raft and retie it; during breakfast the river enters our tent sites; then we move the kitchen and the entire camp to yet higher ground. The velocity of the river quadruples. Down river, a four-foot high standing wave with a reverse curl has formed at a ledge where there is normally a big wrinkle in the water. The roar and the strength of the river are overpowering. Through the watery, gloomy atmosphere the Arctic looks like the end of the world.

Kenai Fjords National Park, McCarty Fjord. Alone. It starts raining the day I expect my airplane, which doesn't arrive because of the weather. It rains hard and steady for two days. I divide my time between the tarp, the tent, and short walks. On the third day it rains harder, the wind stronger. On the fourth day the rain increases to monsoon intensity. In my rain gear, under a double tarp (10' X 16'), I get wet because the entire atmosphere is saturated with water. My tent finally fails and I tarp it, which works. I later learn that in the eleven hours 8:00 AM-7:00 PM it rained a fraction more than five inches.

On the fifth day the rain begins to slacken. Day six is sunny and I emerge from my darkness.

HIKING IN THE Brooks Range. Di and I are headed for a rendezvous point after eighteen days of travel. We've been in a steady cold drizzle for a week but the streams haven't come up. However, the rain intensifies and we awaken to find a flooded stream at our tent door. We must cross three flooded streams in the next two days, as well as make our miles, which include crossing two high passes.

It took an hour to get across the first stream. Soaked boots, wet socks; rain. Hike around the toe of the mountains to the next drainage. Since we broke camp the streams have risen steadily. This next one is full, every braid filled to the brim and running fast, opaque with brown silt.

We cross in boots without socks, and only rain pants on our legs. We pick braids, feel for shallows, moving upstream from bar to bar, avoiding the deeper channels, seeking the shallowest crossing. We pick our way upstream for a full mile before we finally cross the last channel. We dump the water from our boots and squeeze out what water we can, put on our wet socks, put on our polyethylene long johns under our rain pants, and cross willow flats and bog to higher ground.

A violent thunderstorm is moving up the valley. This is very weird: the thunderstorm is embedded in the larger storm system. We scramble to make camp before the heavier storm hits us, and we just get in the tent before it slams through the area.

A respite from the hard rain the next morning, but when we get to the next drainage we find that it remains in full flood, and we repeat the ordeal of yesterday. Once across, we locate the route to our pass. As we cross a large bog to the base of the mountains, the rain resumes, and it intensifies as we climb. The temperature drops.

We climb to the pass in rain, sweating in our rain gear in spite of the cold. As we descend the other side, rain falls in sheets. At the bottom of our descent we slog through a willow tangle growing in a bog. We're almost in, less than a hundred yards from our rendezvous, when we encounter a stream in the willows, a ditch, waist deep and just a foot too wide to jump across.

THESE ENCOUNTERS WERE not, under the circumstances, life-threatening. Nor were they unusual: I selected them as typical problems a wilderness traveler may face. None constitute the makings of stories of high adventure. But all show aspects of nature that can press down on you, slowly and inexorably intimidate you. When will it let up? When will the storm finally break, the cold fog lift, the frigid wind abate? In one sense, nature's relentless indifference intimidates me more than her violence. She has all the time in the world, which fact challenges my character. I must be patient. Patience requires humility. To understand and deal with nature, I must conquer myself.

When nature leans on you this way, the subjective response is all-important. The little nagging fears are as hard to deal with as the big overpowering fears. In my experience, the typical encounter with the wilderness does not include the dangerous and the epic. Rather, the challenges to one's character lie in the long-term, ordinary, daily demands of life. After a week of rain, it takes an act of courage to get out of bed when the pounding of water on the tent intensifies. Fortitude is usually expressed in the small acts of daily life: living in wet socks, sweating in your rain gear during a stiff climb, breaking camp during a summer snowstorm, being tent-bound for days. Perhaps patience is the unrecognized foundation of fortitude.

Of course, courage is one human response to fear. Another response is recognition of the facts, including the fact of our vulnerability, and the acceptance of those facts.

One July, near the end of a five week excursion, we were camped on a river flat in the northeast Alaskan Arctic, in the Arctic National Wildlife Refuge. I had gone out in the morning to climb a mountain and see the country. In the early evening I made my way towards camp, moving downriver along old river benches, mostly alpine tundra with willow thickets in the draws and in patches here and there. I remember thinking, this is a good place to surprise a bear; be alert.

I walked north along the edge of a bench. Our camp was at the base of the bench, perhaps six feet lower, on a tundra flat. I pushed through some willows, and there he was, stationary, pigeon-toed, big-headed and big-bodied, peering down the bank into our camp. He wasn't aware of me. He was watching my family eat dinner.

I ducked into the willows and quickly circled towards camp. As I approached camp I couldn't see the bear but I could see my family, seated on the ground, their backs to the bear, focused on their food. Di looked up with her bright smile of greeting; I responded only by pointing.

The resultant tableau was memorable indeed. All heads swiveled, focused on a point I couldn't see; all bowls and spoons were suspended motionless. Then slow movement. Bowls to the ground; everyone slowly erect; then gradual movement away from the bear, which must have been less than thirty feet away.

I remember Di's response best. She slowly padded backwards, towards the tent, slowly unzipped it, slowly extracted my firearm. I stepped forward into camp where I could see the bear. He was deep-bodied and heavy. (I say "he" because there were no cubs or yearlings present.) Also, he was in no hurry. This bothered me. Bears in that country usually flee precipitately at the first indication of human presence. He was much too casual, too interested. He had been observing my family for much too long. Several minutes had elapsed since I first saw him, and I had no idea how long he had been there before I arrived.

Another half minute, or less, elapsed. His forefeet hit the ground and he slowly bounded away, it seemed to me reluctantly. I could feel the ground vibrate with his weight.

None of us were seriously shaken by this encounter, but it made concrete what I had often wondered: How many times had I been observed by bears or other wildlife as I lay asleep, walked through brush, had my back turned from the world as humans so often do? Humans typically sit in a circle, which often shuts out a view of the world; we are often more aware of each other than we are of our environment; in any case, we certainly know less of what happens around us than do animals. I think that we may be more often the observed than the observers, at least by wolves, bears, and foxes.

ANOTHER LONG TREK; daughter Amy fifteen years old. Two viewpoints.

In the Arctic National Wildlife Refuge; walking upstream, the creek on our left. Amy and a companion hiking about half a mile ahead of Di and me. We spot a female grizzly with a cub in the creek bottom. We want to signal to Amy that there is a bear in the area but she's too far away. We see her briefly on the skyline, then she disappears beyond the shoulder of the mountain.

The bear moves around the area, poking about, grazing, as bears do. Then we lose sight of her and the cub. We pick up our pace, hoping that Amy has stopped and that we can overtake her. Before long, however, we see on the horizon, at nearly the spot where Amy disappeared, the female and her cub running towards us. The cub has no trouble keeping up, though the pace is fast. They run past us at a distance of about fifty yards.

We hurry forward with considerable anxiety. The bear must have come close to Amy and Pedar. Our relief is immense when we finally spot them unharmed on the tundra; but as we approach we see that they are badly shaken. Amy's hands tremble noticeably.

Amy's viewpoint: she and Pedar saw the bear and cub to their left, along the creek. The bear was between 300 and 400 yards away and therefore did not seem to pose much of a threat. However, for some reason, the bear began lumbering across the tundra and uphill on a direct line for the young people.

This was unexpected and frightening. The two humans have absolutely no place to go. There are no trees, of course, no vegetation higher than their ankles, no cliffs to climb. It is worse than useless to run, since running may stimulate a chase response in the bear, and in any case the bear is much too fast for them: a bear can outrun a horse over a short distance.

And so they must stand their ground. They drop their packs and stand upright together to appear as tall and as big as possible. They shout, clap their hands, wave their arms. On comes the bear.

This is the part that is hard to understand. How does it feel to stand up to a charging grizzly, a female with the well-known fierce maternal instinct to protect her cub? No weapon, no place to go, no options. Just stand upright and bold.

However the young people felt, they did it. The grizzly broke off her charge at about thirty feet, turned ninety degrees, and headed along their back trail, where Di and I saw her.

We never could establish why the bear did this. Was she confused by swirling human scent? Did she mistake Amy and

Pedar for caribou, or another bear? Perhaps a male bear had been in the area threatening her cub. It is likely that the female had seen very few humans in her lifetime, and a possibility that she had encountered none, and so may have had no reason to be either antagonistic toward or fearful of humans. In this case nature just seemed to play a wild card, and the youngsters had to deal with the joker in the pack.

ANOTHER EXTENDED TREK, also in the Refuge, with Amy and Jennifer. We had been hiking in very cool weather for four or five days, then the heat set in for a day. We moved upstream through a mountain valley, intending to cross a high pass into another drainage. The temperature must have been in the 80s F. I was bathed in sweat every step of the way, and when we made camp in the afternoon I was quick to wash up, rinse out some clothes, and try to cool down. I sat baking in the oppressive heat, utterly lethargic. Had there been some wind I would have been comfortable, but it was dead calm.

In the middle of the night I heard the unmistakable rustle of snowflakes on the tent fabric. By morning three or four inches of snow had fallen, the gray skies were low, and visibility was extremely restricted. After breakfast we went back into our tents to wait it out: journals, books, naps.

Conditions were unchanged the next morning, except that the snow was deeper. We were less willing to wait it out now—the interiors of the tents were becoming tiresome. We repeatedly studied the unbroken mass of gray cloud, trying to convince ourselves that we could see thin spots or holes, that it was breaking up. In the afternoon we broke camp and walked up the valley several miles and camped at the base of the climb to the pass.

Another tedious night; the storm continued. Very limited visibility the next day. We continued to imagine thin spots or holes in the clouds, and by late afternoon deceived ourselves into believing that the storm was breaking up. We struck camp and headed up the stream-carved gully to find the pass. We climbed into the clouds.

There is a special ambiance to a summer snowstorm, especially when one is hiking in it. I live in a region that is dominated by extreme weather, especially winter weather, and each season has its special emotional tone. In the autumn the first snowfall of the season creates a blanket. This cliché is unavoidable, because it is so apt: the snow not only covers, but it protects and warms, and it silences. It creates a uniform surface, and it muffles and dulls sound. This blanketing effect is enhanced by lowering skies and a severely reduced horizon. One falls back into one's self emotionally, one's world becomes smaller and more intimate. A summer storm has this quality.

Our route was the gully, and we moved easily from rock to rock as if up an irregular staircase. In sections it steepened and was more like climbing a ladder. The packs were heavy and the climb steep but we were ready for some activity and this first phase of our traverse over the pass went quickly.

Visibility was fifty yards at most, and when the creek began to flatten out as we gained elevation we had some difficult navigational decisions. My first instinct was to follow the creek, but we eventually became aware that the creek drained a higher area of mountains to the east, not the pass. We backtracked and decided to reorient ourselves.

Our map was barely adequate. Its scale was 1:250,000, the only scale available from the USGS for that area at the time. We drew some inferences based on brief glimpses of peaks and saddles which occasionally appeared through the clouds, and then set off on a compass course, which we followed for an hour or two. The incessant whiteout, the lack of horizon, became oppressive and claustrophobic. I began to feel trapped.

After three days of storm the snow accumulation was substantial, especially at our higher elevation, and the wind was brisk. In the area of the pass we had been stomping around in snow to about mid-calf. We were not cold, though we were hiking in summer weight clothing; our activity kept us warm, and we had enough warm clothing with us to deal with an emergency; yet it was a psychological relief to find the overcast thinning as we moved along our compass line. My claustrophobic feeling eased, and we could see enough to find landmarks to confirm our position.

The pass, we found, was not a true pass defined by a saddle, but a plateau. The plateau ended in cliffs. The only route down was in a steep creek gully. This channel was a series of waterfalls up to ten feet high, with large boulders. Most of the water in the creek, including the many falls, was frozen. Snow had drifted into the leeward slopes and crannies.

We had no ropes, crampons, ice axes. Therefore our descent was slow and careful; no slips allowed.

By now it was midnight. The storm on this side of the pass was less intense, and a bit more light was coming through the clouds. We could make out bare ground far below us, and I wanted to be there. But the watchword now was "caution"; slow and easy.

We could scramble down much of the upper section, but a series of larger waterfalls, now frozen cliffs, blocked the middle section. We negotiated these by passing our packs down by hand so that we had the mobility to do some scrambling unhampered by weight and bulk. The key thing to remember was to stay off sloping ice.

Eventually the creek gradient eased, we put our packs on, and we walked out onto bare talus. The going remained slow because the gradient, though reduced, was still steep, and the broken talus was large and jumbled. But at least we were on bare ground, we were over the pass, and the storm was lifting.

There was no place to camp in the canyon we entered: rock, rock, rock. So we kept moving, in a hard cold north wind. It was a relief when, after several hours, some vegetation began to appear as we moved down the valley. We camped at the first good location. It was 3:00 AM.

Three and a half days of white landscape, narrow horizons, gray sky, gray rock. What an enormous relief for the eye and the spirit to be back in a world of open horizons, water running free, and lovely luscious living green.

SPINOZA TAUGHT THAT happiness consists of moving from a state of lesser to one of greater perfection. Perhaps I do violence to his philosophy here, but it does seem to me that the impetus for this salutary transition must be courage, and its nemesis fear. Cowardice can affect any part of life, of course, and intellectual and moral cowardice are probably harder to correct than physical fear. In my experience, however, all the aspects of life form a unity. Confronting physical fear forms my character in the moral sphere; intellectual courage informs moral courage and buttresses physical courage; moral courage enables intellectual and physical courage to be expressed in action.

As I wrote in a previous chapter, Jean Craighead George suggests in her beautiful book *Julie of the Wolves* that the three qualities most valued by the old Inupiat were love, intelligence, and courage. Indeed. What else is there?

CHAPTER 6

At Home as a Nomad

In her interesting book *Four Seasons North* Billie Wright discusses the concept of "koviashuktok." This Nunamiut word translates as "the condition of being fully and pleasantly in the present moment." She learned the practice of this concept from a Nunamiut woman, and she and her husband pursued this ideal when they lived for a year in a remote cabin in Alaska's Brooks Range.

The word, and the concept, has resonated for me since I encountered them forty years ago. The wilderness traveler must bear the concept of koviashuktok in mind if his experience is to yield its full value. And with practice, one may, with care and vigilance, bring this attitude to all of one's experience. Unfortunately, for me this last statement is hypothetical: I haven't yet attained koviashuktok throughout my life, partly because our culture does not include this possibility. Our culture has plans for us; to attain koviashuktok requires that we to some extent reject our culture. As long as we chose to live within our culture—and is there a choice?—those plans and patterns are difficult to deny.

One of my friends, unfamiliar with the word, nevertheless comes at a similar viewpoint through the practice of Zen. Other people I know practice some form of quiet time, meditation, or some equivalent. Interestingly, the "equivalent" is often a form of activity, such as running or walking, which may clear the head by using a rhythmic pattern as a focus—or, for some people, clarity is achieved through physical exhaustion.

One obvious distinction separates Eastern and Western approaches to mental peace: the East stresses method, with a devaluation of content: practice first, Enlightenment later. Western philosophy and religion probe first for content, and neglect practice. In the West, philosophers tend to teach that discipline is the result of the enlightenment that follows from knowledge, or by force of will reinforced by knowledge. Religions usually rely on abstinence as a form of discipline: from sex, certain foods, alcohol or caffeine. The model of behavior is sainthood, where beatitude is usually achieved through punishment of the body. These negative disciplines seem unsatisfactory to me. Abstinence may remind me of some religious precept, but to what insight does it lead? If I learn to hate my body, and am therefore somehow led to release the spirit, I am nevertheless merely playing a zero-sum game.

My temperament favors Stoicism, which is based on the Socratic attitude towards life, the foundation of which is that the universe is reasonable and therefore, at basis, good. This profound optimism is, unfortunately, based on faith rather than upon empirical evidence. No matter how often I read Socrates or Marcus Aurelius or Spinoza, I come away with the conviction that the logic does not compel me to recognize an ultimately good universe. For me, in the end, it is a matter of faith, or perhaps temperament, that leads me to that conclusion.

Recently I read a little book on the practice of Zen for beginners; I was also at the time re-reading Marcus Aurelius' *Meditations*. The advice of Shunyo Suzuki (*Zen Mind, Beginner's Mind*) was to put any search for enlightenment aside, and instead concentrate only on the practice of quieting the body and mind. On the other hand, Marcus' book, one I love, was stuffed with Enlightenment: moral advice, rules of behavior, assertions about the ultimate reasonableness of the universe, the need to fulfill civic obligations, and above all, observations on death. But on this reading, I asked myself, yes, but how? Through the force of logic? By sheer will power? Do I consist of content only, and no method?

I RECALL WITH intense fondness one warm July afternoon on Wolf Creek, in the central Brooks Range. My friend Stacy and I had been traveling for eighteen days by foot through what is now Gates of the Arctic National Park and Preserve. We began walking at Anaktuvuk Pass, traveled via Ernie Pass to the Koyukuk, circled towards the Tinayguk River via Cachwona Creek, and camped at Wolf Creek before turning north up the Tinayguk towards Anaktuvuk Pass again.

It rained in the morning and we stayed in the tent. I was in that trance-like state which is the upper edge of sleep, where the mind wanders and dreams but is also aware, on the edge of consciousness, exquisitely relaxed but keenly alert. (Readers of Keats' poems will recognize this condition of relaxed alertness; it is conducive to emotional receptivity and insight.) I slept and slept, dozed and dozed, far beyond what my body required. I dreamed of people and events that I hadn't remembered in decades, events and people that I had forgotten I had forgotten. I was emotionally and mentally transported through time and space. Sleep like this is indeed bliss.

Later, I read. I wrote. I walked along the stream. I stared into space. I did "nothing." I was not bored.

The sky cleared in the late afternoon and Stacy waded to a large rock in Wolf Creek. He sat on it facing west. I too was immobile, my back against a balsam poplar. We must have sat thus for hours, but in truth I don't know how long we sat, because we were not aware of time.

We discussed this later, and agreed that the word "koviashuktok" best named the condition that we had achieved at this point in our trip. We were content to be exactly where we were. We were not going anywhere, not to Anaktuvuk Pass or Bettles or Anchorage, though our travels would take us there. We were where we were supposed to be, fully and pleasantly in the present moment: we were home.

My American Heritage dictionary offers three definitions of "home" that suggest our condition. "*n*. An environment offering security and happiness. A valued place regarded as a refuge or place of origin." For my purposes I would couple the phrase "state of mind" with "a valued place." My home is the place I attach myself to in the wilderness, the ground I walk on, the patch of tundra where I pitch my tent; and it is the emotional envelope that encloses me when I respond to that place. That is where I belong, that is where *I am*. My nomadic existence in the wilderness is entirely consonant with this concept of "home."

CONSIDER THE ELEGANCE of a tent. A lightweight home that is inexpensive; that is weatherproof and bugproof; that requires little maintenance; that always smells good, whether of the must of storage or the fragrance of shifting air; that creates a feeling of independence such as a gypsy or nomad must feel; that brings its occupants together. My fabric home has played a large part in my emotional life, and in the life of my family.

When we pitch our tent, we have a secure place, a nest, a home. If it rains, and if we are tired, there is no such thing as going to bed too early. To smell the air, to hear the rain tap lightly or pound rhythmically, to creep deep into the sleeping bag, to see the children and their mother very near, is to be content. Let it rain all night and into the morning: I could stay there indefinitely, letting the world filter into my mind through a light sleep. I am not only sheltered and rested, but I am also with my family in a primal way, like a pile of puppies.

This sleep is not a period of oblivion. It is a form of experience. During a prolonged rain or snow storm I may be asleep so long that I am rested well before dawn, and I experience the luxury of knowing that I can stay comfortable indefinitely. Listen to the rain, smell the air, hear the birds, absorb the ambience; if I slip away into sleep, I don't shut these things out; rather, they become part of the experience of sleep. I am conscious of sleep itself, I *participate* in it.

I feel the completeness of my rest. I watch my son read, my wife and daughter sleep. Little Amy curls deep in her bag, a soft pocket of warmth, vulnerable and protected. And as eyes open and people stretch, I might have a wrestling match on hand: like a pile of puppies.

PERHAPS KOVIASHUKTOK CAN be attained in a social setting. The conviviality of friends can place me fully and pleasantly in the present moment. But I am inclined to think that silence is most conducive to koviashuktok. I've noticed on my wilderness trips that the quantity of talk diminishes as the trip progresses, and conversely, compulsive chattiness can be positively offensive. Hours, almost entire days, may pass with few words spoken. Silence in this context is not a negative value. It is a positive quality, a necessary condition for clear thinking, mental balance, and emotional receptivity. Too many words may equate with too little feeling. In the wilderness, one must feel well to see well, to be open to the experience.

Our culture prohibits koviashuktok. I lack the ability to be fully and pleasantly in the present moment while sitting at a stop light. Turn on the car radio, and I am further from it than before. Observe the motley spectacle of the roadside, and one's peace is lost. The American "freeway" or interstate is the exact analogue of anti-koviashuktok: noise, restlessness, speed; going there, not being there. A good Buddhist would I suppose not lose his centeredness in a turbulent environment, but where does that leave the rest of us?

IN SOME WAYS, I feel my greatest sense of unease when I am living in my house. However, I paradoxically believe that freedom, and happiness, is being always at home. I imagine old-time Bedouins as being free and happy because, no matter where they were, they were at home. This must be true of any nomad or semi-nomad: pre-contact Yupik and Inupiat, Gwich'in, Mongol herders, Sami.

When I travel in remote areas, every material object I need is right on my back or in my boat. This provides enormous satisfaction. On my back I carry: housing, sleeping comfort, protection from cold and wet, navigational aids, food and the means to prepare it, the means to hunt and fish, binoculars and camera, health aids, and entertainment—even knowledge and wisdom—in books. I have everything I need, not just to survive but to live well, for a month or more. When I live in my house, I "need" several thousand square feet of space, machines such as furnaces and refrigerators, a car, and so forth. Yet in my house I am restricted, confined, burdened by things and customs. It is a paradox that I am freer walking at one mile per hour with a pack on my back than I am driving at fifty-five miles per hour in the comfort of my car.

The price I pay for the freedom of the wilderness is effort, but this is not a zero-sum game; the effort is wholesome in all regards, physical, mental, emotional; the burden I carry is merely an extension of myself.

A late spring camp

In his book on Gandhi (*Gandhi's Truth*) Erik Erickson observes that thinking and walking can be closely connected. He noted Gandhi's habit of walking and talking—and here talking and thinking are virtually identical—and I thought of Thoreau's daily excursions and the fruit they bore. Wordsworth, and many of the English Romantics, were great ramblers, and one is prompted to observe the role of pilgrimages in the world's religions. Socrates did much of his thinking and talking on the hoof, under the open sky, and we can picture Plato's students walking with their teacher through the groves of the Academy, as did Aristotle's students at the Lyceum. Much of Jesus' teaching was done while walking, or standing exposed to the sky. We traditionally teach afoot—hence "pedagogue"—and the prefix likewise refers to "base", as in "pediment." Foundation.

I think that walking and thinking are complimentary activities because both drive forward. Both involve a sense of progression and development. The need to move may be a symptom of restlessness, but I think that it can also serve as a calming focus akin to meditation, with the difference that it draws one out of one's self and forward while also allowing for inwardness, contemplation. I am temperamentally disinclined to practice passive, stationary meditation. (I cannot recall seeing any image of the Buddha afoot. He is in the open, true, though often associated with a well-rooted tree, and his traditional position is seated.) My predisposition is to engage the world outside of myself. I recognize acutely the, perhaps unfortunate, human requirement that one must be intensely involved with one's self, but it seems to me that engagement with the larger world can be an antidote to self-involvement and pride; observation and engagement with what is outside one's self may be a beneficial anti-narcissism.

AT THEIR BEST, science and the scientist must submit to the world and be disciplined by it. This submission to the facts of reality may, paradoxically, be a source of freedom. I got a sense of this when I encountered these words of Albert Einstein's (as quoted in *The New Yorker*):

> Even when I was a fairly precocious young man, the

nothingness of the hopes and strivings which chases most men restlessly through life came to my consciousness with considerable vitality....Out yonder there was this huge world, which exists independently of us human beings and which stands before us like a great, eternal riddle....The contemplation of this world beckoned like a liberation, and I soon noticed that many a man whom I had learned to esteem and to admire had found inner freedom and security in devoted occupation with it.

I think it is fair to say that, by going outside himself and subordinating his self to a larger reality, Einstein was able to check the natural pridefulness that all humans must deal with one way or another (most by succumbing to and reveling in pride, fewer by combating and stifling it, at least to some degree). I think it is significant that a man who, of all men, had a reason to be prideful, was to the contrary most likely to recognize its dangers. Intelligence is often a source of pride, but in Einstein's case he could use his intelligence to get beyond himself to something greater. Of course, he did not say that he was stifling pride, but rather that he was liberated by a contemplation of the great world, and that this gave him security as well as freedom (an interesting paradox); in a word, meaning. He could only do this by keeping himself firmly in harness. Genius without focused work has no value. He had no freedom without his harness. He subordinated himself to the world.

As Plato would point out, Eros is at the root of this sentiment, and I would add, Beauty. I have come to the conviction that all good things spring from Love and Beauty, and that the two together are based on a single Something that I cannot name. Love and Beauty have a common root, and where they exist together, there one finds the Good. These ancient ideas are not merely old clichés and abstractions, for I find them embodied and alive in people and things. I can see them, touch them, experience them. They are palpably real.

Einstein could examine some of the inner workings of the universe using mathematics and science. I cannot do this; his insights and methods are beyond my abilities and reach. But there are other mortals whose ideas, methods, and above all, actions, are within my understanding: the Muries, Bob Marshall, Aldo Leopold, and Sigurd Olson form a sextet of thinkers and doers who lived lives of goodness because they loved the world, and created beauty through their actions and writings. Whatever the arena in which one works, this expression of Love and Beauty must be our highest mission.

Like his scientist brother Adolph, Olaus Murie brought more than logic and method to his researches. I keep his words in a prominent place: "A poetic appreciation of life, combined with a knowledge of nature, creates humility, which in turn becomes the greatness of man." Beauty, Love, knowledge, and the suppression of pride, yield greatness.

It is well known that Margaret Murie attained a kind of greatness through love. Love permeates her book *Two in the Far North*. Bob Marshall and Sigurd Olson inspired people to seek the adventurous life in the wilderness, and their works are filled with love of the world bottomed on an ethical approach to that world. Aldo Leopold in *A Sand County Almanac* and other essays created beauty joined to intellectual activity and rigor, a great accomplishment. I can't think of any other small group who accomplished as much good in the world.

An appreciation of Love and Beauty, particularly in connection to the natural world, is precisely what is missing in our social and economic life. On the other hand, the conjunction of pride and materialism is a fatal connection.

KOVIASHUKTOK: BEING FULLY and pleasantly in the present moment. So I feel when in the wilderness, at home, a nomad, where I can reach outside of myself, forget my nagging ego, and find sources of love and beauty within myself and in the great world. The word "Refuge" in Arctic National Wildlife Refuge indicates a haven not only for the plants, animals, and natural landscape, but a refuge for the human spirit as well. I give thanks to the forces of nature that created it, and the humans who have protected it.

CHAPTER 7

The Refuge in Winter

Most visitors to the Refuge come in the summer, or more accurately, for part of the summer, from mid-June through mid-August. A few trickle in before or after that, backpackers from about June 5 or so, hunters through early September. Most visitors travel by raft, which is only possible or comfortable in the two months I mentioned.

When we visitors withdraw to our other lives, it is easy to forget that life in the Refuge carries on. I have tried to imagine the conditions of life there in the winter—caribou, moose, wolverine, marten, ptarmigan—and it seems unimaginable in its tenuousness and difficulty. And that life includes human existence, Inupiat on the coast, Gwitch'in south of the divide, for perhaps the past 10,000 years, likely more. Most of us, I think, have trouble imagining life in Medieval Europe, or the old Romans, or the ancient Greeks, all relatively recent eras. I have tried to imagine the slow progression of the centuries, the ten millennia or more of human life in the Arctic—8,000 years before the birth of Christ—with its long annual period of darkness and deep cold; and I am provoked and stymied.

SUNLIGHT NORTH

IN 1998 MY FRIEND Heimo Korth invited me to spend part of the late winter with his family on the Colleen River in the Refuge just south of the Divide. I had been planning a cross-country ski trip in the southern Refuge, perhaps beginning or ending at Arctic Village, and I wanted to visit the Korths also, but I didn't want to impose on them or be excessively dependent upon them. This invitation was a chance to mesh the two activities, by staying with them for a while, but then moving on. I accepted his invitation.

I had done many ski treks by this time in my life, but never north of the Arctic Circle, and I knew I had to plan carefully.

My first step was to obtain a 6' X 8' nylon dome tent, not expedition grade. All of my tents were backpacking tents. For this trip, I wanted something big enough to accommodate a wood stove, but small enough to pack in my pulk (a sled designed to be pulled by a skier). I bought a stove of sheet steel about 15" X 12" X 18" with small diameter telescoping pipe. This is often called a Yukon stove. Also two stove jacks: plastic rings, highly heat resistant, that I sewed into the tent and tent fly above where I wanted the stove to be positioned. I put in the stove, erect the pipe, cut the wood, start the fire, and I'm warm.

These were my only purchases for the trip. I packed my winter gear, organized for camping and travel, and packed travel food for three weeks; high calorie food for hard work and low temperatures. For example, I normally eat little fat, but I included a hefty chunk of sausage with my normal breakfast of oatmeal, and another chunk with my lunch. (Nevertheless, I lost ten pounds during the twenty-two days I was in the field.) I also took a cooler of food for the Korths, with an emphasis on fresh vegetables, and protein that would be a change for them, such as shrimp.

I left Anchorage by car for Fairbanks on March 24. It was warming—early spring—in south central Alaska. In the Interior, Fairbanks too was warm, the snow thin, the roads sloppy. I knew that it would not be so in the Arctic.

I stayed in pilot Eric Sterling's hangar. In truth, the hangar was a house, planes and workshop downstairs, facing the runway, the living quarters upstairs. This was a boy's dream, the ultimate tree house, club house, bachelor's heaven.

Eric was one of several pilots who flew support for the Korths over the years, so he knew the vagaries of flying at that latitude at that time of year, and he also knew the characteristics of the Korths' winter airstrip. I knew Eric from a previous trip into the Refuge, when he flew support for our rafting group, and I liked him personally and thought he was a good pilot.

Before we took off, Eric tactfully asked me if I still wanted to do this—at this point I planned to ski from the Korths' to Arctic Village—and I said yes. We left the relative warmth of Fairbanks, and as we flew north we flew back in time, back into winter. Our route north from Fairbanks was very familiar, over the White Mountains, across the Yukon Flats, past the area of Fort Yukon. Eric and I had a pleasant chat over the headsets, and I studied the ground, imagining what I was about to undertake. North of the Yukon River the world was flat, black, white, and gray. Spiky spruce, aspen and poplar flats, frozen bog, tundra, rivers locked in ice. Farther north, low mountains, which were southern extensions of the higher northern Brooks Range, came into view, with ridges stretching north. Sheenjek River. Porcupine River. Boulder Creek. Lake Creek. Pass Creek. Strangle Woman Creek. As we approached the Korths', I could not pick out the cabin—Heimo had hidden it very well.

The approach was typical of bush flying: you're coming in at what seems excessive speed to an area that seems too short and rough for even a small plane. The landing was routine.

I stepped out into another world.

SUNLIGHT NORTH

WHEN A SMALL plane lands on a bush airstrip, there is usually a period of hectic activity. The pilot wants to get unloaded and reorganized, maybe refuel, and secure his plane, which in the winter includes wrapping a cowling cover around the engine to retain its warmth. The passengers want to get oriented. And those waiting on the ground anticipate freight and mail, may have something to send "out," and want to talk to the pilot—what's the news?—and greet the passengers. All at once.

Heimo drove his snowmachine to the plane, pulling a toboggan. (In Alaska snowmobiles are "snowmachines" or "snow-goes".) We unloaded, greeted, joked, exchanged news.

But my first connection was with the air. It was relatively warm, +20 F, but a strong steady north wind felt bitter. (Heimo told me later that a steady north wind was a winter characteristic of this valley.) I told myself to buck up.

We loaded my supplies into toboggans and headed for the cabin, and I got my first taste of Heimo's snowmachine driving: while the passenger sits in the toboggan—a hard flat surface with nothing to grasp—Heimo accelerates, seemingly as fast as possible. For the passenger, there is no way to secure yourself: no hand holds, no seat. You just flop around on the smooth plastic. I eventually developed the method of lying flat and wedging myself tight by pressing my elbows, knees, and feet against the sides of the toboggan. In spite of these constant efforts, on every trip, sometimes forty miles in a day, I was incessantly tossed into the air and thrust in all directions by irregularities in the trail, turns, and accelerations and decelerations. Every bump was transmitted to my body through the hard plastic, wind burned exposed skin, and a steady flow of snow sprayed over me from the snowmachine tread, unless Heimo hit some overflow, in which case I got a dose of water, which quickly froze. And the safest way to cross overflow is to accelerate, which increases the spray. At each stop

THE REFUGE IN WINTER

I emerged from the toboggan as a stiff white mummy. I certainly never complained, and Heimo, bless his heart, never seemed to notice…but he never offered to change places with me either.

But this first trip was short, to the cabin. In time I learned these local trails quite well, but at first the area seemed a maze, along the river, into a slough, then up a narrow trail through stunted spruce, to the cabin site. My confusion was magnified by the wind tearing at me and the steady stream of snow in my face.

The cabin was appropriately small. When one builds with local materials, every log comes dear. The logs need to be located, cut, dried, peeled, transported, and then placed within the wall. The size of the cabin depends partly upon what size logs are available, and partly upon how much volume the builder is willing to heat in the winter, and partly upon the construction of the roof. Since the builder can't use conventional trusses, the span of the roof—the width of the cabin—must correspond to the length of the poles available for use as roofing. One window: windows are poor insulators. A Dutch door, the top half permanently closed during my stay, to trap the rising heat. To enter or leave, push aside the blanket covering the inner face of the door and duck through the lower half quickly. As you enter: to the right of the door, kitchen counter and shelving. Over the door, racked firearms. Looking clockwise: storage for boxes and bins, Heimo and Edna's bunk, shelving and radio on the wall, bunks for daughters Rhonda and Krin, stool, window. In the center, the heart of every northern cabin, a good wood stove. No chairs. I don't know what the exterior surface of the roof was, probably tar paper with sod over it. Moss chinking. Cardboard as insulation placed against the roof poles. The interior dimensions were about 15' X 15', or about 225 square feet.

What happens inside this tiny space in the wilderness? Edna cooks on the wood stove, seated on a stool; excellent meals of pure wild game, pasta or rice, canned vegetables. Two children are home-schooled. Baths are taken, clothes are washed. Wolverines, martens, beavers, wolves, and other fur-bearers are meticulously skinned, stretched, and prepared for sale. Skis are waxed. Snowshoes are repaired. Clothes are sewed or mended. One must imagine the physical and emotional gymnastics required to conduct the daily business of life, and to cohabit harmoniously, in such a space during a seven month winter, when the sun doesn't clear the horizon for several months. At that latitude, when you ask the temperature, "40" means −40, "30" means −30. No need to say "minus," that's a given.

WHEN WE GOT to the cabin Edna and I sorted through the groceries I brought. I doubt if they had had fresh food, other than game, for seven months. The vegetables and fruits needed to be protected from freezing and the meats and seafood needed to remain frozen. I realized that Edna was doing a quick and accurate evaluation of menu choices, combinations and quantities. There were treats in the coolers too; these were subject to careful rationing, though I saw as time went by that no one exhibited any cravings; there was no self-indulgence or gluttony; no one acted as if they had gone through a period of deprivation. The Korths' normal daily diet was one of the healthiest and most satisfying I have ever observed or experienced.

Heimo had a wall tent set up near the cabin, wood stove installed, stoked, and lit. I was exhausted from two days of travel and went in the tent about 6:00 PM and slept through to 6:00 AM, when I rekindled the fire. I sank into a bone-deep coma and had one of the most satisfying rests I can remember.

My first full day on the ground was March 26; morning temperature −12 F. I was determined to stay out of the Korths' way and after breakfast poked around in the woods to select a campsite. I settled on a flat spot about seventy-five yards from the cabin and out of sight, with enough small dead wood nearby to feed my stove without cutting into their potential wood supply. I stamped down the snow, knowing it would set up hard once compressed, and erected my tent. My education continued: the shock cord in the poles had no elasticity at that temperature and got in the way of assembly. I had to solve that problem, which took considerable time, thinking, what if I had to do this under dire conditions? Such a problem would be much more than a mere nuisance.

I assembled my wood stove kit, and built a wood base under it, beneath the tent floor, in anticipation that the stove would melt the snow under it causing the floor to slump. I cut plenty of wood and organized my camp; I saw that it was good.

A winter camp

In the afternoon Heimo and I traveled by snowmachine to

his down-stream cabin. (The Korths rotate between three cabins roughly every three years in order not to deplete one area of game and furbearers.) We stopped at a moose carcass, presumably killed by wolves, to see if any furbearers had been scavenging. Earlier in the winter Edna had caught a wolverine in the area, and Heimo had put out snares for wolves near the carcass. Nothing today. Heimo told me that he had previously caught a wolf there but other wolves had fed on the snared wolf and ruined the pelt. This arouses feelings of outrage in Heimo, as I later saw for myself, when we checked another set and found that a snared wolf was damaged and unusable because it had been partially eaten by his mates. Heimo is a very level-headed and equable fellow, but the waste of a wolf gets under his skin.

About this moose carcass. Many Alaskans claim that wolves are wasteful, insisting that wolves kill a moose or caribou, feed briefly, and leave it as waste. This is ridiculous on its face. Life is hard for all wild animals, including predators. The idea that hundreds of pounds of meat would be overlooked by carnivores is absurd. In truth, they will revisit such a site as long as it is available. A temporary absence from the kill site does not mean it has been abandoned.

At the "lower" cabin Heimo retrieved a second snowmachine that he and Edna had stored there. I thought it was clever the way they had stored it. Machines can be damaged if left on the ground in the open, particularly by bears, who like the chewiness of plastic. Hence the Korths had simply built a log platform about three feet high and just parked it there. Apparently this was high enough to remove it from the range of prowling beasts. After installing a new gas tank (bush dwellers needs master any task) we loaded up two sleds with supplies, the sled Heimo had hauled me in, pulled by his new Ski-Doo Tundra, and another to be pulled by the retrieved Polaris. The supplies were household staples (oats, tea, etc.) to be used next fall. We needed to transport them to the new location now, while ground transportation was relatively convenient.

The twenty-mile return trip was brutal, a stiff north wind added to the speed of the machine. (Heimo and Edna use heavy wolf ruffs, sewn to their parka hoods, as protection against cold and wind and blowing snow; I had a simple heavy winter cap. My face stuck out like a beet. Edna has since made me two wolf ruffs for my parka hoods.) We returned to the cabin from this, my first excursion, somewhat later than expected. Edna was just a bit worried. Snowmachines are reliable, but not completely so. To be caught out at night miles from shelter is serious business. (I later heard her tell about a time that Heimo had to walk all night through deep sub-zero temperatures to get home after his machine broke down.) Dinner was varying hare (the Korths just call them "bunnies"), potatoes, onions, carrots. Delicious.

We visited a bit and I then prepared to spend my first night in my tent. The stove worked fine, all was comfortable (the low went to −18 F). Heimo and Edna came by for a while to visit, partly, I think, out of curiosity—to see how I was set up—partly to check on my safety.

Domestic

My education was continuous. For example, my little stove didn't hold enough wood, nor was it tight enough, to hold a fire all night and I needed to figure out what to wear to bed to stay warm as the temperature dropped. (At –18 F, down booties and overpants in addition to my heavy long underwear. On my torso, woolen underwear and a fleece top. Wool cap.) After several days, as I noticed that my feet were increasingly cold, I realized that condensation had collected in the boot and my felt liner was actually frozen to the inner sole. Hence I needed to dry my felt boot liners every night in the tent loft. I learned that, in the Interior, a breathable canvas or leather boot is much preferable—Edna calls these "kamik" or "gumuk," which words have become the more common "mukluk." Like the rubber-bottomed "shoe-pac" or "Sorel" (a brand name), the canvas mukluk holds a felt bootie and several felt insoles, with plenty of room for several pairs of heavy socks; but unlike the shoe-pac, the mukluk is loose fitting and breathable. Also, I needed to dry my sleeping bag, especially the foot, every morning. During the night moisture from the body's respiration passes through it and freezes on or near the surface, and the ice simply accumulates over time. Without a reliable external heat source –my wood stove—it would be impossible safely to travel for more than a few days at these temperatures because all my essential equipment and clothing would eventually be saturated with moisture, hence laden with ice.

LEARNING CAN BE practical (tent poles, boots); it can also be emotional and condensed into one powerful visual, audial, or sensual memory.

Early in the trip I slipped out of my tent at night to relieve myself. I remember the feeling of isolation—the Korth cabin was well out of sight through the forest—and the bright sky—but most of all the speed at which the cold penetrated my body. I felt exceedingly fragile and vulnerable, a tiny warm envelope that required a hot temperature of 98.6 F to function, which was perhaps 120 degrees warmer than the ambient air. Only a filament of tent fabric and some insubstantial clothing and gear protected me from utter inertia.

Another night the moon was so bright that I think I could have read by it—while in the tent. The moon cast shadows within the tent; indeed, the smoke from the stove cast a shadow. I have never experienced such nighttime brilliance, a combination of a full moon and the white of snow. And quiet. And solitude. The Great Alone.

A WORD ABOUT the Korths.

In this alien environment they are completely at home and comfortable. For most of the winter their environment is much harsher than what I experienced, not only considerably colder by twenty, thirty, or forty degrees (my coldest low was –34 F), but considerably darker. They live north of 68 degrees north latitude, which is 1.5 degrees north of the Arctic Circle. The Arctic Circle, at 66.5 degrees north latitude, receives about two hours of daylight at the winter solstice, though the sun does not rise, so it is considerably darker at the Korths, more than ninety miles to the north. To form a comparison, at Barrow, which lies at 71 degrees north latitude, the sun does not rise for one month before and one month after the winter solstice. So the Korths are between these two reference points. During this time the sky to the south lightens enough to provide some useable light for a few hours each day, less as the solstice nears, more as the winter advances.

Cold and dark are the two inflexible primary facts of winter existence. It takes an enormous fund of knowledge and steady good judgment to be able to survive here, let alone flourish, as the Korths do. The emotional requirements are equally substantial. All successful Alaskans find healthy ways to cope, and for the Korths one key is a daily, healthy, practical routine. Always up by a certain time, always eat breakfast by a certain time, always eat good food regularly, always have some worthwhile task to engage in, whether it is homeschooling, woodcutting, tending the trap line, mending clothes, preparing skins. The daily schedule serves the purpose of providing a necessary structure—it would be very easy in the cold and dark to sink into apathy and lethargy—but the days are not regulated rigidly, on the clock. There is always something to do, but it is rarely the same thing from day to day, and aside from the general schedule—up, eat, bedtime—there is plenty of variety and freedom. No one is on the clock.

The third essential fact is their isolation. They do receive one-way communications from two high-powered AM radio stations in central Alaska. In Alaska, it is common for some stations to devote a part of their time to delivering messages to bush dwellers, always at a fixed time, always reliably. People living in remote locations invariably listen to these messages attentively. The Korths also have limited two way communications with the—extremely rare—passing airplane via avionics radio. But essentially they are on their own for society and safety.

I pondered this when I sat in their cabin one evening. The heart of a cabin is the wood stove, and the eight cords of wood they stockpile for each winter is their interior sun. The tiny cabin encapsulates this heat, retains it; the humans envelop themselves within it; Edna captures some of the heat for cooking; and it is the emotional core of the habitation. The heat could also destroy the cabin and their lives with it. I traced the stovepipe up from the stove through the roof. It was thin-walled, not entirely straight—did the joints fit properly?—the roof poles through which it passed were dry. I didn't think the construction was faulty, merely that there was so little standing between the Korths and celestial cold.

The fact is the Korths are tougher and more courageous than they realize. Their routine existence, what they take for granted each day, would be a life-and-death affair for most people in the modern world. For example, a forty mile round trip to the "lower" cabin to retrieve supplies is routine for the Korths. But if the snowmachine breaks down and it can't be fixed, that could be a long walk. Judging when the ice is thick enough to walk or travel on, maneuvering a canoe in fast water, navigating in poor visibility, swinging a sharp ax tens of thousands of times, hauling heavy loads over long distances over difficult terrain on your back—these are a few examples of many that would befuddle most of us, or betray us into danger.

I will offer one example of Arctic savvy. It is a paradox that in the Arctic (and sub-Arctic) the single most dangerous element in the winter is liquid water. Aside from the problems it can cause with clothing and gear, as I discussed above, it also creates unpredictable travel hazards. I have mentioned "overflow." This is formed when water freezes in shallow sections of streams, causing ice dams to form. But water is still present, and it must flow somewhere, so it flows on top of the existing ice, in turn freezing and often forming layers of ice many feet deep. (During the summer I have observed the remains of overflow, called "aufeis," as much as twenty feet thick.) The overflow may be visible, creeping in a gray sheet across the surface of the river ice; but it can be invisible and insidious, filtering under uncompacted snow that looks perfectly safe. In any case, if the unwary traveler goes into the water, wet feet and legs—meaning wet boots and clothing—can be an extremely serious problem during the winter cold. Water also does things that I can't explain. For example, Heimo and I had travelled a certain stretch of river perhaps five times, and it seemed very stable. But on the sixth trip a section of trail was completely gone. A chasm had opened up perhaps 10' deep, 15' long, with vertical sides of ice, and at the bottom dark water flowed. How could this happen? I don't know. But the fact that our trail led right by the chasm made me queasy. In short, the winter traveler must possess considerable alertness and knowledge in order to stay alive.

And there are many other fundamental skills, based on knowledge and effort, which are necessary nutritionally and economically: hunting and trapping *for real*, not recreationally, are full disciplines in themselves. Heimo must draw on a vast library of knowledge to sustain himself and his family. To pose just a very few questions: How do you find a moose or caribou? Kill it? Butcher it? Transport it? Preserve it for future use? How do furbearers—marten, mink, lynx, wolverine, wolf—behave? Where are they to be found? How can they be captured? This is a small fraction of the total syllabus, which includes everything from how to make a marten set to how to sharpen a chain saw to how to navigate in the wilderness. His reservoir of knowledge and skills exceeds those of any businessman anywhere, and he has more grit and courage. He lives in another world, though, a world of concrete realities and immediate experience, not a world of abstractions. His relationships, be they with the natural world or people, are direct and honest. Lettered people will recall Thoreau's yearning for unmediated experience: "I cannot count one. I know not the first letter of the alphabet. I have always been regretting that I was not as wise as the day I was born." This unlettered man lives it without having read it. Those of us who have read it may not have come to the point of living it. Very few of us have or ever will.

More than any businessman, any entrepreneur, any man of wealth, Heimo is, if anybody can be, a self-made man.

THE REFUGE IN WINTER

ONE OF HEIMO'S PROJECTS, which hung over his head a bit, was to dismantle the camp the Korths had stayed in until mid-winter or a little later. The Korths trap from semi-permanent locations in the Arctic National Wildlife Refuge by permit, and they are meticulous about adhering to its terms. All vestiges of the camp had to be removed, and it needed to be done now—access was impossible after break-up. So we waited for Rick, one of the Korths' pilot friends, to arrive so we could dismantle the camp and ferry the materials by airplane to the cabin where they were currently staying.

The interest here is that the Korths actually lived in this camp through freeze-up and mid-winter. The camp was simply a large wall tent, made of traditional white canvas, heated with wood. They had rigged the usual interior fittings: kitchen counter, cots, storage areas. They also had added Styrofoam sheets to the interior surfaces for insulation. I tried to imagine heating that tent at –40 F and colder, during the dark time. I doubt if I imagined the reality very well.

Heimo told me that he trapped from here afoot, covering many miles each day. The snow pack is normally thin in that country and he could keep his trails packed out simply by walking them. (When I was there, near the end of winter, the snow pack was only sixteen inches, about average.) But his plans during the fall were disrupted when an unusually heavy snowfall occurred. In most parts of Alaska such an event would not be notable, but it was for Heimo in the dry Arctic. (Heimo hates precipitation, snow or rain. It depresses him, he says.) He said he almost gave up trapping and considered moving to "town" (Fort Yukon) for the winter. But apparently the snow settled out or melted down, and they stuck it out. Eventually, though, it was no longer worth their effort to live in the tent and they moved across the divide to a cabin.

IN THE KORTHS' world Heimo casts a long shadow because it is assumed that the final obligations and responsibilities are his. But the three females in the house are not negligible forces. After all, Edna is a Native born and bred, and had grown up in an Eskimo village. I already knew of Edna's resourcefulness from direct observation, but one day I had a chance to talk to her about more personal things. Edna was originally from Savoonga, on St. Lawrence Island, and she showed me some small Eskimo artifacts or keepsakes she had found there, small ivory pieces. A die, in the form of a bird; a sinker, in the form of a fox; a button; a spike; an awl. I think that handling these objects and talking about them awoke good memories of her original home, and her ancestors.

Edna tends her own trap line and is as at home in the wilderness as Heimo. The girls are too. Rhonda, for example, told me in detail and with some pride about the caribou she killed when they were at their fall camp, and she too runs a trap line.

One afternoon I skied with Rhonda and Krin upriver. I was impressed with their powers of observation. Rhonda spotted snow buntings on the ground before I did, and on the return noticed that a small amount of open water had formed in a backwater slough during our absence, a subtle change but potentially significant. She and Krin were as comfortable skiing on a wilderness river against a stiff north wind at −10 F as their contemporaries are watching TV in their rooms while chatting on their private telephones.

PART OF WHAT I did with the Korths had to do with their need to think ahead. Indeed, planning very far ahead is a necessity of bush life. For example, the best time to put in the winter's wood supply is the previous spring, because the spring snow pack allows for easier access to suitable trees, and easier transport of the cut wood, than would occur at any other time of year. Hence, Heimo has noted throughout the winter where the good dead dry trees are, and now he and I, and sometimes all five of us, worked on cutting, hauling, splitting, and stacking dry spruce. Likewise, stocking this cabin required another trip down river to fetch the canoe and motor, a barrel of food, odds and ends such as ammunition and tools, and, of all things, a washing machine, the old fashioned kind with agitator and wringer.

When I think of self-sufficiency in the wilderness, Thoreau immediately comes to mind. I am convinced that Thoreau is much misunderstood; he is so frequently invoked that we often take our knowledge of his ideas for granted; I am convinced that there is more to Thoreau than we realize. For example, do we remember that the first, and longest, chapter in *Walden* is titled "Economics," and that this reflects Thoreauss's understanding that we must establish a rational economic relationship with the world before we can move on to higher things?

The Korths have established such a relationship, and, as with Thoreau, it involves a reduction in expenditures rather than an increase in income. And, like Thoreau, they have substituted self-sufficiency for increased income. But self-sufficiency does not come easy. As I indicated above, it requires, first, intelligence, knowledge, planning; second, it requires hard work. The net result is increased freedom.

For the Korths, as for all of us, energy is the key to life, from the metabolic processes in our cells to the avgas that powers the airplane. However, for the Korths the value of energy is not masked by the ease with which food and fuel are cheaply obtained. Their energy costs are high, and their energy needs are immediately and dramatically essential. One can understand the urgency of this hard fact if one tries to imagine what is required if one must hunt for and kill, or gather, most of one's food. What would or could any modern human do if denied access to groceries? Virtually none of us could meet this most fundamental need.

Even the Korths are tied to the oil economy, though I do think they could do without it if necessary. Nevertheless an important part of their economic calculation has to do with gasoline. All their gasoline is flown in, and what determines the load of an airplane is weight, and gas is heavy. So it must be rationed. Most of it is reserved for the snowmachine, but if in late winter they have a surplus they may run the generator. Why? They are not wired for electricity. Because it runs their one other electrical appliance, a computer, supplied by a school district for home schooling but little used. In truth, Heimo likes his video games, and when I arrived Eric had given Heimo a particularly challenging one. So Heimo itched to get into this game. He dropped a good line one evening. He had fired off the generator the evening before when I was in my tent. "I got involved in a computer game but didn't solve it. I didn't have enough gas."

LIFE'S FUNDAMENTALS ARE usually simple and material. Snow, for example. We have all heard that Eskimos have fifty words for snow and ice because they are capable of making that many distinctions. (We have also heard that the "fifty words" claim should be corrected downwards.) In any case, observing and naming distinctions is one characteristic of being attuned to one's environment. (On the other hand, having the words enables us to see the distinctions.)

I live in south central Alaska, which does indeed have many kinds of snow, but in general the snow has high moisture content, though not as high as snow in warmer areas. ("Cold" is closely associated with "dry" because cold air holds less moisture than warm air.) Alaska's Interior is considerably colder and drier than more coastal areas, hence the snow is less dense, and the snow seems downright weird to a newcomer. For example, though there was only sixteen inches of snow on the ground at the Korths', and though most of it had settled out all winter, it would not support my weight. Even with skis or snowshoes, I bottomed out when attempting to travel on unconsolidated snow. This gave me pause when I contemplated my cross-country ski trek, because I would be moving at the pace of a slow walk.

One homely illustration of this strange dry snow occurred when I decided to wash my hair. I filled a three-quart pot with snow and put it on the stove to melt. That full mounded pot yielded a fraction of an inch of water. (Heimo is part of the National Weather Service cooperative program, and on April 1 he recorded three inches of new snow, which yielded but .06" of water.) In the end it took me nearly an hour to melt a full pot of water. I eventually went through the same process to get drinking water if I couldn't find open water in the river. In such simple ways does the quality of the snow affect your life.

WHEN I FIRST went north I planned a long ski trek to include either a long loop from and to the Korths', or a point-to-point trek to Arctic Village. From my journal: "I'm not sure when I gave up the idea of a big ski loop—probably when Heimo took me up to the East Fork pass route and it had been −34, and the wind was howling, and I looked at the large expanse of overflow on the Colleen, and I was covered in ice from frozen overflow. And there was no sheltering forest. Also I saw that, though the snow wasn't deep, it has no base and is not compacted at all," which, as I mentioned earlier, would make off-trail travel impossibly slow.

It often happens that what one visualizes for a trip evolves into something unforeseen. This is good. During this trip, I spent more time with the Korths than I originally intended. This would not have happened had they not welcomed me, and convinced me that they actually enjoyed my company. As Edna said one day, as I gingerly moved about the cabin to make some tea, "You're not a guest any more. You're Heimo's wolf trapping partner." So we spent our days checking snares (this was a successful year for wolves, Heimo's big money crop), transferring supplies, cutting and hauling wood, putting in beaver sets, and just looking at the country. But by April 8 it was time, and past time, to be off on my trek.

The Korths saw me off in a group, and Heimo skied in my direction when I started north. (He always gets a daily workout of some kind. He even has a running track packed out in the snow.) The girls wanted to see how my pulk worked and how I was equipped. Heimo skied ahead and we passed as he headed back. I thought that he might miss my company—we had worked together very amiably for thirteen days.

The temperature that morning was 0 F and the wind was steady from the north. I was comfortable, and was careful not to move too fast—I didn't want to soak myself with sweat, which would eventually freeze. In the afternoon I started to scout for a camp, and I will let this episode stand as the type.

I wanted a screen of trees to the north as a windbreak. I wanted three or four small diameter dead spruce to use as firewood. And I wanted a level and open space of at least one hundred square feet as a tent site. If there was open water nearby (for drinking and cooking) or a scenic view, so much the better.

One would think that these three simple criteria would frequently occur in conjunction. Not so. I started looking for a camp fairly early, and it took about an hour to find one. I then put on overboots (over my ski boots). I stamped and shoveled (using a snowshoe) a flat area for the tent, and erected it and installed my stove. I organized the interior of the tent (dense closed cell foam sleeping pad, self-inflating sleeping pad on it, sleeping bag with Gore-tex cover, clothing bag, headlamp, books and journal—use a pencil or keep the pen in an interior pocket), then near the tent stamped out a place for my kitchen (small plywood platform for gasoline stove, pots, mug, food bags). I added wax to my skis and stowed them, my ski poles, and the pulk. I then located my dead trees and cut my wood supply (chunks no thicker than four inches and no longer than ten inches) and stacked some in the tent by the stove and the rest outside the tent door. During this process I added clothes as I cooled, and changed my ski boots and overboots for shoe-pacs.

Looking north

Then, my treat of the afternoon, a large mug of tea, and while my dinner cooked a second mug. In April the days are long and I stayed outside until I was ready to write in my journal, read, and sleep. When I went in the tent, I lit the wood stove, using cotton balls saturated with wax as tinder. A tent heats up immediately (and cools immediately) and I put damp boots in the gear loft and shed some clothes. Toasty. Journal. Read. Sleep.

I quickly learned that I needed at least three hours from the time I started looking for a camp to getting myself fed, and in the morning about the same time from waking to travelling. Travelling in the winter requires a lot of time and patience, hard work, and attention to detail. It is difficult actually to be on the trail for more than five hours each day.

It's a great big black, white, and blue land where little seems to be happening. Events therefore stand out sharply: a falcon-like persistent birdcall, but I couldn't find the bird. The difficulty of moving in this strange unconsolidated snow. A persistent deep-throated snarling in the trees one night: marten, I conclude. On several occasions flocks of white-winged crossbills produced a wonderful chorus of song, bringing beauty and life to the silence. A harsh repeated cry during the night—perhaps an owl. A wolf howling in the morning and again at mid-day. A golden eagle, I presume an early migrant. Always, the creeks and the river, with their ice, drifts, and potential overflow: the water is always secretly at work in the Arctic. Spiky spruce trees in the valley, treeless hills, distant mountains. A sky of pale blue, or a sky clouded with ice crystals. A smear of pink or salmon in the evening sky.

ON APRIL 14 I returned to the Korth cabin. The daytime highs had been climbing steadily since my arrival on March 25. The coldest high was −14 F on March 28, the coldest low was −34 F the previous night. On April 13 I recorded the largest temperature change in one day, from −8 F to +26 F, a thirty-four degree swing. The following night it only dropped to +5 F, and as I skied back south on the 14th I recorded +33 F in the afternoon sun. I stripped down to a thin layer of clothes and put on sunglasses. For me it was the first day of spring.

The Korths greeted me enthusiastically when I returned from my seven-day ski trek. I think they were truly glad to see me—I had feared becoming an unwelcome guest. Edna even took my picture—I was surprised that they owned a camera. They filled me in on the news of their doings—a marauding marten had gotten into some meat and was shot, a good bit of wood was stacked. They tactfully vacated the cabin so I could wash—they needed to cut wood, they said—I must have stunk vilely. It was the first time I had removed my clothes in three weeks.

That night I dreamed that I heard a ruby crowned kinglet singing its spring song. In my heart I yearned for spring, and the sea.

When I crawled into Eric's Cessna on April 15, Heimo gave me the ultimate compliment: he invited me to return.

CHAPTER 8

The Most Miserable Trip

I once had the bright idea to do a hiking trip from Walker Lake, in the western Brooks Range, to the headwaters of the Noaktak River. There I would meet my pilot, who would bring in a resupply of food and a double kayak. From there my companion and I would float the river.

This plan seemed reasonable; in fact, even as I write this, it still seems like a good idea. But in the event, this was the one major trip I did that completely fell apart, and left me demoralized, even traumatized, by the time it ended ignominiously, far short of our goal.

MOTHER NATURE HAD a lot to do with our misery. Though we started in late July, the mosquitoes were exceptionally bad—I had expected the mosquitoes to die off by then. Perhaps they were numerous because of the rain: this was an unusually wet summer in northwest Alaska. Also, this area was much brushier than other parts of the Arctic I had hiked in, and the tree line was higher. So for three days we walked through thick brush consisting of tall dense willows and tall dense alder. Willows stands are pretty easy to negotiate—they are slim and limber—but alders present another challenge altogether. They are tough and stiff, and they branch out nearly horizontally, from ground level to at least head height, so they are a formidable barrier. Since we couldn't outflank the thickets by climbing, all we could do was throw ourselves at them: bull through, crawl under, even roll over them. We did this while carrying heavy frame packs and firearms, usually in the rain.

It had rained for some time before we began our trip and it rained steadily during most of these three days. Low areas that would likely be dry during the midsummer were bogs. Bogs were swamps. Swamps became shallow ponds. Rivulets spread out through low spots and insured that as we threw ourselves at the brush we were as often as not standing in ankle deep water. And since it rained so much, each leaf was a little reservoir waiting to dump its load inside our raincoat hoods, down our collars, down our upraised sleeves. And of course the mosquitoes hovered in swarms around our faces incessantly. From the hiker's standpoint, it was the worst of all possible worlds.

We could not locate any good campsites, mainly because of the water.

We could not build a fire. The wood was thoroughly soaked. Eventually, all our clothes became soaked, including spares. We were always wet from the skin out. We dried out a bit overnight in our sleeping bags.

It made no sense to hole up because there was no indication that the weather would change; we couldn't wait it out. Besides, we had to be at Embryo Lake along the Noatak River by a certain date to rendezvous with the pilot.

So we struggled on. On the fourth day we had a stiff walk farther up the creek valley as it steepened and then a very stiff climb to the pass that would take us into the upper Noatak. Again, it rained hard throughout the latter difficult climb, so that our physical labor was aggravated by the cold rain, cold air, cold clothing against the skin of our backs. We camped in the clouds in the pass, and though our situation had its drawbacks, we hadn't had to fight brush either, and there was a grand and spooky beauty up among the clouds and rocks. But real peace evaded us.

Our experience was epitomized for me when we made dinner that night. Some sun came through the clouds and we convinced ourselves that the storm was breaking up. We got out the stove and pots and laid out the food. My companion spread out his sleeping pad to sit on and laid out his wet clothes to dry, took off his wet boots and socks, put on sneakers and dry socks. He was prepared to relax comfortably. And then the rain came again, cold, driven by wind. The joke was on us.

But the next five days were good. We had fair weather and good walking, but more important, excellent terrain to experience, and a lovely clear river to accompany us as we walked. But mentally we continued to look to the future: getting to the rendezvous point, reorganizing our equipment, getting on and down the Noatak.

Once on the river, we were distressed because the boat was overloaded and my tall partner couldn't get comfortable. (We were in a double Klepper, a collapsible kayak.) We didn't have enough time, we thought, to finish our trip within our time frame at the rate we were traveling because much of the upper river was slow flowing. For days we faced dead flat water and oxbow after oxbow. Then the river quickened and we were continually alert, scanning for the right line, dodging obstructions. We had long periods of foul weather and strong head winds, and when we should have been holed up in a snug camp we felt forced to travel because of time pressures. When we should have taken the time to fish, or hike the surrounding country, we instead felt compelled to be on the river. Our minds were always projecting into the future, not living in the present.

The crisis of the trip happened when we were still in the upper half of the river. Our kayak had a rudder that was connected by thin cables to foot pedals. The cables were attached to the rudder with clips. As we approached Atongarak Creek we stopped to reconnoiter for a campsite. We stopped where two branches of the river came together at the foot of an island. We decided to paddle up the other fork to what looked like a good camp, but when we got into the current we found that a clip had come off the rudder and it was jammed to the right. We were trapped.

We were trapped because a very strong eddy formed at the foot of the island where the two branches came together. We came to think of it as a whirlpool. The eddy rotated clockwise. Our boat could only move in a clockwise direction because of the jammed rudder. Hence the rudder was forcing us into the eddy and we had no way to counteract this effect. We capsized very quickly.

In my mind, however, it occurred with excruciating slowness. I remember feeling helpless as the boat circled with the eddy, then a feeling of near despair when I realized that the boat was going over and there was nothing we could do about it.

I had capsized a boat once before in the Arctic and it wasn't so bad. The water was cold but the river was small. It was a matter of clinging to the boat, working it to shore, and drying out. The day was sunny and everything dried quickly. But in this instance clinging to the boat got you literally nowhere because it was stuck in the whirlpool. The stern, my partner clinging to it, lay in the hole in the center of the whirlpool and the bow with me clinging to it circled at a great clip; the bow was considerably higher than the stern. My partner felt closer to death than I did because he felt suction; and because he was lower than the surface of the river he could see little more than surging water. Also, a strong cold wind, which we had been fighting all day, increased the height of the river stacks by thirty percent. He must have felt hopelessly buried in cold water.

The feeling was sickening. The world seemed unreal. I had a feeling of dissociation.

However, it was necessary to act, to force myself to cope, to stay tied to reality.

The usual advice when you capsize is to cling to the boat. However, our boat was going nowhere, the water was very cold, hypothermia was a real threat. I yelled that I was going to release and swim for it.

Also, and this was the one piece of good fortune we had during the entire trip, there was help nearby. Two other river travelers were within earshot. In that country it is very rare to see anyone. The odds against someone being nearby at the precise moment that you need their help are overwhelming. But we had recently encountered Mitch and Ray, travelling in single kayaks, and had travelled in parallel with them today. They were about to make camp upstream of us, at Atongarak Creek. I yelled, they responded. We swam, with great difficulty, from the whirlpool, and struggled towards shore. Because of the cold and rain, we wore several layers of clothes under our PFDs, and rain gear, plus rubber boots, and this sodden burden weighed heavily upon us as we struggled through the water. When I crawled onto the rocky shore, my lungs burned and my muscles did not want to function; I could barely catch my breath and I had to force myself to move at all.

While we struggled to shore, Mitch and Ray, from their single kayaks, tied on to our boat and gradually worked it to shore. They drifted several hundred yards downstream in the process, and we stumbled and staggered downstream after them. My sleeping bag had floated free and Ray generously paddled downstream to look for it, and luckily found it, for which I shall be forever grateful.

It was necessary to camp as quickly as possible to prevent further heat loss. We scoured the area, sopping wet in the wind, for a tent site, then up with the tent, into the sleeping bags, treatment by

Mitch and Ray for shock and hypothermia, an attempt to begin to dry clothing and gear, and then a long exhausted sleep.

We aborted that trip thirty-five miles downriver from that site. The Park Service had established a ranger station at Cutler River and we were able to fly out to Kotzebue from there. During any year prior to 1982 we would not have had that option, for that was the first year that any kind of custodianship in the field was attempted by the Park Service.

Without the assistance of Mitch and Ray, and without the ranger contact at Cutler River, our difficult trip would have become a long, long ordeal. As it was, I had to deal with some very ugly emotions. One was the nagging feeling of time closing in on us. How much food was ruined when we capsized? It is a long way down the Noatak; would the food last? Probably not, and short rations would compound our problems, since we were short on energy as it was. Our gear was intact, so aside from food loss we were fine.

But we weren't fine. I dreaded getting back on the river. As we lay in the tent recovering our strength—hypothermia saps your energy and it takes time for the body to recover—I was deep down bone tired for several days—I felt helpless and lost, bewildered. Despair may not be too strong a word. We did not yet know for sure that we could get help at Cutler River, and in any case it was necessary to get back on the water to get even that far.

Another exceedingly unpleasant emotion was the grinding conviction that somehow I had failed. Other people, such as Mitch and Ray, had floated the Noatak that summer, and had managed to have good experiences. Why couldn't we?

True, there were a certain number of objective hazards, such as rain, alders, and wind that lay outside our control. That our rudder jammed seemed like dumb luck. There were human errors, errors of judgment or oversight. But essentially we failed because of what was within ourselves; or not within ourselves. There was something within us that prevented us from making the essential connection to our environment that is necessary in wilderness travel. Part of that was because we had locked ourselves into too small a time frame. Instead of *being in* the wilderness, we were simply *passing through it* to something else. So we were unable to make the essential connection to our place.

As I have written elsewhere, according to Billie Wright, in her book *Four Seasons North,* the Nunamiut word "koviashuktok" translates as "the condition of being fully and pleasantly in the present moment." I find this pithy definition to be immensely provocative. It has practical, concrete applications. The conjunction of "fully," indicating complete immersion, and "pleasantly" as a consequence of that immersion, is important. It is reminiscent of Thoreau's continual attempt to live only what was life, and to eschew what was not life. My essential failure on this trip was to look too keenly to the future instead of looking intently at my present situation. I did not allow myself to be immersed in the immediate activity in that space at that time. True, Mother Nature placed considerable obstacles in our way. Nevertheless, life can only be lived now; we live tomorrow only when tomorrow becomes now. The essential failure of that trip was my failure to live properly, to think and act and judge properly, and it may be that, in those parts of my life where I have failed, it is for the same reasons.

Knowing how to live is truly an art. The key questions, for someone with a Western viewpoint, are, "What to do?" and "How to do it?" As Thoreau pointed out, if we allow ourselves to be absorbed by frivolous, unimportant detail we will fritter away our lives. We must instead attend to what is important…and only that.

And, as the Stoics taught, we must maintain a sense of proportion. My emotional life was grim on that trip, particularly after capsizing the boat, because of my lack of proportion. I forgot my true place in the world. I failed to see some things, I overemphasized others. I lost my center. I forgot who I was.

Optimistic footnote: in later years I did descend the Noatak successfully, and was able to cancel some of my shame and embarrassment. The river has changed. The last time I descended the river I could see no trace of a strong eddy or whirlpool just below Atongarak Creek.

CHAPTER 9

The Old People

I went to the wilderness looking for adventure, and instead learned the importance of self-discovery; on my quest for self-discovery, I learned that I wanted redemption; from the wise and the old, I learned that redemption is impossible.

Redemption from what? I am economically secure, in good health, and a citizen of a strong and wealthy nation. I have security, and choices. I have "everything."

In his important book *The Invisible Pyramid*, Loren Eiseley quotes Samuel Taylor Coleridge: "A Fall of some sort or other…is the fundamental postulate of the moral history of man. Without this hypothesis, man is unintelligible; with it every phenomenon is explicable. The mystery itself is *too profound for human insight* [emphasis added]."

WHEN I REACHED Arctic Village after crossing the Brooks Range in 1974, I learned that down river lived two old people who were revered by the Gwich'in and whites alike as survivors from the time before European-American contact. I remembered.

In 1977, I did another walking trip in the area with a friend, which began and ended at Arctic Village. Sam left, and I spent a few days with a young Gwich'in in Arctic Village. I was keen to learn about the Gwich'in and the ways of the north, and the subject of Gwich'in history came up. I told Ernest of my interest in the two old people. It so happened that the next phase of my trip was to float down the East Fork Chandalar River in a double kayak with another friend to the Yukon, and then part way down that stream to the village of Beaver. How would I find the old people? Ernest squatted and drew, from memory, a map in the dirt, which I transcribed to paper. He cautioned me to get into a slough upstream of their cabin, because the cabin was off the main river behind a gravel bar. He included other instructions and landmarks, which I carefully noted.

After five days of floating, we pulled into the slough that flowed beneath the bank at the Franks' cabin. That map scratched in the dirt was completely accurate.

SARAH AND JOHNNY Frank were ninety five and ninety seven years of age in 1977, which means that they were born about 1880. (Of course, no written records were kept among the Gwich'in. However, Johnny claimed to have been born in 1880, even narrowing it to the day, October 18.) Although Europeans had been in Alaska for some time, the Russians mainly to the south and west, the New England whalers on the north coast, and others chasing gold, the Gwitch'in youths of Sarah and Johnny were pre-contact, because of their extreme isolation.

I have tried to visualize growing up, to young adulthood, in the aboriginal past. It is not enough to say, "They lived before electrification," or "They lived before paved roads." Their isolation was total. They did not know that New York or Paris existed, that a Civil War had been fought in North America, that trans-Atlantic cables were being laid, that the industrial world was expanding rapidly. They had never as much as seen a road, or heard about or seen money. I find this pre-contact world extremely hard to penetrate. It requires an act of the imagination that requires us to shed our culture, a difficult or impossible thing to do. Sarah and Johnny lived their early lives before the Fall.

The author in front of the Franks' cabins twenty years after his first visit.

When we secured the kayak and walked up the bank to the cabin, we met two vigorous and enormously self-reliant people; two people who had been formed in the Dreamtime and had lived to see something of after the Fall.

They were in the cabin and I think we startled them a little. They wouldn't expect visitors, except by motorboat from downstream, or by bush plane, which they would have heard.

Their first thought was to be hospitable. Three girls were staying with them, Lucy, Connie, and Melody, granddaughters, and they were soon sent off with pails. They returned later with berries—for the guests.

Sarah did not attempt to communicate in English. She indicated by gesture what she intended—sit down here, for example—or Johnny translated. Johnny did not speak English any too well, and I reflected that they would have heard English for the first time as young adults, and would have taught themselves the language, one which had no common root with theirs.

Johnny was the talker and the firebrand, the natural leader, the boss; Sarah deferred, probably gladly on this occasion, since our presence likely created some discomfort in their lives.

My companion Paul went downstream to fish. I was more interested in the old people.

Their faces peer at me as I write. Their photos have been on the wall beside my desk for more than forty years.

They are seated outside their cabin, against the log wall. The day is sunny. Johnny looks out from under a hat brim, his mouth a strong horizontal gash, strong chin, large aggressive nose, a lean face. His face projects determination and strength; a serious face.

Sarah is close beside him. She is hatless, and her gray hair is neatly parted. Her head is tilted left, her shoulders are rounded. Her mouth is not quite horizontal, there is a slight uplift beneath the cheeks. The chin is strong but not aggressive, the nose ample and rounded but not large. Eyebrows slightly lifted, forehead slightly wrinkled, as if quizzically. I see here a combination of strength and love.

The interior of the cabin was like all Alaskan cabins everywhere: wood stove, firewood, kitchen counter, central table, sleeping area. No partitions, no easy chairs. The tools of life were hung in handy places on the wall: ax, saw, hammer, coat. Johnny, a great smoker, apparently could not part with his cigar boxes—they lined one wall; but his pipe was his companion.

THE OLD PEOPLE

Johnny was a great talker, laugher, and storyteller, and so we talked; or rather, Johnny talked and I listened. Foremost among the conversational topics was religion and language. Much of what I heard I inferred, listening to ideas filtered through broken English, but I heard Johnny speak about the first white man he had ever seen, as a young man, one or several whites who appeared one day along the river, and I tried to imagine the enormity of their advent. (According to Sarah's transcribed memory, they were probably Archdeacon Hudson Stuck, Bishop Bompas, or a Mr. Moody.) From that moment, an entire culture was to be permanently altered, certainly damaged, perhaps destroyed. (Sarah: "None of the people they [the preachers] met knew about God.... They say there was a God. The news spread quickly and people started praying for each other....They cried and prayed for each other. Even women were praying. They didn't know there was a God. So when they heard about it, even the women were crying and praying. I remember them crying and praying." Sarah doesn't say, but perhaps it was the question of Hell and salvation that brought them to tears. It seems likely that their introduction to western culture began with fear.

I began to recognize the great tragedy of deculturation. We live in our culture as fish live in water; our culture forms and determines us to an extent that we ourselves do not recognize; our sense of ourselves as completely autonomous individuals is an illusion; to destroy the culture was to destroy or damage the individual.

I am reminded here of a story someone, I think Sam Sam, told me in Arctic Village. He said that one day a man showed up in Arctic Village to travel into the wilderness. He had a goat with him. He left Arctic Village with his goat and disappeared; no one ever learned what happened to him. This man, said Sam Sam, was *a black white man.*

This story brought home to me that the most important defining trait we possess is our culture. In the dominant European culture, we are tempted to think that this man's foremost traits were the genes that determined his appearance. The Gwich'in knew, however, that what defined this man was his culture, regardless of his appearance. Even the genes that dictate our outward appearance are nugatory. Misunderstand the culture, and you misunderstand the individual; destroy the culture and you destroy the individual.

Johnny showed me his Bible, of which he was very proud, and he claimed with even more pride that he could read it, and he did so, pointing to the words on the title page and declaiming, "Holy Bible." (Years later I was to learn more of the importance of Christianity to the Gwitch'in. In her transcribed memories, Sarah was asked if Johnny went to school. "He never went to school, and neither did I. He taught himself by learning to read the Indian Bible. Lots of times we met white men....He could understand what they were telling him from reading the Indian Bible. He taught himself how to read using the abc's.")

It was time to move around. Johnny took me outside. We stood face to face beside the cabin in the bright sunlight, his face close to mine, and he launched into his stories. They were tales of ancient times, and I could just barely follow him. At first I thought he was narrating first hand experiences, and I tried to question him, but he impatiently moved ahead in his narrative. I eventually realized that I was hearing of ancient battles and terrible and strange monsters of some mythical time, stories heard by Johnny as a child, very likely from his grandmother, and carried around in his head for nearly a century.

He also, I realized, included some personal history in his story telling, and he made no transition or distinction between the mythical past and stories of his life, which were without exception narratives of travel and hunting. I remember one story of a caribou hunt, and particularly an image of Johnny as he told it: he raises his firearm to shoot, and *releases* the bullet the way an archer releases an arrow with two fingers. He made a "puff" with his lips—no explosion, no recoil—just quiet stealth.

Gwich'in hunting grounds

The third kind of narrative was Biblical. I suppose that Johnny's Bible stories came from sermons he had heard: Moses climbed a mountain every bit as big as Denali to fetch the tablets; when a crowd of people were hungry Jesus took a couple whitefish and fed everybody; Moses' people had trouble in the wilderness, mainly because they were out of grub; Joseph told Pharaoh that the lean cattle meant that spring wouldn't come, it would stay cold, they should build caches.

WE STOOD THERE, Johnny talking steadily, for hours, the entire afternoon and into the evening. Paul took the photos I have mentioned, and we sat beside the cabin for a while. Johnny explained that he loved to associate with birds, especially in the winter. One time he was feeling particularly unwell, and the birds came to visit. He and Sarah fed them—hardy northern chickadees—and the birds lit on Johnny's shoulders and hands. A great weight was lifted from his chest; Johnny became well and happy. He was certain that there was a spiritual, healthful connection between himself and his avian friends. They healed him. I am willing to believe it.

A boat skeleton, left by one of the last of the Old People

Paul and I slept in a spare cabin, and Johnny and Sarah were up before us. She had cooked eggs and the grayling Paul had caught. After breakfast we packed up and headed down river, and I regret to this day that we left nothing of value behind for them. I wanted to stay longer, but I don't regret staying for only twenty-four hours, because we would only have been a trial to them.

I don't think that the last aboriginals are the last link to a lost Paradise, but I do think they are the last to live before the Fall, and that the Fall is more than a metaphor. Johnny and Sarah fell into Time, that most ruthless and relentless of human inventions. As Loren Eiseley phrased it, they "entered upon what we may call history."

Years later I found the excellent book edited by Craig Mishler that preserved many of Sarah and Johnny's words: *Neerihiinjik [We traveled From Place to Place]: Johnny Sarah H`aa Googwandak [The Gwich'in Stories of Johnny and Sarah Frank]* (1995, Alaska Native Language Center, UAF, Fairbanks). Mishler has compiled a fascinating account of the old people, in their words, translated from the Gwich'in into English by the Gwich'in descendants of Sarah and Johnny.

Johnny narrates his stories, such as I have recalled above. He recalled his grandmother, who was crippled when he was a boy. "During the winter when we traveled, my father used to haul her around in an animal hide blanket....He packed her around on his back when we were traveling in the summer....My grandmother knew all the stories from a long time ago....From the time she got up, she sat by the fire and told story after story all day long. She told stories of all the old time wars. She did this day after day. Even when there was no one sitting by her."

Johnny does not say that he learned his stories from her; he does not say that the entire store of Gwich'in myth and history was carried this way; but it must be so. Johnny does not say, "I am the last."

I could not talk to Sarah when I met her, but thanks to Craig Mishler I have since learned that she had much to say, not about myths and monsters, but about her experienced past. Several themes appear repeatedly through two hundred pages of printed memory, but all the themes have one root: the scarcity of all the material resources of life, but particularly and most importantly, food. We hear her say repeatedly, "Life was hard then."

The import of this understatement is hard to grasp without first-hand experience. A few years ago (see Chapter 7) I spent three weeks in late winter on the south slope of the Brooks Range, in the Colleen River valley, Sarah's birthplace. I traveled on skis, and camped in an 8'X10' nylon tent that I equipped with a small wood burning stove. Fuel was abundant, and I had a good saw. I also had good clothing, good cook pots, a good sleeping bag, and good sleeping pads. I had an excellent food supply, and much else. Without exception, every item of my gear was purchased with money.

For one three-day stretch the low temperatures were in the -30s F, and the highs were sub-zero. On the coldest day, March 28, the low was -34 F, the high was -14 F. The average low temperature over three weeks was -8 F, the average high was +12 F, and the average daily temperature was +2 F. There were more than twelve hours of daylight.

When the north wind blew down the river, and the wind chill plummeted, I pondered the extreme hostility of this winter environment, and tried to put it into perspective.

I was traveling during relatively balmy conditions. What is it like in mid-winter, when the sun doesn't rise at all? What is it like in December, January, February, when the low temperatures may be well below -50 F, and daytime highs may be -40 F or colder?

And then: take away my food supply, my equipment, all my synthetic goods. Put me in a situation where *everything*, absolutely

THE OLD PEOPLE

without exception, is to be found in the environment and crafted by someone in the family group from natural materials.

And then live a "normal" human life that includes childbirth and child rearing.

The Old People had the knowledge, the strength, the character to survive here. Indeed, they did more than survive, though they did not flourish. They lived on the tiniest of margins; starvation was always a threat, and the accumulation of material wealth an impossibility.

Sarah says, "It was hard," and that phrase encompasses all her experience, but does not bring home the reality.

THE OLD PEOPLE did not lose a Paradise when the Europeans came, but they did Fall into something that was destructive and frightening: Time.

The great thinker and writer Ernest Becker has written somewhere that obsessive-compulsive behavior is the disease of modern man. We hear the term "obsessive-compulsive" often, but it took me years to puzzle out a workable meaning. I wanted to define "obsessive," and I wanted to define "compulsive," and I wanted to put them together to arrive at a full definition. In short I misunderstood Freud's use of the language. I eventually came to see that the two parts of the term are inseparable, and my personal working definition became: "This term describes behavior in which a person is convinced he has no choice; his emotions tell him that he must behave in a certain way; a variation in the behavior is felt to be impossible. This need to conform to a certain behavior has the force of taboo. Even though this feeling of absolute need is purely emotional, it is often accompanied by intellectual rationalizations for the behavior."

As Ernest Becker observed, we humans are capable of robotic, mechanical activity performed on a frighteningly massive scale, day after day, by many millions of people, over and over and over again. A view of commuter traffic is the best contemporary illustration I can think of to illustrate this obsessive-compulsive behavior. The same cars, the same routes, the same routine, the same cup of coffee, the same radio thrusting the same noises and words into our brains day after day; always the same. While we drive to work, we are at work. We live in the world of Time; we mark time; we waste time; we save time; we kill time. We begin the day with an *alarm*, and we end the day by setting one; we are on the clock even when we sleep.

A far more horrifying example is the behavior of armies, and their auxiliaries, such as the extermination squads of World War II.

A more amusing example is Charlie Chaplin's movie *Modern Times*.

In a *New Yorker* cartoon, one train commuter says to another, "Now that I've been let go, the commute is all I have."

The philosopher Josef Pieper has discussed a similar idea in his essential book *Leisure, the Basis of Culture*, where he points out that all of European (let's say modern Western) life is subordinate to the demands of work, in a society where work is a totalitarian activity that permeates every moment of existence. When we are not at work, we are preparing explicitly or implicitly for work; our "leisure" time is not leisure at all, in the sense that it is a time free for the development of human beings, but is instead simply time away from work, a negative quality; when we are not at work we are thinking about work, preparing for work, escaping from work. Surely this is an obsession that controls our personalities and behavior; we feel compelled to act this way; we think we have no choice. If our behavior is challenged, we say, "Well, we all have to make a living." In truth, our culture has decided for us how we are to behave. We are creatures of our time who live within Time.

SARAH SAYS, "In those days when a child was born they never recorded the birth date. So we never knew when they were born as time passed." Each child was born out of time as we know it.

IN MY LIFE, there were two Falls.

Like most people in our culture, I learned that the Fall occurred soon after Creation, and involved the disobedience of our mythical parents. Their redemption, and ours, lay in atoning for this original sin. This is the theological root of Christianity.

I came to read the myth differently. To me, the importance of that story lay in the idea that once-upon-a-time there existed a pre-industrial, even pre-agricultural, period of intellectual innocence which *Homo sapiens*, because of his aggressive character and aggressive intellect, destroyed. This heedless destructiveness was part of the development of European civilization, with its political wars, its religious wars, its ruthlessly stratified social organization based on human exploitation. This culture was exported to the New World, which we Europeans soon burdened with the sins of the Old World, beginning with mass murder, torture, and slavery, and continuing on to include environmental destruction. Human exploitation and environmental exploitation went hand-in-hand in both Americas.

The Fall of my personal knowledge, the second Fall, is the Fall as described so eloquently by F. Scott Fitzgerald in *The Great Gatsby*, and by Loren Eieseley in *The Invisible Pyramid*. For Fitzgerald, we European-Americans were given the gift of a fresh new world, and shat upon it; for Eiseley, we were driven by an aggressive intelligence obsessed with technology. In both views, our behavior is driven by radical economic materialism implemented, in Eiseley's view, by technology.

Jared Diamond, in *Guns, Germs, and Steel*, offers a mechanistic explanation of how Europe conquered the world. This is an important and useful book, though his method does not allow him to probe the sources of human motivation. One of Diamond's main points is, if you have the technology of destruction you will inevitably use the technology of destruction. One reason why Europeans conquered the world was because they could. This is worth noting, but what was the motivation? I think that the most ruthless of the Europeans, the Conquistadors, were motivated by a gross materialism that resembles our own; and, like ours, their aggressive materialism was buttressed by their religion.

Much more complete is Frederick Turner's *Beyond Geography: The Western Spirit Against the Wilderness*. Turner recognizes that the European thrust into the Western Hemisphere and beyond was motivated by a number of forces, including religion, and that the tools of conquest were guided by ideas and dogmas. All sources agree, however: the conquest of the world by Europe was not merely one fact among many; it was a profound tragedy.

An intellectual understanding of the mechanisms that enabled Europe to conquer and colonize the world is one thing; a subjective, emotional response to Paradise Lost, or Paradise Befouled, is also necessary. Fitzgerald's Nick Caraway would recognize these words of Turner's, discussed earlier, about growing up in America: "A feeling of American loneliness began to insist upon itself, a crucial, profound estrangement of the inhabitants from their habitat.... Neither in proverb nor in history have we been able to come to loving terms with what we call home." Sociologists have studied and explained this phenomenon; modern philosophers have recognized and analyzed the modern experience of alienation and angst; the fact of estrangement and alienation can also be discovered in economics, demographics, psychology, history, literature, and, perhaps most broadly and intensely, in the best of our popular culture, in movies such as *On the Waterfront* or *Chinatown*, in the lyrics of Bob Dylan and Bruce Springsteen, or in the blues generally. I feel it, have felt it, all my life. Surely Eiseley, Turner, and Crawford are not unique. There is something wrong about the behavior of our culture vis-a-vis our earth. There is a basic disconnect between people and the ground they walk upon. This is not just a simple environmental problem. This is a profound ethical problem that reaches deep into our personal lives, our politics, our economic behavior. Who are we? What are our deepest, most important connections? Surely we are or can be more than T. S. Eliot's hollow men.

F. Scott Fitzgerald knew the rich of his time, who are the rich of our time, of all time, from ancient Persia to Rome to the Conquistadors to the plutocrats of capitalism. In *The Great Gatsby*, Tom Buchanan, graduate of Yale, is one of the entitled rich whose ignorance is impervious to correction. "I read somewhere that the sun's getting hotter every year," said Tom genially. "It seems that pretty soon the earth's going to fall into the sun—or wait a minute—it's just the opposite—the sun's getting colder every year." If this sounds like the ignorance and confusion of another privileged Yale plutocrat and recent American president, his ideas on "family values" are equally vacuous and typically false. The philanderer and libertine speaks from the depths of his privileged hypocrisy, "Nowadays people begin by sneering at family life and family institutions...," yet Tom and his wife are responsible for the deaths of two people, and the destruction of much else. Nick reflects, "They were careless people, Tom and Daisy—they smashed up things and creatures and then retreated back into their money or their vast carelessness...and let other people clean up the mess they had made." They have run America, they do run America.

Fitzgerald knew very well the tragedy of having destroyed Paradise through our own bad behavior. Nick again:

> I became aware of the old island here that flowered once for Dutch sailor's eyes—a fresh, green breast of the new world. Its vanished trees, the trees that had made way for Gatsby's house, had once pandered in whispers to the last and greatest of all human dreams; for a transitory enchanted moment man must have held his breath in the presence of this continent, compelled into an aesthetic contemplation he neither understood nor desired, face to face for the last time in history with something commensurate to his capacity for wonder....Gatsby believed in...the orgiastic future that year by year recedes before us....So we beat on, boats against the current, borne back ceaselessly into the past.

Of course, European and American cultures have many facets, including the ethical and creative. In contrast to the Tom Buchanans of the world are the committed, ethical citizens, the ones who clean up the messes, or try to prevent them from happening. For example, the rich and powerful, in the form of corporations large and small, devastated much of Pennsylvania, ruining its land with strip mines and coal waste, and ruining its streams with mine drainage and industrial pollution. I recall this vividly and painfully from my youth. Now the mess is being cleaned up with public and private money, and public and private labor. Much of the effort comes from committed volunteers. As Fitzgerald accurately said, the rich destroyed things with their "vast carelessness" and let other people "clean up the mess they had made." Fortunately, some people are good enough—very fine indeed—to strive to redeem their environment; unfortunately, "messes" are still being made, and the people who make the messes are still looking for ways to avoid cleaning up after themselves. I am trying to get my mind around the ethical problem of how the ruthless wealthy can destroy a place and walk away with the money, and the ordinary but committed citizen can find it in his heart to undo the harm with no financial end in view. What motivates these secular saints to spend large parts of their lives working for the good? How do they calculate their interests? What gives them the moral clarity to be able to see their true self-interest, while the exploiters are only able to see their immediate and narrow self-interest? I have trouble convincing myself that altruism actually exists; perhaps I am wrong.

All the great religions and ethical systems have taught us that the lowest form of human existence is lived at the material level; that we must raise ourselves above matter. Yet in our society gross materialism yields power, and we paradoxically invest the most materialistic people with the most important roles of leadership, elevating those with the least ethical understanding to the highest social spheres. Those who are devoted to materialism have this in common: a devotion to the lowest level of human and ethical development. In Inupiat society, social standing is determined by how effectively one contributes to the community; the most highly respected person may live in the least of the huts. One is prized according to what one can do. So it was with Sarah and Johnny. They were respected and honored not because they laid away wealth, but because they knew how to live.

Perhaps those who work for the good are motivated partly by a sentiment expressed by Eiseley. What is the human predicament? "How nature is to be reentered; how man, the relatively unthinking and proud creator of the second world—the world of culture—may revivify and restore the first world [the world of nature] which cherished him and brought him into being." Living at this ethical level is significantly higher than living at the level of gross materialism. How do we get there?

ENVIRONMENTAL EXPLOITATION is usually accompanied by human exploitation, as the history of our music records. The songs of Woodie Guthrie are part of a tradition carried on by Bob Dylan and Bruce Springsteen; all three chronicle the deep and profound disconnect between Americans and their land, and the equally profound disconnect of ordinary Americans from economic and political power. This tradition is so deep that you can recall some of these lyrics from memory right now; I need record no examples. We often hear the word "dispossessed" used in this regard: Native Americans dispossessed of their original holdings, small family farmers dispossessed of their land, workers dispossessed of their jobs. A sense of loss is a strong, dark undercurrent beneath the American Dream. One version of the American Dream is based on the idea of happiness through economic gain; equality of economic opportunity results in social justice, we claim. If this is what the American Dream is, our social and economic system produces far too many losers and not enough winners, the American Dream is a lie, and the larger idea of social justice is a simple impossibility.

SARAH'S LIFE WAS dominated by the search for food, and by caring for people—which all translates into hard work in a most difficult environment. The hardest part no doubt was the dark time: the long sunless period each year when the cold makes the earth stand still.

Yet when I peer into her ninety-five-year-old face, I don't see the face of suffering. Her skin is relatively smooth, her facial muscles are relaxed, her body is at rest, she is calm. Obviously she is robust, still living in the wilderness, and she has some years yet to live. She seems happy. For all her hardships, and though she lived under the constraints of a harsh environment, she lived in a world of personal freedom. The Old People gave themselves to life. They knew they were not in charge of fate. The future was uncertain, they lived on their strength and wits, they knew that the ultimate facts of life were beyond their control. They stepped forward into the unknown every day. This is not "freedom" in the abstract, but freedom in the concrete; freedom without fear.

As Becker said of our culture, we are obsessive-compulsive because we are willing to trade today's freedom for tomorrow's safety. Without even being aware of it, I made my bargain, trading the present for the future, at least to an extent. Sarah could never imagine the obsessive-compulsive world of the commuter, the world of totalitarian work, the world of Time. For that I envy her.

AN ANCIENT philosophical debate revolves around the question, Does change occur? Parmenides said not, that the surface appearance of things may deceive us into thinking that the world changes, but that this is an illusion; the foundation is fixed. Heraclitus thought that change was inevitable, that the second time you dipped your foot in the river, the river had changed in the interval; it was not the same river. We have enshrined the former view in the cliché, "The more things change, the more they stay the same." The Stoics, however, understood that the world was in a state of flux, and that humans had to understand this and accommodate themselves to it.

Loren Eiseley has eloquently explained that *novelty* is one characteristic of the process of evolution. The very fact that life exists at all may be the ultimate novelty; the development of life from inorganic matter is perhaps the ultimate mystery and anomaly. The proliferation of millions of species into every environmental nook on earth is one of the wonders of the universe. But there is another aspect of novelty as well. With every new adaptation, every new evolutionary development, a fork in time is reached and something is discarded forever. In evolution, what is gone is permanently gone. There is only the future.

In his essay "The Star Dragon" Eiseley wrote these bold words: that scholars have come to recognize that the skulls of *Homo sapiens* represented "the dropped masks of the beginning of Nature's last great play—the play of man." He is not referring to a religious Apocalypse, an Armageddon, but to the scientific fact that the process of evolution had arrived at a great paradox: it had created a creature that had the tools to escape biological evolution. "He had done so by the development of a specialized organ—the brain—whose essential function was to evade specialization. The tongue and the hand, so disproportionately exaggerated in his motor cortex, were to be its primary instruments." We thus passed out of evolution into history. We passed into Time. This indeed is the Fall of man, this is the source of our tragedy. With our consciousness we became aware of time, death, and the search for meaning.

Our great brain has allowed us to develop a "fantastically accelerated social evolution induced by industrial technology," and since Eiseley wrote these words the acceleration has only increased.

Where is the tragedy? Simply this: by becoming conscious creatures when we left the path of evolution, we substituted thought for instinct. Where once instinct was the basis of behavior, we became the responsible, conscious initiators and judges of our actions. We needed to develop an ethical structure to match our technical ability, and we have failed to do so. While our technology has been steadily accelerating, our ethical development has advanced slightly, if at all, in the last five thousand years. Not only have we failed to advance beyond the ethical frameworks established by the world's great religions, we haven't even lived up to those original teachings. Christianity itself has not understood, absorbed, and implemented the teachings of Christ. And on the secular side, the ethics developed without a religious base, the teachings of Socrates, say, or Spinoza or American pragmatism, are studied, understood, and practiced by a small minority. No wonder the Romantic yearning for a better, purer past, based on healthy instinct and innocent emotion, has such a strong appeal. But *Homo sapiens* cannot indulge in nostalgia, that destructive, enervating emotion. Our only ethical choice is forward. We can only step into the future. The ethical structures we create may one day be our glory, or our shame. One ponders this in fear and trembling.

Loren Eiseley died in 1977, the year I read his fine book *The Invisible Pyramid* while traveling in the Refuge, in the area of Johnny and Sarah's home; I visited the Franks that summer. Johnny Frank died on December 27, 1977, five months after I visited him and Sarah. My biological father also died that memorable year, in the autumn of 1977.

Sometimes Fate, or Chance, presents us with situations that embody a strong symbolism. I thought of the passing of the Old People with sadness, and I looked back through time with yearning and regret. The passing of the Old People was an irrevocable fact.

Done. Forever. I intend to fully cherish their memories, to learn from the past, to feel what is behind me.

But I moved forward from that point. My children too learned to cherish the wilderness, particularly the Arctic National Wildlife Refuge, home of caribou and grizzlies and wolverines and birds, and the home of Sarah and Johnny. Like Sarah Frank and Margaret Murie, they learned to live lives filled with love for what is good, love for what is wild, and love for what is human. Courage, intelligence, love. For my part, I intend to fight human incursions into what is good to the extent that I can. The world that we shape will soon be our past and our grandchildren's present.

South of timberline

CHAPTER 10

Time Past: The Evolution of an Attachment

I write this in late December 2017, more than forty-four years after my first Refuge trek. My planned trip in June 2018 will be my forty-fifth year of travel in the Arctic National Wildlife Refuge.

My attitude towards wilderness travel has evolved as the years have passed. In 1974 I was ignorant and my son was fourteen months old. I can still hear his piping voice as he and his mother saw us off at the train station in Anchorage.

By 1989 I had accumulated considerable experience, and my children, now aged fourteen and sixteen, joined me, as did my wife Diane, for the first time. Now there was a family connection.

I started guiding in 1990. My motive was simple: I had accumulated considerable experience and it was time to share it. Profit was secondary, even tertiary. I had tired of keeping the experience of the Refuge to myself. I was starting to repeat myself and I needed some stimulus for growth.

In 2006 I led my last commercial Refuge trip, down the East Fork of the Chandalar River, with Bob and Nick Clarke and their young friend Dan. I have travelled with Bob and Nick since 2005 and they have come to mean a lot to me. That 2006 float was a demanding and rewarding trip, but the most valuable part was seeing how Nick had grown into a vigorous outdoorsman, and a young man who will carry on the tradition of wilderness preservation.

Since 2006 I have travelled with small groups of friends, and always with Diane. Now I am filling in places on the map where I haven't walked, which usually requires that I also cover ground I am familiar with, always a pleasure. Piecing out a new route for next June—as I write this, my current project—generates considerable anticipation.

So, WE LOOK back and we look ahead. One backward look is particularly pleasurable.

In 2003 daughter Amy took my place as a trekking guide. She was recovering from a persistent illness and part of her recovery was maintaining a connection with the wilderness. Her recovery was emotional as well as physical, and was certainly successful, because she did not lack strength, as we shall see.

Amy had one client in a three passenger Cessna 185, so Jeremy jumped at the chance to occupy that seat. Their plan was to start hiking on the upper Sheenjek River and head straight north.

Amy and Kim eventually headed for the coast—Kim had that as a goal—while Jeremy left them after several days to travel on his own. Amy and Kim had to grind out hard days of at least ten miles per day with no rest days and heavy packs. In the meantime Jeremy peeled off for the various Aichilik drainages, the Jago, and the Okerokovik.

Three of the four members of our family were now leading parallel and separate lives in the same area of the Refuge, because a day after they flew into the Refuge, I too flew in, to the Jago, to begin a solo trip. A thirty-year-old sentiment was in the back of my mind, because during my first trip in 1974 the Jago was the site of our first, and most difficult, river crossing, and our first pass. From here we made the difficult descent into the upper Aichilik valley. I remember that pass as the crux of our 1974 trip. After that descent there was no going back.

In 2003 I explored the upper Jago alone, walking to the south, then returning north to the drainage that we followed to the Jago-Aichilik pass—barely a pass—in 1974. On June 14 I hiked into the fine alpine valley below the pass and made a camp at a place where Jeremy couldn't miss it if he passed that way.

The next day I started up the valley. I tried, as I walked, to draw forth those old memories, now thirty years dormant. But the present intruded: as I hiked upwards I heard insistent bird calls, and saw across the valley a jaeger harassing, of all things, a sheep; and was delighted to see the sheep butt upwards at the jaeger! Twenty or so sheep were nearby on another slope. An unusual wildlife encounter, reminiscent of another time, when I observed a short eared owl tracking a fox, and the fox jumping for it, and of course failing to catch it.

Not long afterwards I saw movement above me. A human. It had to be Jeremy—it was! He had climbed his route out of the upper Aichilik yesterday, the 14th (and a difficult scramble it was, steep, with snow drifts), looked for me at the pass, came down to the first good camp site, and later saw my tent when he scanned from a ridge.

We ascended together. We exchanged news, of course, as we walked upwards, past his camp, then he descended again to break camp while I pushed on to the pass for the sake of the memories. I then descended to him and we continued down to my camp, where he spent the night. We visited through the morning of the next day, when he departed to continue his journey. He calculated that if he walked through the afternoon he could substantially shorten his future daily mileage.

From my journal: "He walked off at about noon or a little before. I watched him go; I thought he would look back from the knoll, and he did; we waved. I felt sad and joyful. I remember how intensely I missed him in '74, loath to part from him and delighted to see him again. Now, thirty year later, we rendezvous here, of all places. A wonderful and pleasing symmetry. We only part for a week, but perhaps wilderness partings mean more. I carried that farewell with me all day."

My time in the Arctic has evolved, from blundering exploration, to expanded knowledge, to establishing family connections, to a period of guiding. Now I travel with friends. We are relaxed in our approach, as befits people who are in their seventh decade of life. We pick good routes, we carry our weight, we walk our miles. We are savvy enough to know what is good for us and what is too much. We balance knowledge of the past with discovery of the new.

What next? More. I know that a time will come when I can go there no longer, but before then perhaps I will travel there with my grandchildren. I would like my bones to be left there in some unknown place, but that is unlikely to happen. As the forty-fifth anniversary of my first trek approaches, I will find a way to celebrate. Probably by doing more of the same.

Near the end of that memorable 2003 trip, on June 22, I sat in camp at the southern edge of the coastal plain by the Jago River looking north. The day was clear, the warming air shimmered with heat waves. On the distant horizon I could barely discern, through the deceptive coastal plain atmosphere, one, two, three

TIME PAST: THE EVOLUTION OF AN ATTACHMENT

shapes. As they neared I saw that they were human; then I could see the backpacks; then three vigorously striding figures, coming in from the North; full circle, so to speak.

So the future is imbedded in the past, and as time passes it unfolds into the present.

Clear, clean Arctic water

High country stream

The last of the spring snow

TIME PAST: THE EVOLUTION OF AN ATTACHMENT

The green of early summer

A surprise in the cold dry Arctic. American dippers nest in this green haven

Upper Junjik River

The mid-Junjik River

UNAVOIDABLE CONSIDERATIONS

EXPLANATORY NOTE

The following four essays are an attempt to explore why many people in the United States are indifferent to our environmental needs; and an attempt to find a corrective. Why include these essays in a book about wilderness travel? Because we cannot, much as we would like to, separate the existence of wilderness from social and political influences. Such purity does not exist. Indeed, the existence of wilderness, and other green space, relies on political decisions, like it or not. Some of the political references in "How the Curse of Materialism Killed the Old Alaska" may seem dated, such as Senator Ted Stevens' removal from the Senate in 2008, but those events from the past are still in play because of their results, and those results will persist into the future. We can be thankful that good environmental legislation will also persist into the future.

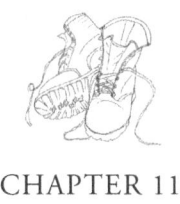

CHAPTER 11

The Curse of Materialism

"We may see the small value God has for riches, by the people he gives them to."

Alexander Pope
Thoughts on Various Subjects, 1727

"Send me some of it [gold], because I and my companions suffer from a disease of the heart that can be cured only with gold."

Hernan Cortes, to Moctezuma's ambassadors,
as quoted by Frederick Turner in *Beyond Geography*

"I wish to speak a word for Nature, for absolute freedom and wildness, as contrasted with a freedom and culture merely civil—to regard man as an inhabitant, or a part and parcel of Nature, rather than a member of society. I wish to make an extreme statement, if so I may make an emphatic one, for there are enough champions of civilization...."

Henry David Thoreau,
from "Walking"

"There is no wealth but life."

John Ruskin

The wilderness traveler inevitably must deal with the simple existential question that is demanded of all humans: Why am I doing this? Opponents of wilderness like to characterize us lovers of the non-motorized outdoors as privileged and egotistical users, anti-democratic elitists, who want to keep wilderness as the playground of the few. These slurs are buttressed by an understanding of "recreation" as something frivolous and much subordinate to the "real" world of work. Serious people who do the "real" work of the world would not have this time to waste. I suggest, however, that "recreation" is very serious and vital. The word is *re-create*, "*v.t.* to create anew; *n.* an act of recreating or the state of being recreated." Creating, or re-creating, one's self is the most important task faced by the individual.

For Thoreau, every excursion was a life-or-death matter, because one was incessantly confronted by the challenge of *living*; and because every moment was charged with ethical significance. He writes in *Walden,* "Our whole life is startlingly moral. There is never an instant's truce between virtue and vice." In his essay "Walking," he speculates that one etymology of the word "to saunter" is "*sans terre*, without land or a home…but equally at home everywhere….For every walk is a sort of crusade….We should go forth on the shortest walk, perchance, in the spirit of undying adventure, never to return—prepared to send back our embalmed hearts only as relics of our desolate kingdoms. If you are ready to leave father and mother, and brother and sister, and wife and child and friends, and never see them again—if you have paid your debts, and made your will, and settled all your affairs, and are a free man, then you are ready for a walk."

How we live our lives is our most important business. Stepping forth, our feet on the ground, to face what comes to us, is no trivial matter. When we do so, then, we must question our motives and means.

The wilderness traveler confronts, and must deal with, two worlds: one's self, and the world of matter. We must deal with the latter on multiple levels. Of course, there is the material world of weather, water, and topography. However, there is also another layer of the material that is fundamental to the experience, and that is our relationship to the larger culture and its economy. We visitors to the wilderness are among the rich of the world. As visitors, what is our relationship, not just to the wilderness, but to our wealth? Can we establish a genuine, honest, unhypocritical relationship to the wilderness without also clarifying where we stand in relation to our privileged economic position? We lovers of the wilderness probably have a touch of the Romantic in us; we probably contain a dash of some kind of Idealism. I find that those impulses may be at odds with our materialism. I know that I need to resolve these contradictions within myself.

I know of three kinds of materialism. Philosophical materialism holds that all existence is identified with matter: everything either is or comes from matter.

Economic materialism stresses the desire to possess wealth. It emphasizes that every aspect of one's life is affected by the possession or acquisition of wealth: wealth in the concrete (the castle on the hill) or the abstract (the numbers on the quarterly statement). One's worth as a human being—as in the phrase "he is worth X number of dollars"—is literally based on this kind of wealth.

The third kind of materialism has no name that I know of. I will call it "the materialism of the utilitarian object." This view stresses the value of an object in and of itself, regardless of its market value. This view recognizes that owning a physical object doesn't necessarily reflect a person's "worth." This view, unlike philosophical materialism, is compatible with spiritualism. This view also prompts the question: can a physical object have *intrinsic* value? Of course not, say the economists; everything has a price. True enough, I suppose, but must that value be expressed in money or determined by markets? Can a vital utility create intrinsic worth?

Decades ago my wife Diane bought two cooking pots for camping. She paid $.35 for them at the Salvation Army thrift store. I can't begin to estimate how often they have been used, the number of places they have been, or, most important, the value of the essential function they have performed. I place a very high value on those blackened and battered old pots, yet they have no economic value at all. I doubt if I could give them away. Yet their function has been absolutely vital, and I love them for what they are.

We "Idealists" often forget that Alaska's aboriginals were, in this sense, very materialistic. What value would a five-gallon food tin have for an aboriginal Eskimo? A sturdy metal container, relatively durable, that can withstand the heat of a fire? That can be put to a wide variety of uses? That is beyond their means to manufacture? Such an object would be priceless, an heirloom. This is true simple necessary materialism, the materialism of the utilitarian object, when the value of the *thing* is understood. Our garbage dumps are full of such objects.

WHAT I CALLED "economic materialism" above of course dominates our culture. It is commonplace to observe and condemn our materialism, and to say that money is our God and religion. I fear that we have heard these sentiments so often that they have lost their force. Yet these words are truer than we realize. They are *profoundly* true, and it is important that we grasp their import.

We read that Roman Catholicism dominated every detail of an individual's life during the Middle Ages. (The writings of

Johann Huizinga are particularly valuable on this subject.) The sacraments, of course, were the most important and visible religious expressions, but each day, even each hour, had religious significance; one's entire life was an expression of religious symbolism. Roman Catholicism so completely permeated each individual's life and behavior that it was apparently impossible for most people even to begin to visualize any alternative. People lived within that culture as fish live in water or people in air: it was a medium that was so intimately entwined with one's life and embedded within one's mind that its power was both total and unconscious. It controlled and determined behavior to such an extent that we must conclude that these people were largely unfree. They lived out their lives according to the template that they were born into, and all beliefs and behavior were determined by the Church unto the least detail.

Modern American materialism has precisely the same controlling power over us, and we are equally unfree, and unaware of our unfreedom. Of course, like a citizen of Medieval Europe, we are free to salt our food or not, drink wine or not drink wine, select this or that article of clothing. But in the significant aspects of life we are just as trapped inside a closed system as the least of the Medieval peasantry. We are the slaves of an unconscious dogmatism

Our modern materialism takes three forms:

1) The enlargement of the self through conspicuous consumption. Thorstein Veblen's apt phrase is more pertinent now than ever. It's not just the Cadillac that people must display, it is the Hummer; it is not just the big house on the hill, it is the castle on the mountain in Colorado; it's not just the second home, it is the third or fourth mansion. And it is not just the Hearsts and Vanderbilts, it is anyone at all who has been able to get a big enough piece of our economic expansion. We chew up land and spend resources on objects of no utility, houses that sit empty, simply to satisfy an unrecognized emotional drive. Unfreedom.

Our conspicuous consumption is meant for display, and is aggressive. The most repellent vehicle of them all, that takes up the most space and is the most wasteful, the Hummer, is made for warfare; the big pickup and the big SUV are near cousins.

2) Money and power are equivalencies. For a certain kind of egotist the attainment of power is an irresistible drive. It is those egotists whom the popular culture most admires.

3) We are accumulators and hoarders. We invest our emotional lives in our things. Things substitute for actions; i.e., substitute for living. What does a woman do if she plans a wedding? She *shops*. Pregnant? *Shops*. You prepare for parenthood—the advent of a human being—by buying things. Or read a magazine devoted to, say, hunting. The real story is in the advertisements. How do you become a hunter? By buying an ATV, by buying a trailer for the ATV, by buying a large truck to pull the trailer for the ATV, by buying a garageful of doodads to go along with the truck and the trailer and the ATV. And so on. It never ends. And does our outdoorsman actually put his feet on the ground in the forest? Observe animals and their behavior? Learn what plants and birds live in that habitat? Obtain fulfillment through connection with the world that he and his prey inhabit and share? Not likely. He is a consumer first and last, and it is a requirement of his existence that his life be mediated by his purchases, that they serve as a substitute for experience.

As I write these words, on December 23, my fellow citizens are fulfilling their civic obligation of shopping. A newspaper article this morning adopted the theme of instructing the reader what to buy—since buying is an obligation—at "the last minute," for "that hard-to-buy-for special somebody." Yesterday the newspaper instructed parents how to buy gifts for their adolescent children, apparently a specialized skill. The helpful author included a list of electronic paraphernalia and goods designed firmly to cement the youngster's materialism; objects that would help the adolescents keep their distance from reality. Now I write again, on December 28, and the newspaper instructs its readers how to dispose of their junk. One article deals with the critical problem of creating storage space for all our acquisitions; another deals with how to get rid of stuff now that we have lots of new stuff. The challenges of the materialistic creed never end.

It is ironic in the extreme that there has never been a religion or a widely respected ethical system that placed a high value on materialism. On the contrary, it is very nearly a universal truth that, of all the values to which humans cling, materialism is of the least value, the least worthy of respect, the least satisfying emotionally and intellectually and spiritually. Yet we have devoted ourselves to this most worthless of value systems; the Rich are the Saints whom we emulate; and Alan Greenspan was for decades the Prophet closest to God. His voice was, as they say, oracular. The power of this materialism in the United States considerably outweighs all the spiritual force of Catholicism and Protestantism and Mormonism; the vaunted power of the Evangelicals is as nothing compared to the materialistic creed; for they too are materialists. Whether it is the vast wealth of the Vatican and its many branches, the extensive business network of the Mormons, or the Evangelical belief that wealth accrues to the saved, economic materialism trumps theology in practice, regardless of the austerity preached by the creed.

As for the less-than-rich, or even the poor: they too follow the creed of materialism as much as anyone, for they want to obtain vicariously what the rich already have. Their televisions are tuned to the "rich and famous," their tabloid gossip is all about the rich, they know them by their first names. Celebrities thrive only because they have an audience; and their audience has substituted vicarious existence for actual experience, which, in truth, is the implicit purpose of television, and now other forms of electronic entertainment as well.

IT IS VERY difficult to escape the materialistic trap for the simple reason that our culture wields nearly overwhelming power over us. This statement will be very difficult for many people to accept. We have been taught since we were old enough to understand language, and we have come to accept as an article of faith rather than empirical knowledge, that we are "free." We have also been taught, with the same insistence, that the individual is the sacred unit of social life. The social organism, we think, is secondary to the importance of the individual, and by accepting this as a truism we usually fail to recognize its immense delusive power. We have an unjustified faith—and it is no more than a faith—that we are nearly absolutely free and autonomous individuals, whereas in fact we are intensely conformist in our behavior and very dependent upon the larger society for support and sustenance. Even our nonconformity follows certain protocols and is a projection of one pre-packaged image or another (rebellious redneck, rebellious biker, rebellious driver-of-muddy-pickup-truck-with-loud-muffler, rebellious listener-of-rap-music-with-heavy-base, on and on.) More than a century and a half ago Alexis de Tocqueville observed that Americans were uncommonly conformist, and so we continue to be. We are in fact a nation of imitators, and we imbibed conformity and materialism with our mother's milk, or to be more exact, in front of the television set, and later, from numerous electronic sources. Most of these images—biker, rapper, bad boys of one kind or another—have nothing whatsoever to do with freedom, but rather with rebellion; and even fantasies of rebellion are imitations. In fact, the rebel is the most slavish conformist of all: they all look interchangeable, they wear the uniform. But the question should not be which rebellious posture to assume; the real question is, What do you do with the freedom you have? The American rebel wouldn't know what to do with himself once he realized that he is free. He wouldn't know whom to imitate.

AN ASSUMED CONTRAST and conflict between wilderness and civilization controls a large part of our debate about the value of wilderness and about the importance of certain kinds of economic growth. Both sides in the debate accept the dichotomy of "wilderness" versus "civilization." This dichotomy is the single major theme in Roderick Frazier Nash's influential book *Wilderness and the American Mind*, often referred to as the definitive history of the wilderness movement in America.

This dichotomy exists in the *language* of the debate but not in the reality of the facts, is therefore false, and skews the debate about the value of establishing additional wilderness areas and protecting existing wilderness.

First, let us assume that there really is such a conflict. If so, then we must declare a victor: civilization has won! Its victory was complete a long time ago. It is impossible to say exactly when that victory occurred. In the Eastern hemisphere, many centuries ago; in North America, one likely date would be the closing of the frontier in the mid-to-late nineteenth century as noted by Frederick Jackson Turner. In any case, in our nation of 320 million people (and increasing rapidly), in a nation of aggressive economic activity, and in a nation committed to the materialistic creed, the idea that the existence of wilderness somehow threatens civilization is an absolute absurdity, as is the idea that continued economic growth depends upon the invasion of wilderness.

(The first time I saw Hoover Dam, I was overwhelmed by its absurdity. I had never before been to Las Vegas, and the moment I walked down the jet way into McCarran I knew I had entered a sick place, a place built, first, upon crime, and second, upon human fallibility and vice. I was at Hoover Dam about two hours later, and my first thought was, we destroyed these canyons so that the moral sump of Las Vegas and its close relative Los Angeles could burn the electricity and waste the water. This forms the most complete contrast I can imagine when I think of wilderness versus "civilization." The Bureau of Reclamation still has a plaque in place stating how important the dam is; it actually says that they "made the desert bloom." There is in fact no blooming in that desert, neither biological nor metaphorical, except the blooming of neon, cement, buildings, vice, the artificial emerald of golf courses, and human exploitation.)

Second, the term "civilization" needs to be defined. Just as the term "development" is often a euphemism for "destruction," just as the term "growth" often means "loss," so much of "civilization" as we know it is in truth "barbarism." Mountaintop removal in the coalfields, interstate highway construction that levels the severest topography, and longwall mining and its subsequent subsidence, are three examples of barbarism directed at the crust of the earth. Mercury from coal fired power plants, chemicals imbedded within foods, and poisons distributed into the air from vehicles and industries, are three examples of barbaric behavior directed towards humans. The destruction of estuaries and wetlands, the loss of topsoil, and the pollution of fresh and salt water, are examples of barbaric behavior directed at the base of our ecosystem and food supply. Western forestry practices, drawing down the aquifers of the southwest, and animal grazing in arid regions, are three examples of barbaric activities directed at the sustainability of life in fragile environments. The confused hodgepodge of ugly business establishments that have enveloped almost every town and city, the vast sprawl of housing developments, and the excrescences of services at major highway interchanges, are three examples of barbarian chaos. And perhaps the most barbaric activities of all: we drive large aggressive vehicles, we casually consume and waste enormous amounts of energy, and we are changing the climate of the entire globe. This behavior is not only destructive, it is aggressively so; it is violent; and the violence is performed by ordinary people who are very nice, who consider their behavior to be normal. Well, their behavior *is* normal. That is exactly the problem. I suppose that many of them consider themselves to be environmentalists.

My Random House unabridged defines "civilization" as: "An advanced state of human society, in which a high level of culture, science, industry, and government has been reached." And my American Heritage dictionary adds the words "intellectual development," and in another definition, "Cultural or intellectual refinement; good taste." Neither dictionaries anywhere include "High ethical development" in their definitions. I suppose the word "civilization" in the narrow sense is neutral. It simply identifies the culture under discussion regardless of the value of the culture; in the strictest narrowest sense all are of equal value. What I mean here, however, is not free of value. I am assuming that civilizations are bad, good, better, best. And I am concluding that when we compare American "civilization" to wilderness, and suggest that wilderness should yield to "civilization" and be consumed by it, we are in fact participating in the degradation of the Earth. For example, it is one thing to transform the earth into, say, Italian or French agriculture; it is something else again to develop an agricultural system that often resembles mining more than husbandry.

The creed of materialism is the driving force behind this litany of destruction. The practitioners of this creed, be they the American auto industry, the mining industry, the energy companies, real estate and construction firms—on and on, industries too numerous to list—oppose every corrective, they attack every step forward, they erect every possible obstacle to right behavior. Loren Eiseley called us "the world eaters." And so we are.

As for the supposed conflict between wilderness and civilization: it takes a civilized people to establish and defend wilderness. Barbaric economic behavior stands opposed to wilderness. The conflict isn't between wilderness and civilization, but between wilderness and barbarism. Wilderness and civilization are wholly compatible.

America is not an abstraction. America is a real concrete place. Unfortunately, patriotism as it is commonly practiced appeals to our love of the abstract America, the America suggested by abstract nouns such as "liberty" and "freedom." But true patriotism expresses love for the real thing: the ground we walk upon, the air we breathe, the water we drink, the lives that we share the planet with, including our fellow citizens. I challenge the world-eaters to actually love, in practice, the real America, rather than behaving as if they have contempt for it. If you love America, you don't poison it or damage it. If you love America, you express that love through your actions, not through abstract words that refer to abstract concepts such as "liberty" and "freedom"—abstract nouns that name conditions that we often avoid in practice. Beware: when we embrace the abstraction we lose the ability to see and experience what is real.

THOREAU'S PHRASE "in Wildness is the preservation of the World" inevitably comes to mind here. I am inclined to think that, in truth, our preservation will also depend on reforming our agricultural practices, protecting our water, creating efficiencies in transportation, energy consumption, and manufacturing, and providing for economic justice. But, as usual, Thoreau had a more radical—that is, more fundamental—idea in mind.

Thoreau's phrase is to be found in the essay titled, appropriately enough, "Walking." "In Wildness is the preservation of the World. Every tree sends its fibers forth in search of the Wild. The cities import it at any price. Men plow and sail for it. From the forest and wilderness come the tonics and barks which brace mankind. Our ancestors were savages....I believe in the forest, and in the meadow, and in the night in which the corn grows....Give me a wildness whose glance no civilization can endure." (For Thoreau, the word "savage" is not a slur. Here, it simply acknowledges our history.)

As I mentioned above, one argument against establishing legally protected wilderness is that it is for the elite, a playground for the rich, a haven for the few. The truth is, the "elite" are vacationing at a Club Med and the rich are planning their fourth mansion, this one in Colorado, on a mountain with a view: everyone can see it. As for wilderness being a haven with few visitors, this is true. I do not see why that should be considered a criticism.

I know that entering the wilderness helped to make me whole. The wilderness taught me about myself. It taught me my physical strengths and limitations. It taught me how to think, and how to make judgments. It taught me to develop my character, such as learning patience, and at least recognizing the importance of humility. (It is so difficult to quench pride, that I am hesitant to say that I learned humility.) It taught me several aspects of love, and how to sharpen my intellectual curiosity. I know that it taught these qualities, and much more, to my children.

So I am left with an apparent paradox: in my experience, the wilderness is a very human place. Contrary to what its critics say, the wilderness is not a place in which people are aliens, or that is intrinsically hostile to people, somehow inhuman. The wilderness is a good place to be human. Thoreau was right: Wildness—including wilderness—is necessary to the preservation of the world, the human world: civilization. In the most radical, most basic way, it is the surest anchor we have. Would you rather anchor to that, or to the creed of materialism? Can I say, "In television is the preservation of the world?" "In money is the preservation of the world?" "In computers is the preservation of the world?" "In cars is the preservation of the world?" "In evangelical and fundamentalist religion is the preservation of the world?" "In commercial sports is the preservation of the world?" I am trying to insert into Thoreau's phrase what our culture pays most attention to, and they only sound ridiculous. Thoreau was right. Our wilderness areas are environmental banks, our residue of savings from the biological past. They are places in which our ancient memories reside, perhaps places that our teenage "gamers" and electronic addicts will turn to some day when they decide that they want to deal with reality. When our culture grows up to a higher level of understanding, when the creed of materialism gives way to a deeper, more mature ethical knowledge, when we reach a greater understanding of what it is to be human, our wilderness, if we preserve it, will be waiting for us.

THE MATERIALISM I learned in the wilderness is the materialism of the utilitarian object. I am hesitant to insist that any human artifact has intrinsic value, but I do know that the utility of some things is so important that they are very nearly priceless. My cook pots. My tent. My boots. My rain coat. When I travel in the wilderness, I try to imagine the needs of the Old People—how do you stay alive at –40 F? No, that's not right. Simply staying alive is not enough. How do you maintain your essential humanity at –40 F? How do you give birth? Suckle a baby? Raise toddlers? Prepare adolescents for maturity? Maintain the social fabric? The material foundation for such a life must have been precious beyond words; precious beyond money.

When in the wilderness, I discard the trivial. This is brought home to me when I reflect on what my mind may have dwelt upon before I start a trip, and then again after I get into a trip. Before a trip, I might think about car repairs or bank statements, buying a lawn mower or fixing a washing machine. But once in the wilderness each and every one of those concerns evaporates. They are so trivial that during a wilderness excursion I have trouble recalling what I once thought was important to me. I remember a phrase that I recite to myself as a mantra when I walk: "Only a few things are important." It is strange how easily I forget such a simple injunction when I return from the wilderness.

I remember what is materially important when I am in the wilderness—my fleece pullover, my sleeping bag, my stove, my pack—and I place a proper valuation on those items. I envision transferring that attitude to my life within the civilized world. How do I place a proper valuation on any material object? How can our culture come to value its things properly? One way is the Thoreauvian way, as mentioned by the essayist Curtis White: attend carefully to each object we handle, every nail that we drive. Live with a strenuous *alertness*.

We need to think about what we *do*. We need to think about our actions rather than our possessions. Even the most committed materialists must know somewhere inside themselves that investing their emotional lives in their things cannot produce happiness. You cannot *be what you possess*; instead, *you are what you do*. The Old People knew this, and they valued the person who could *act*, not *display*. The deep commitment to the materialistic creed has a large obsessive-compulsive component to it. We feel an overwhelming need to pile up a stash against the future, both in the abstract form of money or in the concrete form of things. But life isn't static, it has no end point short of death, there is no ideal state to attain. Life is for the living; but the materialist surrounds himself with dead objects. Of all creeds, it is closest to death, and produces death through its violence.

How to escape a binding ideology, a dogma that has the force of religion?

I try to circle back to what makes me happy.

I KNOW THAT the best antidote for anything that ails me, including materialism, is to do something of value. Who am I? *I am what I do*. What establishes the quality of my life? *The quality of my actions*.

This commitment to activity is, however, personal. I will not save the world by preaching this advice. But still, our world does need to be saved; it does need to be transformed. How can we transform ourselves into something better than idolaters of the Thing?

I think it must occur incrementally, in the same way that conservationists have indeed changed the world for the better during the previous century. When I feel overwhelmed by the corruption of our economic lives, when I think of the clever men in suits who have impoverished all of us by manipulating our laws, regulations, and economy, and the energy companies who controlled the Executive Branch during the first eight years of this century, and the right-wing commitment to a sterile ideology, I remember what conservationists have accomplished, and what America's most powerful economic forces have been unable, in spite of their power and best efforts, to undo. In the area of public lands, we have our parks, forests, monuments, and refuges, threatened but more or less intact. In the area of environmental protection, we do have clean water and air laws, and they have survived waves of right-wing attacks. The coastal plain of the Arctic National Wildlife Refuge has not been drilled, though it will continue to be threatened until it gets wilderness status. And we sometimes forget what can happen at the state and local levels. Much good can come from the other levels of government. The good fight doesn't have to be fought only in Washington, D. C.

The commitment to environmental protection is the precise antidote to the creed of materialism. A commitment to the environment and a rejection of materialism both appeal to a higher ethical standard; both challenge our culture to be better than what it was; both challenge the individual to reach inside himself and find a way to grow. Our movement towards a higher level of ethical behavior will occur in a multitude of small ways. Jared Diamond writes a book called *Collapse* that recognizes that humans are rational creatures, able to make rational decisions, and points out in concrete detail what decisions are necessary to our survival. The Rails-to-Trails Foundation continues to get trails built, one of the most salutary developments of the past thirty years. The Nature Conservancy continues to find land to preserve; Audubon Alaska continues to use science effectively to advocate for environmental protections. California can use its power to lever the nation towards higher automobile fuel standards and lower greenhouse gas emissions. As Gregg Easterbrook has written, the only reason why we haven't solved the greenhouse gas problem is because we haven't tried. It takes legislation. Scientific and moral suasion to that end is a real hope.

The list of effective organizations is too long for me to enumerate. One example: I know of one small, impoverished town in western Pennsylvania that was able to build a trail corridor and preserve a significant piece of acreage as high-quality forestland while also attacking the formidable task of cleaning up mine waste left behind by a cut-and-run coal company. It took decades of very hard work and commitment to accomplish what they did. They haven't finished yet; they are still moving forward and they continue to have ambitious plans. They did not do this as people of wealth and privilege; Apollo, Pennsylvania isn't Ann Arbor or Madison; but they did it anyway. You probably have never heard of the Roaring Run Watershed Association; but whenever I think of them I am heartened, and filled with admiration. Good things can be accomplished. There are very, very good people in this world. I am reminded: despair is a sin.

In good farming practices is the preservation of the world; in the protection of water is the preservation of the world; in good forestry is the preservation of the world; in the practice of honorable politics is the preservation of the world; in economic justice is the preservation of the world. In Wildness is the preservation of the World.

Thoreau traveled to the wilderness, but he spent most of his time in a tamed small town and a domesticated rural environment. In truth, an infinitesimally small portion of *Homo sapiens* lives in the wilderness. In my case, most of my outdoor hours are spent in places that in fact straddle the wild and the civilized. I love my ski trails, my bike trails, my walking trails. I love my urban parks and greenbelts. I am unusually fortunate to live in a city, Anchorage, Alaska, that has many effective park and trail advocates, and that includes an exceptionally large amount of green space, and which borders a very large wilderness park. Because I spend a large part of my year in the wilderness, and another large part of my year in environments touched in various ways by civilization, I am acutely aware that the values of nature may affect us in many ways and from many directions. In the quote from Thoreau's "Walking," we observe that he recognizes this. He believes in the forest, but also "the night in which the [domestic] corn grows," and his hut on Walden Pond was an easy stroll from the village. Nature can be present in our lives in many ways, and true wilderness and carefully husbanded land do not necessarily form a mutually exclusive contrast. Aldo Leopold knew this. His early career in the Southwest eventually came to focus on the value of wilderness and resulted in the nation's first legally designated wilderness, the Gila. However, his subsequent work in Wisconsin, as documented in his *For the Health of the Land,* was devoted to conservation on privately held land that was used for forestry and agriculture. This latter interest was as prophetic as his interest in wilderness and must become one of our first concerns. It avails us little if our wilderness enclaves, regardless of their size, are surrounded by deteriorating air and land and water. Most of us spend most of our time in an environment that in one way or another is crafted. We need to focus on the nature of the husbandry that we undertake. Like Thoreau and Leopold, we must recognize that the preservation of wilderness and the nurturing of more civilized places are complimentary.

THOREAU HAS SOMETHING to tell us about philosophical materialism. Not surprisingly, his keen insight is the result of a wilderness excursion. I quote extensively from the "Ktaadn" chapter of *The Maine Woods*:

"Perhaps I most fully realized that this was primeval, untamed, and forever untamable *Nature*, or whatever else men call it, while coming down this part of the mountain. We were passing over 'Burnt Lands,' burnt by lightning, perchance, though they showed no recent marks of fire, hardly so much as a charred stump, but looked rather like a natural pasture for the moose and deer, exceedingly wild and desolate, with occasional strips of timber crossing them, and low poplars springing up, and patches of blueberries here and there. I found myself traversing them familiarly, like some pasture run to waste, or partially reclaimed by man; but when I reflected what man, what brother or sister or kinsman of our race made it and claimed it, I expected the proprietor to rise up and dispute my passage. It is difficult to conceive of a region uninhabited by man. We habitually presume his presence and influence everywhere. And yet we have not seen pure Nature, unless we have seen her thus vast and drear and unhuman, though in the midst of cities. Nature was here something savage and awful, though beautiful. I looked with awe at the ground I trod on, to see what the Powers had made there, the form and fashion and material of their work. This was that Earth of which we have heard, made out of Chaos and Old Night. Here was no man's garden, but the unhandselled globe. It was not lawn, nor pasture, nor mead, nor woodland, nor lea, nor arable, nor waste land. It was the fresh and natural surface of the planet Earth, as it was made forever and ever,—to be the dwelling of man, we say,—so Nature made it, and man may use it if he can. Man was not to be associated with it. It was Matter, vast, terrific,—not his Mother Earth that we have heard of, not for him to tread on, or be buried in,—no, it were being too familiar even to let his bones lie there,—the home, this, of Necessity and Fate. There was clearly felt the presence of a force not bound to be kind to man. It was a place for heathenism and superstitious rites,—to be inhabited by men nearer of kin to the rocks and to wild animals than we. We walked over it with a certain awe, stopping, from time to time, to pick the blueberries which grew there, and had a smart and spicy taste. Perchance where *our* wild pines stand, and leaves lie on their forest floor, in Concord, there were once reapers, and husbandmen planted grain; but here not even the surface had been scarred by man, but it was a specimen of what God saw fit to make the world. What is it to be admitted to a museum, to see a myriad of particular things, compared with being shown some star's surface, some hard matter in its home! I stand in awe of my body, this matter to which I am bound has become so strange to me. I fear not spirits, ghosts, of which I am one,—*that* my body might,—but I fear bodies, I tremble to meet them. What is this Titan that has possession of me? Talk of mysteries! Think of our life in nature,—daily to be shown matter, to come in contact with it,—rocks, trees, wind on our cheeks! the *solid* earth! the *actual* world! the *common sense! Contact! Contact! Who* are we? *where* are we?"

This remarkable passage reveals to us the psychological mystery of philosophical materialism. One would not expect to find it in a writer who is usually classified as a Transcendentalist with (perhaps erroneously) Romantic leanings. The passage begins in mild confusion caused by the strangeness of this wilderness environment, and ends with existential dread at the alien material world we inhabit. I know of no other passage in literature that shows the emotional turmoil, even despair, to which epistemological confusion can lead us. Annie Dillard struggled with the same problem in *Pilgrim at Tinker Creek*. How can we connect to a world of matter, vast, alien, mysterious; frequently dreadful;

indeed, often monstrous? And the paradox is that we ourselves are material—"What is this Titan that has possession of me?"—and so are left in awe of ourselves and perhaps as alienated from ourselves as we are from the world of rocks and wind.

The wilderness has induced this feeling in me also, a conviction that Nature is prone to confusion and chaos; its indifference is total, because it is Matter, and Matter cannot care. This confounds us; our difficulty in defining ourselves is intensified; the human paradox is magnified; and Thoreau is led back to the eternal questions, Who are we? Where are we? The bubble we live in, wrapped up as we are in civilization, with its cultural dictates and material protections, can be pricked. Gaining a view of Chaos and Old Night may be as close to transcendence as we will ever get.

WHILE WE AMERICANS congratulate ourselves on being the richest country ever to exist, we shield ourselves from other more important truths. These have to do with the size of our population, including our rate of population growth, the distribution of our wealth, and our ability to be happy.

I quote Jared Diamond (*Collapse*, Viking, 2005, pp. 511-512):

"The 10 countries with the most people (over 100 million each) are, in descending order of population, China, India, the U.S., Indonesia, Brazil, Pakistan, Russia, Japan, Bangladesh, and Nigeria. The 10 countries with the highest affluence (per-capita real GDP) are, in descending order, Luxembourg, Norway, the U.S., Switzerland, Denmark, Iceland, Austria, Canada, Ireland, and the Netherlands. The only country on both lists is the U.S.

"Actually, the countries with large populations are disproportionately poor: eight of the 10 have per-capita GDP under $8,000, and five of them under $3,000. The affluent countries have disproportionately few people: seven of the 10 have populations below 9,000,000, and two of them under 500,000. Instead, what does distinguish the two lists is population growth rates: all 10 of the affluent countries have very low relative population growth rates (1% per year or less), while eight of the 10 most populous countries have higher relative population growth rates than any of the most affluent countries, except for two large countries that achieved low population growth in unpleasant ways [China and Russia]. Thus, as an empirical fact, more people and a higher population growth rate mean more poverty, not more wealth." Thus does Jared Diamond counter the argument that "the more people, the better, because more people mean more inventions and ultimately more wealth."

The *Scientific American* devoted its September 2005 issue to "Crossroads for Planet Earth." This single issue is one of the most important compendiums of facts and concepts that I have encountered in a long time. A particularly interesting article on demographics, ("Human Population Grows Up," Joel E. Cohen, p. 48), includes some interesting facts that places the United States in some very odd company indeed. "Virtually all [global] population growth in the next 45 years is expected to happen in today's economically less developed regions....Half the global increase will be accounted for by just nine nations. Listed in the order of their anticipated contribution [to population growth], they are India, Pakistan, Nigeria, Democratic Republic of the Congo, Bangladesh, Uganda, the U.S., Ethiopia, and China. The only rich country on the list is the U.S., where roughly one third of population growth is driven by a high rate of immigration." One might well add, that the high rate of immigration—the U.S. at this writing accepts more immigrants annually than all other nations combined—is driven primarily by economic considerations rather than by humanitarian impulses. According to Michael Lind in *The Atlantic,* the immigration law now in effect, passed in the 1990s, was heavily influenced by business lobbyists. A high level of immigration (between 1.2 and 1.8 million *legal* immigrants per year, somewhat less after 2007, driven largely by coat-tailing family members into the States) makes for larger retail markets and cheap labor, which helps to lower salaries and wages and undermine the unions. Why go offshore if you can bring offshore labor onshore? So our policies stab workers in the back—our own fellow citizens—make the middle and lower classes poorer, and place additional stress on our own institutions (schools for example) and the environment (through increased consumption and construction). (Keep in mind that these numbers refer to *legally sanctioned* immigration: what the lawmakers and their lobbyists *want.* Illegal immigration is a separate issue.) This aspect of our culture is driven by the materialistic creed and has little—just a little—to do with humanitarian impulses.

The United States has chosen not to follow the path of Sweden, Norway, Finland, Iceland, Switzerland, et al, towards stability, but is heading willy-nilly into unknown territory. *The Atlantic* and the *Scientific American* both ran a summary of an important study (Adrian White, University of Leicester) that attempted to measure happiness around the globe. The findings indicate that a list of the happiest countries correlates closely with Jared Diamond's list of the wealthiest countries per capita; the exception is the United States. We recall that these countries are small and well organized. Apparently, a certain minimum level of material wealth is necessary for happiness, but doesn't guarantee happiness. Social and economic justice, and personal security, are also necessary. An example of economic justice is knowing that you are getting a fair share of the nation's wealth. An example of personal security is knowing that you will receive health care.

THE CURSE OF MATERIALISM

I find it unsettling that the United States made the "A" list for wealth, but only the "B" list for happiness, and ranks with the most populous, and wretched, third-world countries in population growth.

EARLIER IN THIS essay I asked the question, How could I escape the trap of the materialistic creed that controls our national life? My answer for myself was to deflect my attention from *things* to *actions*. My suggestion for the culture was to re-dedicate ourselves to the world we live in, to connect with the physical environment we inhabit, to find meaning in the natural world we are blessed with and should assume responsibility for. In other words, to find it in our hearts to love something other than ourselves.

Curtis White makes an additional suggestion, to be found in his excellent essay "The Spirit of Disobedience," (*Harper's*, April 2006, p.31). He correctly observes that America is not primarily religious, but materialistic; he also asserts that capitalism trumps Enlightenment impulses. "Capitalism has not believed and does not believe in the authority of Christ's spiritual vision nor does it feel constrained by Kant's Enlightenment ethic, which argued that human beings should be treated as ends, not means."

Like me, Curtis White finds inspiration, and answers, in Thoreau; not Thoreau the Transcendentalist, but Thoreau the Radical: neither Republican nor Democrat, neither Conservative nor Liberal. When we are in dire need, what do we do? We should "return to the fundamentals of being human.... [Thoreau's] answer would imply at least three things. First, a refusal of the world as it stands. Second, a recommitment to fundamentals. What does it mean for a human being to need a house? Food? Clothing? [What I have called "the materialism of the utilitarian object."]

Third, an understanding that to stand before the questions of these fundamentals requires spirit. Thoreau called it awareness. I make my home with *this* plank. I make my food with *this* seed. This awareness is really a form of prayer, and our culture is nearly bereft of it…. When we…share an impulse that separates us from a state not only distracted but apparently bent on its own destruction, and when we can again confront work in a way that reconnects us spiritually with human 'fundamentals,' then we will have recalled life from the culture of death…. We need to work inventively—as Christ did, as Thoreau did—in the spirit of disobedience for the purpose of refusing the social order…and putting in its place a culture of life-giving things."

The curse of materialism is that it condemns us to live in a "culture of death," in which we invest our emotional and intellectual and physical selves in dead things. As for me, I must be vigilant, like Thoreau, because "Our whole life is startlingly moral. There is never an instant's truce between virtue and vice." I must always remember: keep your feet on the ground.

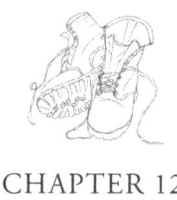

CHAPTER 12

How the Curse of Materialism Destroyed the Old Alaska

Our national dedication to material wealth has a strong political component. When my wife and I came to Alaska in 1970, the construction boom associated with the building of the Trans-Alaska Pipeline had not yet occurred, hence the oil (and money) from Prudhoe Bay had not yet started to flow, and I was pleased at the quality of our government in Alaska, including both major parties. During the 1970s, when the Viet Nam war, and then Watergate, had soured many people on the possibility of good government, and when high oil prices and inflation had caused many people to doubt the future, I thought that Alaska was an exception. We were functioning under good government. I was convinced that people came to settle in Alaska for love, not money.

Even in urban Anchorage one could sense the old Alaska not far away. Perhaps the best indicator that the old Alaska was nearby was the fact that Alaska Natives were viewed with considerable respect by the "dominant culture." True, there was a dark history that Alaska Natives were and are keenly aware of, mainly the abuses perpetrated upon them in the schools, some BIA, some missionary. There was the forced relocation of Aleuts (Unangans) during World War II. There were certainly episodes of injustice and racism in our past, and the recent exposure of Roman Catholic sexual exploitation revealed that Alaska Natives were among the most abused. But Alaskan history was relatively benign compared to what Native Americans had experienced in the rest of the United States, and at that time, before Oil, relations between Alaska Natives and the "dominant culture" were relatively good.

As soon as the oil started to flow many things changed irrevocably. Oil wealth has brought many material benefits to Alaska, but I think that the bad far outweighs the good, because political corruption followed immediately. People chased the oil boom north, and our population doubled in the decade of the 1970s. The nature of the electorate changed because of the change in the work force, resulting in a strong right-wing shift. When that change happened, attitudes towards Alaska's Natives also changed, creating a rural-urban split that now seems unbridgeable. ("The rural-urban split" is our term for the Native subsistence way of life in contrast to the urban world that has little connection to the old ways. New urbanites brought their attitudes with them, and though they knew little of the Alaska Natives they did have opinions about how those Natives should behave. This split has a racial component, and we have had more than our share of hate crimes.) The building of the Trans-Alaska Pipeline pressured the United States government to settle Native land claims throughout the state, and Congress structured the Alaska Native Land Claims Settlement Act so that the Native regions became corporations, managed for profit, with the Natives as shareholders. This corporate model dictated much of Native life thereafter, though the corporate model had nothing to do with their histories. The flow of money into the regions and villages was changed, as was the way that that money was spent. I conclude, from news reports and public discussions, that as a consequence native culture was changed and damaged from within as well as from without.

For me, a powerful symbol of that change was the introduction of television service to the villages in the 1970s. For many, perhaps most, people, television is a necessity, and wouldn't it be an advantage if the villagers could benefit from television just like everyone else? Wouldn't it be churlish and condescending to object? Yet the advent of television simply prefigured and intensified the invasion of the "dominant culture," and I find it disheartening to watch village kids trying to be like kids elsewhere instead of being themselves, be it the Chicago Bulls gear, the headset thumping with rap, or the obsessive "gaming." (The original name of the television network was RATNet—really—later changed to the Alaska Rural Communications Network.)

The most important change for all Alaskans, but particularly Natives, was in their and our connection to the land. I saw this in reference to my own life when I visited the Korth family (Chapter 7), because it was apparent that their connection was real: their food came from the land, their cash (via furs) came from the land, their heat came from the land, most of their building materials, including and especially their dwelling, came from the land. On the other hand, everything I relied upon came from a factory far far away, even my (highly processed) food. And food is our most fundamental connection to the world. I was merely a tourist; my income had nothing at all to do with the land; my connections to the land, though heartfelt, were based upon esthetics and a desire for adventure rather than necessity; emotionally I was after something authentic, but I would not find it as the Korths had. I was too "wealthy," too comfortable. They are among the very few people left in Alaska who have an authentic connection to the land, a connection based on subsistence.

WE ALASKANS OFTEN hear about the claims of Alaska Natives that their food is sacred, that their connection to their food is spiritual. We hear the words, but do we understand what they mean? For a westerner to understand the importance of food at the subsistence level, I suggest a thought experiment.

If you are a Christian, recall taking Communion. If you are not a Christian, imagine it. This act is the most important sacrament; it is the heart Christianity. It involves the ingestion of blood and flesh. Some sects settle for the symbolism of the act, others believe in transubstantiation: that the wine and bread are literally transformed into the blood and flesh of Christ. In either case, the closest a Christian can approach to the divine is to take it into their mouths, route it through their digestive systems, lodge it within their cells. The divine then is as intimate as anything possibly can be.

Hence, a Christian should be able to see more clearly than most people why our connection to food can be literally spiritual; why for the Old People the plants and animals of Alaska are not merely nutriment and energy, but are part of a spiritual connection as well. The spiritual connection to the land is neither a superstition nor a metaphor.

All of Native life revolved around food; which statement seems foolishly obvious. After all, isn't that true of everyone? It is not, because for a subsistence hunter the fish and animals must be studied carefully and understood well and the knowledge remembered and transmitted, be it of a caribou or a moose, a seal or a whale, a duck or a goose, a Chinook salmon or a char; and the methods of hunting must be refined intellectually and practiced with diligence and courage. (Try to imagine killing a caribou, a moose, a whale, without firearms; animals that are fleet, wary and potentially dangerous.) This same process must occur for the gatherers of the household or village. Add to these essential skills the ancillary ones of transportation and building, tool making and sewing, and we see that subsistence is complex and difficult, requiring high intelligence, hard work, courage. And love for the land.

The subsistence way of life survived contact with the dominant culture until past the middle of the previous century, but with the advent of Big Oil and Big Money this ancient web of knowledge was quickly damaged. The destructive force was and is cash, for one of the several powers of money is that it substitutes for many other things. Money can substitute for skill and knowledge, for it can be traded for goods that someone else has made or obtained, including food, and it represents a surplus of wealth, something that not all of the Old People had. Thus did economic materialism damage the subsistence way of life, and as subsistence disappears the culture disappears, for they are in fact identical.

Subsistence is still important to Alaskans, though it means something different for Natives who live on the land and urbanites who hunt. For the latter, there is no recognition that one's culture and one's manner of obtaining food are intimately connected. Indeed, in the dominant culture the connection between food and our essential lives has been severed, and hunting is a sport, at best a supplement to store food.

On the other hand, traditional Native subsistence is absolutely vital, spiritually and materially, to the survival of those cultures. It is not a sport. It is a life-and-death matter. But it is apparently dying. Money has substituted for the old ways, and the villages are becoming less and less sustainable, as they become increasingly dependent on the cash economy, and the knowledge required to hunt and gather disappears. One of the best examples of this trend was during the winter of 2008-2009. As we all recall, oil had spiked to $150/barrel, which drove up the price not only of gasoline but, more importantly in the north, heating oil and diesel (used in the villages for electrical generation). If there was anxiety in Iowa or Ohio about the price of energy, there was even more anxiety in the villages, because the cost of fuel in remote areas is already several times higher than in locales that are easy of access. News reports claimed that people were actually leaving the villages for Anchorage and Fairbanks because they could not afford to stay in their homes.

This situation was and is grotesque. Here were people whose ancestors had mastered the skills necessary to live on the land, and had done so for at least ten thousand years. Their vast library of collective knowledge ensured that they could extract every necessity of life from their environment, as they had done for millennium before the advent of the dominant culture. But now they felt that they could not live in their ancestral homes. They were and are so tied to the global market for oil that life without oil was for some unimaginable.

In the event, the price of oil dropped, and the villages were not depopulated, but the point remains: subsistence is on the brink of extinction.

Alaska news sources regularly run articles on obesity, and we predictably read that we Alaskans are fatter than the national average, which isn't surprising—we are a red state—but what is dismaying is that obesity is actually worse in the bush. One would think that a more demanding life would counteract the effects of modern food. Not so. Sweet drinks sell well in village stores, in spite of their high price. These heavy items are flown, not trucked, into the villages, at enormous cost. Of course, much of that air freight is subsidized by the federal government. You, dear reader, are paying to ship soft drinks to villages where obesity, hence diabetes, is a problem for people who once could draw all they needed from the land itself, including food that was (and is) free of refined sugar and corn syrup, hormones, antibiotics, excess fat;

food that would be classified as organic by most standards; food that would command top dollar in the best restaurants.

WE HEAR HOW the people of Kaktovik, on the northern edge of the coastal plain of the Arctic National Wildlife Refuge, desperately need the oil money expected to result from drilling there; they don't even have sewer! So we are told; and we sympathize. But we don't hear that they are part of the North Slope Borough, a huge borough which has taxing power over Prudhoe Bay and surrounding oil fields, or that the Borough is installing a sewage system in Kaktovik that in 2006 was priced at about $1 million per household ($60 million), or that the Arctic Slope Regional Corporation, whose membership roughly corresponds to the Borough's, is a billion dollar enterprise that has nine subsidiaries. One of these, ASRC Federal, in Greenbelt, Maryland, has eight additional subsidiaries, all designed to do business with the Federal government, for which work they get, by law, preferred (no-bid) contracts. Another subsidiary, ASRC Construction Holding Company, has six subsidiaries. This Corporation does business throughout North America. In 2006 the Arctic Slope Regional Corporation generated $1.7 billion in revenue; in 2009, $2.3 billion. We are told that we must drill the coastal plain of the Refuge because these impoverished people are just scraping by.

The official position of the North Slope Borough and the Arctic Slope Regional Corporation is that there should be no official wilderness designations in the Alaskan Arctic. They also are convinced that the polar bear should not be listed as an endangered species. The existence of wilderness, and protection of the bear, would both be an onerous restriction of their freedom.

If anyone comes from the wilderness, it is the Inupiat. If anyone knows about the white bear, it is the Inupiat. Yet the Inupiat's official political and corporate spokesmen and spokeswomen scorn protection of both the wilderness and the bear, not because these designations would restrict their subsistence activities—they would not—but because they could—maybe—restrict the development of oil and gas fields.

In an opinion piece in the *Anchorage Daily News*, January 23, 2011, a spokeswoman for ASRC claims that the Interior Department's designation of the Arctic coast as critical bear habitat would "catapult the quality of life in rural Alaska back to Third World conditions." By which she means that protecting the bear *might* pinch the Borough's and ARSC's revenue stream somewhat. She claims elsewhere in the article that protecting the bear "may force Alaska Natives to abandon our ancestral villages in search of new work to support our families." In other words, as far as this ASRC spokeswoman is concerned, subsistence is in fact dead. And most outrageously and insultingly, she claims that protecting the bear "may well be the 21st century's version of removal and termination for Alaska Natives." For this rich and powerful modern corporation to equate itself with the victims of the worst Federal policies practiced against Lower 48 Native Americans is deeply offensive and deeply cynical and obviously completely false. And to claim that "removal and termination" will occur because the bear would be *protected* is a grotesque inversion of reality. One would think she and the Inupiat corporation she represents would be distressed because of the possible *loss* of the bear, rather than being distressd at its protection!

Unlike most Native Americans of the Lower 48, who managed to survive genocide, relocation, active hostility, and neglect, (the attempt to establish "removal and termination" as official Federal policy), the North Slope Borough has considerable assets.

HOW THE CURSE OF MATERIALISM DESTROYED THE OLD ALASKA

At 88,817 square miles, it is larger than 40 of our states. Its population is only 6,752 (2009), so the considerable revenue the Borough and Corporation generate is certainly not spread thin. In fact, the median household income in 2009 was $82,015, compared to Alaska's $66,953 (city-data.com). "Removal and termination" indeed.

Much of the Arctic National Wildlife Refuge lies within the North Slope Borough. I have heard rumors that the Borough is considering requiring permits of visitors to the Refuge.

IF THE SUBSISTENCE life is based on the land and the sea, why would their first concern be to amass more money? Why oppose wilderness, when wilderness is their ancient foundation?

A PERFECT SYMBOL of confused material values is the Barrow, Alaska, high school football team, established a few years ago. Barrow is the capital of the North Slope Borough. It advertises itself as The Top of the World. When we think of the Inupiat, we often think of Eskimo whaling, and their struggles with the International Whaling Commission to maintain their subsistence hunt for bowhead whales. Indeed, the football team is called the Whalers.

Think about the cost of any football program: equipment and facilities; coaches; adjuncts such as cheerleaders and their coaches; and above all, travel. Most football teams board the bus to get to the game. Not in Barrow. For every away game, an entire team and its support staff must travel long distances by air—there is no road access whatsoever—on very expensive travel routes either to or from Barrow. (Barrow played six away games in 2010). Aside from the cost of airplane travel, there is the need for food and lodging and all the necessities of travel at the destination. In the Lower 48, we expect these kinds of travel expenses with large Division 1-A football teams, which generate quite a bit of revenue; but in Barrow, these expenses are to play a *high school* football game! (To get an idea of distance: Barrow is the farthest north community on the mainland of North America; all of mainland Canada is south of Barrow.)

In the spring of 2006 the team traveled to Florida. Had a great time.

A Florida benefactor decided to supply the team with an artificial turf field.

As reported in the *Anchorage Daily News,* August 19, 2007: "Barrow's new field was trucked from a Dalton, Ga., facility….The rubber mulch that goes underneath the field came from Seattle…. After arriving in Anchorage from Tacoma, Wash., the field and its components were trucked to Fairbanks…[and then] to Deadhorse along the Haul Road [which services the Trans-Alaska pipeline]." From there it was flown to Barrow. Keep in mind that it is about 1200 miles from Tacoma to Anchorage and about 800 miles from Anchorage to Barrow. These are not easy miles.

The Florida benefactor "was particularly touched by donations from senior citizens on tight budgets." An official from the Native Corporation that installed the field gave a speech in which he opined that "we have in place a football field for our youth and community members as a whole to assist in combating the many social ills that attack, destroy, and kill the character of a sound mind and body of a person."

I find this confusion of values to be breathtakingly bizarre. The Barrow Inupiat have decided that the way to save their youth from destruction is to adopt America's game. They must think that they cannot do so by reaching into their own traditional culture.

HOW THE CURSE OF MATERIALISM DESTROYED THE OLD ALASKA

I FIND IT HARD to fault the Native Alaskans, and particularly the Inupiat of the North slope, for this predicament. When the push to build the pipeline—the largest construction project in history, greater than the Egyptian pyramids, greater than the Roman aqueducts, greater than Angkor Wat—required the clarification of title of all lands along the proposed route, and thence the entire state, Alaska Natives and the North Slope Inupiat in particular knew that they must seize the chance to settle their own claims with the Federal government. The Inupiat knew that they were in a power relationship with the dominant culture, particularly the federal government, and that this was their chance to get what they wanted. They understood that in the dominant culture power was expressed as political savvy. The Inupiat were and are politically savvy. They were and are committed to acting in their self-interest and, given the history of the relationship between native peoples and the United States Government, they had no reason to act otherwise. They, together with all Alaska natives, were able to engineer a land claims settlement that seemed ample, at least at the time.

Perhaps there were unforeseen consequences. That the native corporations were locked into the western business model may have been one of them. Another may have been that the acquisition of wealth accelerated the very trends that native elders were trying to forestall: the loss of the young people to television, drugs, pop culture, and urban life. On the one hand the corporations required men in suits, office buildings, national and international travel, college educations, lobbying, political sophistication, economic sophistication, houses in the suburbs; on the other hand, village elders were and are struggling to preserve the knowledge of the past and pass it on to young people whose interests are elsewhere. Straddling the two cultures looks nearly hopeless. The young villager who attends college knows that there is little demand for a college education in the village. On the other hand, if a young person wants to devote his life to subsistence in the village, why pursue a formal education? The two sets of skills and attainments simply don't mesh.

BY 1980, WITH the ascendancy of Big Oil, the political process in Alaska was largely right-wing and corrupt. A state with a strong Democratic history had gone from being blue, or purple, to bright red. The right wing has demagogued the tax issue to the point that mentioning a tax is equivalent to proposing an unnatural act. The legislature incessantly squabbles over the state budget—there is never enough money, it seems—but individuals and households still pay no tax, and we get more federal money than any other state or territory per capita. It is fair to claim that Alaska is the wealthiest of the fifty states. (Because of our foresight in establishing a Permanent Fund, following the leadership of moderate Republican Jay Hammond, we have accumulated a savings account that was approaching $40 billion prior to November 2008.) Senator Ted Stevens and Representative Don Young are (or were, before 2008) impervious to political challenge because they delivered an astonishing amount of pork to the state. Of course, they are adamant about opening the coastal plain of the Arctic National Wildlife Refuge to oil drilling. We Alaskans never have enough money.

I notice when I travel Outside that rich benefactors have contributed substantial institutions to certain communities; Andrew Carnegie's libraries and museums are but one example of many. In Alaska our edifices rarely name benefactors who spent their own money on some contribution to the community. Instead, we name our buildings after people who spent *someone else's money*, such as Ted Stevens Anchorage International Airport, or a new, fabulously expensive, and unnecessary bridge across Knik Arm from Anchorage, to be called, according to one influential advocate, Don Young's Way. The late Senator Stevens suggested that name. You, dear reader, if you live in the Lower 48 states, have been paying for Don Young's Way, and Ted Stevens' Way, for a long time. (This proposed bridge will supposedly pay for itself. We shall see.)

When Alaska decided to dedicate itself to money, the Old Alaska died, and that death included part of the old native cultures as well as the old life of self-sufficiency as practiced by migrants who arrived here just prior to me. Now we are dedicated to milking the federal treasury, and our political heroes have their hands firmly on its teats.

These are the basic facts of Alaska's politics: the late Ted Stevens (R) was appointed to the Senate by a Republican governor to replace a Democratic senator. Don Young (R) was appointed to the House of Representatives by a Republican governor to replace a Democratic representative. Lisa Murkowski (R) was appointed to the Senate by her father, who had vacated that seat upon being elected governor, and therefore had the power to replace himself. (Rod Blagojevich, once governor of Illinois, would go to jail for proposing to do something similar, but Frank Murkowski's behavior was legal since it was allowed by the Alaska constitution. Blagojevich didn't actually sell Obama's Senate seat; he just talked about it. Blagojevich just wanted cash. The Murkowskis wanted and got much more than that. Lisa Murkowski has been re-elected twice.) Thus was our entire three person congressional delegation, prior to 2008, appointed to their positions, and in two cases the seats changed parties, since the Alaska constitution did not require a replacement to be of the same party as the person vacating that seat. (That has since been corrected by referendum.) Once the power of incumbency was seized, the lucky winners' futures were assured, and the shift in party dominance was permanent.

The new Governor Frank Murkowski also had the power to appoint the replacement of Lisa Murkowski, who vacated her State House seat to accept her father's appointment to replace him in the United States Senate. Ted Steven's son Ben had previously been appointed to the State Senate, where he quickly gained power and influence, eventually serving as Senate president. These are the salient facts of modern Alaskan politics. Power, money, patronage, and nepotism substitute for democracy.

The man whom Don Young replaced was Representative Nick Begich, Alaska's popular Democratic Congressman in the late 1960s and early 1970s. Nick Begich won three congressional races and last retained his seat in November 1972, when he beat Don Young with 56% of the vote to Young's 44%. He accomplished this landslide victory even though he was dead. He was a passenger in an airplane that disappeared on October 16, 1972 into Alaska's wilderness. The plane has never been located.

Don Young's official biography pridefully outlines his political history in some detail. We learn that he taught in a log school heated with a wood stove, and that he is a licensed mariner, that he worked in construction, on and on, but we don't learn how he came to occupy Begich's seat in the house. It completely skips Begich's death and Young's appointment to Begich's seat, mentioning only that Young won a special election in March 1973. The biography elevates Young to Congress without context; an Immaculate Election.

Sometimes justice is done, however belatedly. On 4 November 2008, Nick Begich's son Mark Begich, two-term mayor of Anchorage, beat Ted Stevens in the Senate race. The vote was close, in spite of Steven's seven felony convictions of failing to report goods and services received, as required by law. (Since then the Obama justice department has nullified results of the trial, deciding that the prosecution had withheld important facts from the defense. Many Alaskans have chosen to claim that Stevens was "exonerated;" in truth, the justice department decided not to retry him, presumably because of his age and long service in the Senate. Bill Allen, the man who provided Stevens with $250,000 of unreimbursed goods and services, was head of a pipeline service company and did most of the bribing I mention below. He was Ted Stevens' good buddy. According to unrefuted reports in the *Anchorage Daily News*, he was also a sexual predator. His name is prominently displayed in downtown Anchorage on the statehood monument, where he is declared to be a "Founder".)

Alaskans have a great tolerance for corruption. As I write, eleven Alaskan politicians and business figures have been convicted of or pleaded guilty to bribery or related charges. Most of the bribes had to do with legislation favorable to oil companies. One ex-legislator awaits trial. At least three more public figures are under investigation. Of those convicted or under investigation, all but one, a lobbyist, are right-wing Republicans. Alaskan voters could have figured out for themselves what was going on: that for the past three decades the oil industry was in control of the Republican legislature. But Alaskan voters would not act. It took Outside forces, the FBI and the Justice Department, to begin to clean up our mess. All of these corrupt people, without exception, would like to see the Arctic National Wildlife Refuge go under the drill; indeed, would drill anywhere under any circumstances, if drilling yielded wealth. For nearly three decades Alaskans have been delighted to have people like these, people without moral direction and without a sense of the public good, direct the fate of our state.

Another example of Alaska's weird political world was when Walter Hickel decided to be governor for a second time. (He was governor of Alaska when Nixon chose him to be his first Interior secretary.) In 1990 Arlis Sturgulewski won the Republican primary for governor fair and square. A group of Republicans decided, for obscure reasons, that she should not be governor, and at the last minute Republicans Walter Hickel and Jack Coghill joined the Alaska Independence Party. Running as third party candidates, they won a plurality of the vote, becoming governor and lieutenant governor with slightly more than 30% of the vote. Hence, our state Executive Branch was controlled by men who had committed themselves to the Alaska Independence Party Platform, the first and most important plank of which demands independence from the United States. Meanwhile the Federal pork, of course, kept coming in. It has averaged about $7,000 per person, every man woman and child, during recent years; the highest subsidy in the nation. So much for independence.

The comedy continues. Before she was in office two years, Governor Sarah Palin resigned. Of all people, who is in the best position to do good things for the State of Alaska? Why, the governor, of course. What reason did Palin give for resigning? That she could do more to help Alaska if *she was not governor!* This is another bizarre inversion of reality that Alaskans accept as normal. Of course, we all know that her real motive was to pursue celebrity and wealth; and she has certainly done nothing for Alaska.

SHENANIGANS SUCH AS these are not taught in our high school government classes. Our students are taught an entirely different description of how government works, at both the state and federal levels. How many years will it take for them to suspect that the Senate might not be the world's greatest deliberative body after all, and that countries like Iceland and Sweden, Finland and Denmark,

HOW THE CURSE OF MATERIALISM DESTROYED THE OLD ALASKA

Norway and the Netherlands, and, particularly in its treatment of its First Nations, Canada, just might have an edge on us in political, economic, and social justice?

I HAD CONSIDERABLE trouble adjusting to the loss of the Old Alaska. I knew that something immeasurably valuable, in particular the health of the Native cultures, was irrevocably damaged, and that much of the worst of the modern world was taking root here. But there was still the wilderness. And as many Alaskans descried the establishment of wilderness, and other protected lands, in the Federal and State systems of public lands, I turned to those places for emotional, intellectual, and physical sustenance.

When all is said and done, our economic dogmas and our political convictions must mesh with our approach to wilderness and the environment. Given our national propensity for the grossest sort of materialism, and our tolerance of poorly functioning political systems at both the Federal and State levels (at least in Alaska), it seems a miracle that we have been able to accomplish as much as we have. It is a fact, though, that the existence of wilderness cannot be sustained by feelings of nostalgia; wilderness cannot be a retreat for the introverted Romantic. Is it too much to wonder if perhaps there might be a feedback loop in play? That the visionaries, private and political, who once protected our wilderness, and established our environmental laws, might have created the conditions for national improvement? That if we make a better natural world, we might be able to make better people? That a better environment might contribute to social justice? After all, humans and their environment form a continuum. I know that the chance to experience the natural world has made me a better man. Might that not be true of everyone? What if our political leaders, so often divorced from the realities of the physical world—engulfed in the artificiality and insularity of government, especially in Washington—and tempted by the illusion of their self-importance—were to develop a love for Anchorage's and America's excellent trails and extensive green spaces, and a love of all of Alaska's—and America's—lands? Not an abstract, theoretical love, but a love based upon concrete experience? Would he or she thereby become a better person, and hence a better leader? I suggest that this isn't just silly whimsy. After all, Alaska's most beloved governor, Jay Hammond, was of all our governors closest to the land, and he was a conservationist and a Republican, a combination that has disappeared and, one hopes, could be resurrected. We encourage our young people to get outdoors, go to camp, do something adventurous and strenuous. And with good reason. Those times in the outdoors shaped me. I suspect that is true of most of my readers. Virtually every person I know well and respect has a substantial bit of green in their past and in their hearts. Do weary adults have such callouses on their souls that they are impervious to the green earth?

I cannot let the curse of materialism deaden me, strangle me; life is not in dead things but in actions. In Wildness is the preservation of the World, and of myself; and of Alaska Native culture; and maybe even Alaska. I am what I do and only what I do. I can't reform society, but I can reform myself.

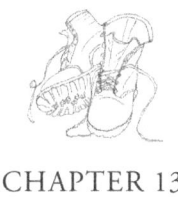

CHAPTER 13

Toward an Ethical Advance in Conservation

"When the last individual of a race of living things breathes no more, another heaven and another earth must pass before such a one can be again."

William Beebe

I claimed in another chapter that economic materialism is the belief that controls our national ethical life, as did Catholicism in Europe during the Middle Ages; that this belief is so fundamental that it is unquestioned, unexamined, and even mostly unconscious; and that the only escape from it, at the personal level, is activity: engagement. *Actions* must replace *things* as the focus of our lives. True, there are some people embedded in our culture who manage to rise to a higher level; and we do say words that indicate that we are aware of the problem, such as "money is our God," or "we worship the dollar," but these are clichés, spoken without conviction or understanding.

Re-reading Aldo Leopold's "The Land Ethic" recently, I was struck by certain parallels he developed in the more specific realm of ecology. One of his main points is that we lack an ethical, social, or political mechanism whereby we recognize our connection to the land, and therefore we are unable to connect to the land. Our ethics have not evolved to this point.

The question is, How can we bring about this advance, this next step?

One bit of good news is that, in the years since Leopold wrote his essay, major advances were made in conservation, and not just in the establishment and enlargement of protected enclaves such as parks and refuges, but advances in protecting the commons: water and air. And these advances were not merely legal. Ethical advances did change and improve the way individuals see the environment and act towards it. The importance of environmental protection is now the norm accepted by a majority of people. The right-wing backlash against environmental protection is a sign that environmentalists have been successful.

But it is time for another step forward. Even though environmental protection is embedded in law and society, we all know that the protections we have are not enough. Individuals must change; society must change; politics must change. We have changed for the better before; we can change for the better again.

This is a hard nut to crack. Saying the words, and saying them over and over again, is not enough. Preaching is not enough. Fear is not enough. How do we gain a purchase on this problem? How do we close the gap between thought and action?

LEOPOLD WRITES: "There is as yet no ethic dealing with man's relation to land and to the animals and plants which grow upon it.... The land relation is still strictly economic, entailing privileges but not obligations."

We divide land use into two realms: public and private. Public lands may or may not be managed according to ethical standards. That depends on which bureaucracy controls that land, and what kind of policy is being pursued in the executive branch. The private realm is at the mercy of the owner's self-interest, the owner's personal conscience, and whatever community pressure can be brought to bear (such as zoning requirements or tax incentives). During his time at the University of Wisconsin, Leopold became increasingly aware that we need to focus on private lands as well as public lands and wilderness. His concern was prescient: today half of the United States, about one billion acres, is made up of privately owned farms, ranches, and private forests (*Audubon,* May-June 2012, p. 57).

Leopold would likely be pleased with the growth of land trusts, such as The Nature Conservancy, which have created a number of hybrid agreements governing the use of land. These trusts bridge the gap, at least to some extent, between public and private interests. Their activities are invaluable.

Aside from these relatively small protected tracts, much or most of our land is still being abused, as is our commons: air and water. It is a shame, and it should be a crime, that we still treat our air and water as if they are private property, subject to casual abuse, "entailing privileges but not obligations."

(There are at least three other concerns. One is consumer excess, which wastes resources; another falls under the general heading of "casual indifference," such as littering; the third could be named "habitual ugliness," to include negligent behavior such as strip development and ugly signage. Some of this can be corrected by law, but most must be corrected by a change in individual behavior.)

LET'S START WITH two situations familiar to everyone.

The first is the utility smokestack. Controlling what comes out of that stack is a concern of government and hence is already potentially under control, depending on the will and goodwill of government. This is a political problem. We already have a way to fix the problem if government has the will to do so. It is difficult for consumer groups to act in this area, though it has been done. It is also difficult for individuals to act because it is difficult to get off the grid, and doing so doesn't fix the problem. This has to be primarily in the hands of government.

Compare this with another pipe, the one sticking out the back of our car. True, government has the potential to control emissions and establish mileage standards. But once I buy that gasoline, it is my gasoline, and I can do with it what I will.

Economists claim that high gasoline prices serve to reduce the time that vehicles run, and I am sure that the over-all statistics bear this out (and a recession has the same effect). It is also true that our energy is priced too low. But pricing energy to reduce consumption does not result in an ethical transformation, though it may result in a salutary change in behavior in the short run. (A young woman I know bought a used, nearly new Prius cheap; the seller was quick to unload it as soon as the price of oil dropped—wanted to move "up" to something big.) When oil was $150/barrel and gasoline more than $4/gallon, I frequently observed vehicles in Anchorage, Alaska idling away while the occupants shopped or stood in line at the Post Office, and this when the temperatures were mild. These drivers were likely upset with the price of gasoline, and would no doubt be reluctant to set dollar bills aflame, but the vehicles were running nevertheless.

If, as the economists say, human behavior can only be altered by price, then we can make few claims for human ethical advance. That view is even more disheartening when we observe that many people don't respond to price anyway, staying with old habits instead. It's as if people don't know that their gasoline is transformed into something else, that what comes out the tailpipe is invisible and therefore doesn't exist. Maybe if we added a coloring agent to the exhaust people might realize that what we burn actually goes someplace: the atmosphere.

In my state, government workers are even less likely to shut off their vehicles than are private citizens. I often see this carelessness among drivers for the military, the Municipality of Anchorage, and the State of Alaska, particularly the Department of Highways. (I also see it among drivers working for private businesses.) They show up for work, they turn on the truck, and it runs all day regardless of the actual work it is doing. This is literally incredible; and bizarre; and deeply irrational; but true.

I chose this example of behavior not because it is our most important problem—fuel consumption by the shipping fleets, land and sea, is far more significant—but because it illustrates the difficulty of altering human behavior in the most simple and obvious ways. Is it difficult to turn the key to Off? Of course not. Does it make economic sense not to? No. Is there any advantage gained by not doing so? None whatsoever. Yet the behavior persists.

People are often irrational, and the economists are often wrong. Appeals to reason and thrift are insufficient. We must find another way.

Homo sapiens, however slowly and fitfully, have managed to make ethical advances during the development of what we call "civilization":

Criminal law replaced the code of revenge.

The blanket of the law replaced the patronage and protection of powerful benefactors.

Governments replaced local tribes and chieftains.

People who do the work of the world gained power within the economy.

The significance of individual rights became recognized within the body of law.

Governments extended legal protections to lands, waters, and air.

We came to recognize that if governments are legitimate, they themselves must be held to the constraints of law.

I intend this list to suggest examples of reform. Of course it is not comprehensive.

I suspect that most of us think that religions are the source and cradle of ethical behavior. If so, this is an error. In the words of E. R. Dodds, an historian of antiquity, "I need hardly say that religion and morals were not initially interdependent, in Greece or elsewhere; they had their separate roots. I suppose that, broadly speaking, religion grows out of man's relationship to his total environment, morals out of his relationship to his fellow men." (*The Greeks and the Irrational*, p. 31. By "total environment," I suspect that Professor Dodds is referring more to psychological and social needs than to the natural world, except to the extent that the natural world was a threat.)

I am willing to accept that once upon a time, three or four thousand years ago, the rise of the world's great religions did eventually constitute an ethical advance and served to regulate human behavior for the better. But I can think of few ethical advances *within religions* since then. I am willing to exempt Buddhism from this judgment, and the very few saints that manage to practice their religion in some pure way, be they Christian or Hindu or something else. But for the most part religions have abdicated any responsibility in the area of ethical *advance*, and when they have been suborned to right-wing and fundamentalist uses they have led the retreat back to barbarism. In particular, fundamentalist and evangelical Christianity has been doggedly hostile towards any ethic of conservation or environmental protection. And some who are eager for the apocalypse look forward to the day when the earth is burned to ashes and they can look on from heaven at the damned. Why practice conservation if you yearn for the end of the earth, the sooner the better? How can you love the earth if you look forward to the day when it and everything on it burns to cinders? Indeed, if one is psychologically eager for apocalypse, one must be profoundly alienated from the World and from the Creation. As Frederick Turner pointed out in *Beyond Geography*, Christianity became an *historic* religion, within linear time and divorced from connections to the Earth and our myths; Paradise was lost; and the Church "set its face resolutely forward in the hope of recovering in an apocalyptic future what it had once had in the past" (p. 65). Or, in the condensed language of Jorge Luis Borges, "'Heaven' is a projection of nostalgia."

In the world of myth, before we fell into Time, there was no Ideal of Heaven, and no idea that Eternity and History were separated. We moderns, occupants of history, live within lineal finite time, a trap that we can only escape with death; and so Heaven can only exist for the dead; we can only be truly happy after we are dead.

This Christian view is entirely opposite of what one experiences in what I call the real world, when one is truly at home in the world, and particularly in the wilderness; all I need of home and the only glimpse of eternity I need or want.

AT BEST, RELIGIONS protect the status quo. Oberve that my short list of seven reforms above all occurred within the secular realm; none were religious initiatives; yet all were essential. On the other hand, at their worst religions may advocate violence, terror, and destruction, and I am not just referring to the Taliban. It wasn't so long ago that Europe and the Near East were torn apart for centuries by the wars of the Christians.

One example of the ethical irrelevance of fundamentalist Christianity is the Ten Commandments. Fundamentalists offer the Ten Commandments as the ethical foundation of life and often aggressively demand that they be placed in public places, contrary to the First Amendment. Yet what does the list of ten include? In the area of everyday human relations, a mere five injunctions, obvious to anyone: murder, adultery, theft, lying, and covetousness (which means respect for property). Add respect for parents, and that is all we have as guides to everyday behavior. The remaining four deal with subordination to the divine will: idolatry, monotheism, blasphemy, and observing the Sabbath. Apparently many fundamentalists think that this list is comprehensive; we can stop here. But in fact most people learn a much more nuanced ethical system than this by the time they are in elementary school. Of course Christianity as a whole has developed a much more comprehensive and sophisticated system of ethics than that list of ten; but the fundamentalists don't seem to know that, and they are the religious vanguard in the United States, a primary driver of right-wing politics; a western mirror of Islamic fundamentalism.

If everyone were Christ-like, I wouldn't be writing this essay and we would have a paradise here on Earth; and, I think, that paradise would include ethical behavior towards the natural world, though I can't quote Christ on that subject and may be wrong. I respect the ideals of behavior that religions offer. But most Christians do not in fact aspire to be Christ-like; the ideal is beyond them. Therefore we must be concerned with what religions do *in practice*. In the area of creating a healthy relationship between humans and the earth they inhabit, they don't do much. What is missing? Love. Where is the love? Why is it missing?

In his essay, Leopold repeatedly uses the word "violence" to describe what we actually do to the land; and he uses the word "love" to name the relationship we should have with the land. We must recognize that we practice violence towards the earth not only routinely and aggressively, but often unthinkingly, through mere carelessness and ignorance, and that we need to eliminate this violence by discovering or rediscovering the source of love of the earth that we should naturally feel.

TO REPEAT: IF we examine my short list of social improvements above, we observe that major ethical advances have occurred in the secular realm, not by the agency of religion, but by law. This raises the question, Is the law driven by an ethical change within society, or is ethical change driven by the law?

One clear advance that has occurred since the seventeenth century is the development of scientific knowledge. The human brain is indeed an astonishing thing, and it is easy to see that, though our ethical development is sluggish, our scientific development is rapid, wide, and deep. And of course our scientific knowledge has been quickly adapted to technological uses.

Knowledge and ethics must be closely connected. It is a truism that unguided scientific and technical knowledge can be put to evil ends; it is less commonly observed that "ethical" ideas that are unformed by knowledge can be profoundly evil. One reason why our ethical development is glacially slow is because we have failed to link ethics and knowledge. Indeed, much of the bad behavior we suffer from in this tired old world of ours is because of the inflamed minds of the ignorant, be they Islamic terrorists clinging to pre-scientific Medieval beliefs, or the willfully ignorant Americans who think Obama is a Moslem or that the idea of global warming is a conspiracy. In the second case, the ignorance is self-imposed: people believe what is false because that is what they want to believe. The former case is more interesting. The Islamic terrorist illustrates very clearly my point about the disconnect between scientific/technological knowledge and ethics. They rely heavily on many forms of sophisticated technology; they fly in jets and they use sophisticated phones; but their ethics are as primitive as their technology is current. The two important areas of human behavior don't connect.

Plato taught that Eros drives our search for knowledge (or wisdom, or whatever the best modern term is). We desire knowledge, we love knowledge, unless this natural process is perverted in some way.

I find that I stand outside the material world, peering at it, wondering of what it consists, and above all, desiring to connect with it somehow. But there is a barrier between my subjective view and what I am convinced is a world that exists objectively. That gap must be bridged somehow. In the words of Loren Eiseley, "Nature remains an otherness which incorporates man, but which man instinctively feels contains secrets denied to him."

For me that objective world has two components, both of which can serve as the bridge I need. The first, because it is most readily accessible, is beauty. The world as given to us is inherently, intrinsically beautiful. I do not accept the notion that beauty is strictly subjective (I am not discussing art here) because I recognize that I spring from the world I observe; I am an extension of that world; and so I must be in harmony with it. When I experience the beauty of the world, I feel that harmony.

On the other hand, as a conscious being I have the power to stand apart from the world; hence my subjectivity. In moments of despair, particularly in the face of death, or at times of emotional turbulence or apathy, I may feel alienated from it, like this character in John G. Neihardt's excellent book *When the Tree Flowered* : "Sometimes I rode all day, but there was nothing. Everywhere the valleys were empty, and if I stopped to listen, they would be listening too. The hills looked, and did not know me."

But I know that my biological history leads me back to the world. I see the beauty of the world because I am of that world. In the depths of my cells this is where I come from. The world will know me.

The objective world offers beauty; it also offers knowledge. Paradoxically, we humans, because of our subjectivity, are in a position to examine the world precisely because we stand outside of it. Our subjectivity separates us, sometimes painfully, from the world, yet that very subjectivity allows us to examine that world. This painful split can be reconciled, however. Just as we can contemplate the world aesthetically because we and the world are of the same substance, so for the same reason can we derive immense satisfaction from gaining knowledge of it. We are separate from the world but we are joined to the world.

In another chapter I discussed Albert Einstein's explanation of why he was eager to harness himself to the discipline of scientific inquiry. It is worth our while to examine his words again:

"Even when I was a fairly precocious young man, the nothingness of the hopes and strivings which chases most men restlessly through life came to my consciousness with considerable vitality....Out yonder there was this huge world, which exists independently of us human beings and which stands before us like a great, eternal riddle....The contemplation of this world beckoned like a liberation, and I soon noticed that many a man whom I had learned to esteem and to admire had found inner freedom and security in devoted occupation with it."

The "huge world" is not just a riddle, but an "*eternal* riddle" the contemplation of which offers not just "freedom" but also "security." The apparent paradox of simultaneous freedom and security is resolved when we consider that this world of Einstein's is the *only* world there is, and though it may be mutable its riddles are eternal. I think that Einstein recognizes that this huge world of his is his one and only home; he is *of* that home; hence his security.

We, like Einstein, are akin to the world in both regards: akin in that we sense its beauty, akin in that we have access to its knowledge. Hence our freedom. Plato's Eros—love—is the linkage.

WHAT STANDS IN the way of this love of the world? Many things, but most fall under the heading of human egotism.

In the words of Olaus Murie, scientist and a founder of the Wilderness Society, "A poetic appreciation of life, combined with a knowledge of nature, creates humility, which in turn becomes the greatness of man."

This statement has three parts, all equally important.

The vaguest is "a poetic appreciation of life." I will take that to mean that at least some humans can find some emotional connection to the natural world, and that connection can be expressed in human terms—in language—and that love and beauty are the basis of that connection: appreciation. We are inevitably reminded of the Romantic response to nature: that if one were receptive, nature could arouse a response in the observer; that in fact the receptive observer becomes an active participant in that transaction because of that response. We attend to what nature has to offer, and nature in turn penetrates our sensibility. This alertness to the power of the natural world is a truth of Romanticism, and indeed transcends Romanticism and culture. The key is: how to be receptive? Especially in a world where most people insulate themselves from the natural world, choosing instead an electronic environment.

Murie's phrase "a knowledge of nature" is easiest to parse and hardest to achieve. Love and beauty are potentially open to anyone who can bring themselves to the point of being receptive, but gaining knowledge, be it the knowledge of the scientist or the knowledge of the hunter-gatherer, is much harder to achieve, requiring arduous study of the knowledge we inherit, and persistent effort in the attempt to discover knowledge for ourselves.

And finally, why would "humility" be the "greatness of man"? Aren't we taught that greatness is the result of conquest, achievement, or some measurable and public success? Are we not taught that pride is a virtue not a sin? And that humility is for fools? Christianity correctly identifies pride as the worst of the seven deadly sins; but how many Christians actually turn this teaching upside down, scorning humility as a posture of weaklings and promoting pride in all its forms?

I am not aware that Olaus Murie adhered to a formal religion, yet his conclusion corresponds to the teachings if not the practice of every major religion and most secular ethical systems. The relentless pressure of pridefulness does indeed indicate that humility in the face of the natural world constitutes "the greatness of man," since pride is so difficult to suppress.

There is another side to humility that is more important. The suppression of the prideful ego is a negative quality, however salutary. But there is a positive side to humility, because in Murie's view it is the result of appreciation and understanding. When we appreciate and understand nature we recognize its greatness, and our consequent humility is merely a recognition of reality. It is great, we are small. To learn this is an achievement. We need to establish a perspective. We need to understand the proportions of things. When we do, humility is inevitable. We must be humble as we stand before nature, which is Einstein's "huge world," the universe; and though Einstein had every reason to be prideful, humility is I think his accomplishment, his greatness. The scientist, all of us, must subordinate ourselves to the facts of this world; we must accept first that we don't know. "I don't know" may be the most important words in the language.

I READ IN today's newspaper how chickadees survive prolonged periods of cold in the sub-Arctic and Arctic, where they must deal with more than eighteen hours of darkness, during which they cannot find food; when temperatures of -30 F are frequent, -40 F common, and colder than -50 F not unusual; and when the most difficult part of winter may extend for four or five months.

In a nutshell, if you will: before winter, they cache large quantities of food, mostly seeds, in thousands of hiding places; they locate these cached seeds in time of need; they eat enough during the day to add ten percent to their body weight and lose that ten percent during the long night (for me that would be a seventeen pound weight fluctuation every day!); they do this day after day, and if they run out of energy just once they are dead. This vulnerable little fellow weighs less than half an ounce but is able to survive the Big Cold and the Big Dark. Dramas like this are being lived around us every day.

As Rachel Carson wrote, "Most of us walk unseeing through the world, unaware alike of its beauties, its wonders, and the strange and sometimes terrible intensity of the lives that are being lived around us." What is required for us to see? In two words: the *scientific attitude*. We are surrounded by many tens of thousands of species, some microscopic, some gargantuan, and most with a life cycle as surprising as the Arctic chickadee's. But if we can't see them, or don't try to see them, or reject knowledge about them, we fall into the trap of pride; we focus on ourselves instead of facing outward to the larger world; we stare at our little screens instead of the world in front of us. Instead of achieving "the greatness of man" we lapse into the pettiness of man. Hence, the official position of the State of Alaska is to oppose the protection of almost any endangered species, be they polar bears or beluga whales—the state would rather see the species disappear than pass up a chance—just a chance—at any profitable activity. This utter lack of empathy is chilling and should horrify my fellow citizens, but it doesn't. And when the protection of the coastal plain of the Arctic National Wildlife Refuge is discussed, the official position of the North Slope Borough, home of the Inupiat, past masters of the Arctic, is that legally protected wilderness, the wilderness of their ancient ancestry, is bad, though legal protection as proposed would not interfere with their traditional subsistence activities.

OUR LACK OF empathy can be truly monstrous. I was reminded of this while re-reading Loren Eiseley's essay "Man: The Lethal Factor," first printed in *American Scientist* in 1963. This may be Eiseley's most pessimistic essay. He traces in rough outline our species' change, from small groups of families or small tribes, few in number, to today's technologically advanced and very numerous sophisticates. He particularly deplores and fears our ability to make nuclear war, which, given the policies of the United States and the Soviet Union at the time, would likely lead to the extinction of life on earth. He points out what I did not have the wit to realize at the time, as a high school junior: the United States and the Soviet Union did not merely put their own populations at risk because of their national nuclear policies, but they put at risk the lives of all humans in every country on the planet. And so the Norwegians, the New Zealanders, the Kenyans, the Ecuadoreans, everyone, were at our mercy and helpless as we held the knife to their throats. "The evil man may do has this added significance about it: it is not merely the evil of one tribe seeking to exterminate another. It is, instead, the *thought-out* willingness [emphasis added] to make the air unbreathable to neighboring innocent nations and to poison, in one's death throes, the very springs of life itself." Not only were we willing to put all humans at risk as a consequence of our policies, but the entire natural world also, all the myriad glory of our abundance of species, perhaps unique in the universe, the living result of millions of years of evolution. He observes that in all the studies of the results of a nuclear war, it is difficult to find "a word spared to indicate concern for the falling sparrow, the ruined forest, the contaminated spring," and he writes that he "is just primitive enough to hope that somehow, somewhere, a cardinal may still be whistling on a green bush when the last man goes blind before his man-made sun....[And] if we have mishandled our own lives...it seems a pity that we should involve the violet and the tree frog in our departure.

"To perpetrate this final act of malice seems somehow disproportionate, beyond endurance. It is like tampering with the secret purposes of the universe itself and involving not only man but life in the final holocaust—an act of petulant, deliberate blasphemy." For this evolutionist knows that species come, species go, but life itself continues; if *Homo sapiens* were content merely to destroy itself, life itself could continue to evolve into the indefinite and unknown future with all its possibilities. The blasphemy that Eiseley recognizes is that the elimination of life is the elimination of all future possibility. It is an affront to Creation itself. This profound egotism and its attendant lack of empathy is a dark sin.

Dear reader, you may object, But there was no nuclear holocaust, the policies worked, and the United States and the Soviet Union have developed a way to coexist. Indeed. But as I read Eiseley's words it came home to me that we have been devising other kinds of holocausts even as the nuclear threat seems to have diminished. A nuclear holocaust would occur in minutes, hours, days; we can picture vividly its consequences; and our fear is immediate and palpable. But we have in the meantime set in motion another holocaust which may be nearly as deadly but which has unfolded in slow motion; hence we have trouble visualizing its consequences because they seem distant and abstract; and we feel little fear because we lack the imagination to understand, and for many we lack even the will to acknowledge reality.

It came home to me with a shock that Eiseley's words could apply just as well to this real holocaust, already well underway; a holocaust devised by us; a holocaust that will cause the people of innocent nations to suffer; a holocaust that will not be limited to those who caused it but will transcend species and national borders; a holocaust that is within our means to correct or slow; but a holocaust for which we have not taken responsibility.

I characterized this holocaust as slow motion, though we know that in geological terms it is very sudden and fast. It only seems to be slow because of our restricted human time frame. Our loading of the atmosphere with carbon was, at the beginning of the industrial revolution, merely thoughtless, but since science has identified global climate change as the result of human activity more than thirty years ago, it has been deliberate. When I read Eiseley's words, I realized that once again the United States is putting the human population of the world at risk, and is also putting the rest of the Creation at risk, for no good reason.

Again, dear reader, you may object, The United States is not the only consumer of energy and cannot be solely responsible for climate change. This is true, though we have been the largest consumer of energy for a long time. But we are not assuming sole responsibility. Instead, we are assuming no responsibility whatsoever. Indeed, my senior Senator, as ranking Republican on the Senate Energy Committee, proposed in February 2013 to increase oil drilling, keep prices low, keep consumption up, and prevent any cap on carbon. Our local newspaper characterized this in a headline as a sweeping energy policy. In other words, Lisa Murkowski, like so many powerful politicians on the political right, wants the United States to pursue an energy policy which will certainly make things worse. So much for assuming responsibility for what we do.

In the past there has been a pattern to reform. For example, reformers in the 1960s identified tobacco as being a very significant health hazard. The tobacco industry responded with a public relations campaign making the preposterous claim that tobacco is harmless. Yet they were able to stall action for years, and when Congress finally acted all we really ended up with was a requirement to post a warning on packaging. (In the meantime, this most harmful of all drugs remains legal, while we wage "war" on less harmful drugs, thus keeping their price high and enhancing profits for suppliers, while neglecting the real problem, which is the demand side.) Also during the 1960s, DDT is identified as a poison which is destroying the base of the food chain, driving predators such as falcons and ospreys towards extinction, and lodging within the bodies of humans; the manufacturers respond with a public relations campaign claiming that the poison is harmless; action is delayed for years; but finally Congress acts. Again: refrigerants are identified as the agent destroying the ozone layer; the manufacturers spend much money denying the truth, because they can add to their profits for every year of delay; and Congress finally acts, however belatedly.

One would hope that the problem of carbon emissions would, at worst, follow this same trajectory. At first it did: strong evidence, denial, public relations campaigns from the energy companies. But, unlike the other reforms I cited, industry resistance did not erode in the face of the facts, nor did resistance from the right wing. Instead, denial intensified, and laws that may have a bearing on climate change, such as the Endangered Species Act, were attacked. Never in my lifetime have I witnessed such political intransigence about such an important matter. This denial of reality must be calculated and cynical, because I cannot believe that otherwise intelligent people, if they were indeed people of good will, would consent to the perpetuation of such a catastrophe. What intensifies my bitterness, as a respecter of science, is that in every case I mentioned above, there were scientists-for-hire who were willing to pervert science for their personal profit; and journalists who were willing to weigh the words of these few against the knowledge of thousands of reputable scientists.

OUR PATHWAY TO developing a proper ethical stance toward our world is the path of love coupled firmly to science. This is the pathway of Thoreau, John Muir, the three Muries, Aldo Leopold, Sigurd Olson, Loren Eiseley, Annie Dillard, and the millions of anonymous biologists, scientists, birders, fishers, hunters (at least some), and lovers of our parks, green spaces and wilderness; but it is not the pathway of those who shape our economy and our politics. Those powerful people collectively are utterly divorced from the citizens they are supposed to represent and protect. This is well known, and because our national politics has collapsed, I began this essay with the intention of finding another way into a better future. Perhaps, I thought, there is some way to bypass a failed political system. Instead, I have simply circled back to the status quo. At the level of politics and society, I can't find any way forward except through the methods of the past: establishing a body of law designed to protect people and their world. And that body of law will not be established until we heal our diseased body politic. And I do not know how to do that.

I CAN ONLY remember the fundamental Thoreauvian truth: reform begins with myself. I must attend carefully to the life I live—what I am doing *now*, at this very moment—I must attend alertly to every detail of my life, perhaps thereby attaining authenticity—and I must avoid abstractions and generalizations—in other words, I must avoid habits that lead me away from life rather than towards life. I am what I do.

CHAPTER 14

Value is Inherent in Nature

Dear reader, I ended the previous chapter stumped, at an impasse, nowhere to go. I was somewhat depressed about our current inability to see our way forward as a society towards a better environmental future, though I know that many, perhaps most, individuals possess an environmental conscience. It's the larger institutions that won't move forward. Two and a half years after starting that essay I encountered an article in *The New York Review of Books* (April 4, 2013, pp. 67-74) titled "Religion Without God," by Ronald Dworkin. This first chapter from his book of that title, since published, provided the missing pieces in my thinking. It also brought into clear focus, and gave new depth to, the writings of Emerson, Thoreau, and many another of the authors I admire and rely upon, and invited me to try to throw a net around Spinoza as well, and even to read the Romantics, particularly Wordsworth, in a brighter light.

I was tempted to skip the article because my interests center neither on atheism nor on conventional religion. But Dworkin begins with a more fundamental, indeed radical, collection of ideas that I found immensely exciting and fruitful.

What is the actual basis of the human connection to nature? And is that connection objective or subjective? By "nature" I mean that which we may call The Creation in its entirety, not just the birds and the bees and the trees. And the question of objectivity v subjectivity is crucially important, because resolving that difference establishes the truth or falsity of my viewpoint.

Dworkin writes, "We are part of nature because we have a physical being and duration: nature is the locus and nutrient of our physical lives." In the language I have used, we are of nature; we are part of the continuum of nature; nature is our source. And the key paradox of being human: "We are apart from nature because we are conscious of ourselves as making a life and must make decisions that, taken together, determine what life we have made." Because we are conscious, we have the existential choice of determining the details of our lives, which may include the choice of separating ourselves from nature and determining our own evolutionary path. Though this separation may be illusory.

Nothing new here. Many thinkers, including my beloved Loren Eiseley, have dealt extensively with this apparent division within the human organism. Dworkin's advance is the next step forward, clarifying the question of objectivity v subjectivity in the area of human values. This is the key.

The common and dominant viewpoint, I am convinced, is that ethical and aesthetic judgments are purely subjective and therefore arbitrary unless they are grounded in something rock-solid: an omniscient and omnipotent deity which (who?) authored and established those values. Absent a divine author, such judgments are, we are told by deists, simply arbitrary and therefore likely to be wrong, even evil. Hence the fundamentalists' horror of secular humanism.

Dworkin's great advance is to argue convincingly that ethical and aesthetic judgments can be objectively established without the authority of a deity. Indeed, he argues, a deity cannot have authored those values. They stand alone, and carry all the objective authority of the other major subjects of human scrutiny, science and mathematics. The scientist and mathematician may stand in awe at the wonders of nature—the universe—and in the same way and for the same reasons we can all stand in awe at nature's goodness and beauty. These are intrinsic, not human inventions, not projections of ourselves onto the natural world.

I have been "accused" of being a Romantic by friends who consider themselves "hard-headed realists." We have all encountered the term "hopelessly romantic," as if it were an affliction, however silly, of which we should be cured, but are too stubborn to relinquish.

On the other hand, scientists are among the realists, and can take satisfaction in their efforts to establish truth. Their efforts are often laborious, tedious, time consuming, expensive, and occasionally heroic. They dedicate themselves to establishing the objective fact. I think that they also know that behind the fact is Something awesome (in the true sense of the word), mysterious, exciting; something that may fill one with "fear and trembling," or delight and joy.

It is a mistake to suppose that this noble endeavor is at odds with Romanticism—with value. Indeed, they are precisely complementary.

Neither science nor mathematics require the ultimate justification of a divine source, though indeed a deity can be introduced as a deus ex machina. As Dworkin points out, "We find it impossible not to believe the elementary truths of mathematics....But we cannot demonstrate either the elementary truths or the methods of mathematical demonstration from outside mathematics." We cannot trace mathematics to the creation story in the first two chapters of Genesis; we cannot claim a divine source for mathematics. And we cannot claim that mathematics is a purely human invention. Mathematics tracks too precisely with The Creation for that. Yet the human organism has an innate capacity for logic and mathematics. Mathematics is inherent in nature; it is also entirely human; hence we are in this way intimately linked to all of creation. We are of the same substance. (Note the word substance. This word of the rationalists, particularly Spinoza, is inevitable and necessary.)

So it is with science. The scientific method is a human invention, yet the facts and theories and laws of science as stated in human language are independent of human thought: objective. What happens in our thoughts and actions when we practice the scientific method corresponds precisely to The Creation. Yet this activity and this correspondence cannot be traced to a deity. A god didn't do it. The laws of the universe are inherent in the universe.

Thus it should not be at all surprising that other areas of human thought are likewise inherent in the universe. The sense of beauty is I think the most accessible of these values, because we have all experienced it to some extent. (I am not attempting to discuss art here, but the beauty inherent in The Creation.) Surely everyone has experienced this delight, if it is only a whiff of cut grass or a snatch of bird song as we hurry to the urban bus stop. Just a fragment of such beauty can reverberate with us regardless of the turbulence and insularity of our days. A sparrow on a window ledge surely penetrates the consciousness of the crustiest urbanite.

Bird song is perhaps the clearest and most universal illustration of the pervasive, innate beauty of The Creation. How can it be that this descendant of the reptilian world has evolved ways of vocalization that are so akin to, so appealing to, this mammalian organism? Birds and humans resonate to the same wave lengths, the same cadences, the same melodies, even the same harmonies, on occasion; indeed, the same passions. This beautiful production is closely akin to human music, which is akin to mathematics.

Yes indeed, responds the realistic skeptic, and those passions happen to be territory, food, and sex. Just so. But why in such beautiful form? And why in a form so appealing to the human ear? Indeed, *why is it that we can identify such noise as beauty?*

So it goes with the rest of the natural world. I thrill to the beauty of a spreading birch tree. I am also delighted by the maple, the hemlock, the southern live oak; by the Arctic tundra; by the desert. One may claim that this is a matter of conditioning, that I have simply learned this. The desert dweller thrills to the desert, the steppe dweller to the steppe; but remove me from my sub-Arctic home and I too can thrill to the desert, to the steppe, to the tropics. We love what we are accustomed to, but we can also love all of The Creation. We have that capacity for love, but the beauty is not merely within ourselves. It is in the world. We are akin to it. It is intrinsic; and, like mathematics and science, need not be traced to a deity, unless one again introduces the divine as a deus ex machina.

When I first experienced the Arctic tundra, I felt that I was coming home.

Dear reader, observe how I slid from a discussion of beauty to a discussion of love. Thus are beauty and eros inextricably mixed.

The aesthetic value of The Creation is at once the most accessible and the most neglected of the two areas of value. Most accessible, because readily available to any and all of our senses; most neglected, because we may take it for granted, or shut it out entirely. And when we interact with the world to shape it, change it, we are willing to sacrifice beauty as if it were an unnecessary luxury instead of being integral to The Creation.

I fear a growing insensitivity to beauty, as beauty is sacrificed to "development," and we push the sources of beauty, plants and animals and landscape, aside; and as we grow a body of citizens who are mostly urban, and seem increasingly to spend their lives staring at the palms of their hands, wires projecting from their heads. I fear that one form of connection destroys another form of connection.

OF THE TWO areas of value, the ethical is the most difficult to establish as being inherent in nature, because, of the four areas of human understanding—science, mathematics, aesthetics, ethics—the latter seems most subject to human whim. Indeed, I have in the previous chapter called for an advance in our conservation ethic, and I have mourned the fact that our ethical development is so tardy. But how can we advance if it is already there?

And therein lies the answer. It is present, but not entirely manifest.

I must make clear that I intend to dismiss from my consideration a multitude of actions that we usually place under the heading of ethics: religious taboos such as not eating pork, or avoiding alcohol or caffeine, or practicing religion according to certain forms; sexual behavior in its multitude of forms, most dictated or prohibited by the culture in which one finds oneself; cultural customs such as dress or use of the voice or standards of etiquette which seem to carry ethical weight but do not do so in fact; traditions and customs generally.

What is left? We are left with the standards that a person of good will applies to himself and to others. To fall back on the cliché: you know it when you see it. That in itself is an indication that it is inherent, innate. It is religious.

This sounds simplistic, shallow, unempirical, and arbitrary. But listen to Dworkin (p.2):

> Many millions of people…have convictions and experiences similar to and just as profound as those that believers count

as religious.... They feel an inescapable responsibility to live their lives well, with due respect for the lives of others; they take pride in a life they think well lived and suffer sometimes inconsolable regret at a life they think, in retrospect, wasted. They find the Grand Canyon not just arresting but breathtakingly and eerily wonderful. They are not simply interested in the latest discoveries about vast space but enthralled by them.... They express a conviction that the force and wonder they sense are real, just as real as planets or pain, that moral truth and natural wonder do not simply evoke awe but call for it.

But what of the details? What constitutes a universal, intrinsic ethics in fact and in practice? How *do* we know it when we see it? (In the previous chapter I pointed out what it is *not*: a checklist of forbidden actions, such as the Ten Commandments.)

A simple thought experiment should suffice. Dear reader, you have read many ethical thinkers: Socrates, Plato, Aristotle, Jesus, writers on Buddhism, Montaigne (though he would likely not claim to be an ethical teacher), Spinoza, Kant, Neitzsche (yes, I am convinced that he was one such). You read that justice should be the goal of society; or that one must first recognize and correct one's ignorance; or that one must not perjure oneself; or that an ethical death is preferable to an unethical life; or the Golden Rule; or the Categorical Imperative. You read the words, and you say, This is true! Perhaps a logical argument buttresses the words, but in fact the logical argument is secondary. You know—you *recognize*—the truth of the words the instant you read them.

Other great thinkers embody their wisdom in fictional characters. You know Pierre's moral worth, in *War and Peace*, by observing his behavior, even when he fails to see it himself. You know Levin's superior worth, in *Anna Karenina*, even as he thinks he is struggling in a moral swamp. You clearly recognize Alyosha's keen moral sense, in *The Brothers Karamazov*, even as he is struggling with uncertainty. You recognize Huckleberry Finn's steady moral compass, though he is barely in his adolescence and considers himself to be a moral weakling. These characters are not "merely" fictive. They are life. They are us.

Thoreau wrote, "Our whole life is startlingly moral," as indeed it is. How do I know that? Dear reader, how do *you* know that? You read it; you know it.

Thoreau was no systematic moralist, but his entire body of work is based on a profound moral insight: that our lives are, or should be, part of the continuum of the natural world.

Thoreau's companion and teacher, Ralph Waldo Emerson, was perhaps the greatest exponent of the idea that value, including ethical value, is intrinsic in nature, and that aware individuals are equipped to tap that knowledge, because the human mind is of a piece with nature. Emerson's attachment to Transcendentalism is well known, and scholars generally treat Transcendentalism as a subset of Romanticism. I have wondered if, in Emerson's case, the word Transcendentalism may not be exactly right, because it may be that we do not need to transcend ourselves to gain insight. It may be that we instead need to recognize and intensify *what we already are*.

"Trust thyself. Every heart vibrates to that iron string." These are among Emerson's most memorable words, from the essay "Self-Reliance." They ring true. But why? As much as his words appeal to me, I have had the nagging question always in my mind, How does he *know* this? Is it a matter of mere faith? His own personal intuition? Where is the *certainty* of his faith? Is it just the result of a persistent optimism?

He speaks indirectly to this point near the end of his essay "Nature," Second Series. The final three paragraphs are enigmatic, and the final two verge on the ecstatic. Emerson recognizes that nature can be remote, can turn her back on us, just as Jehovah presented only his hinder parts to Moses. "Quite analogous to the deceits of life, there is, as might be expected, a similar effect on the eye from the face of external nature....Must we not suppose somewhere in the universe a slight treachery and derision? Are we not engaged to a serious resentment of this use that is made of us?....One look at the face of heaven and earth [a treat denied to Moses] lays all petulance at rest, and soothes us to wiser convictions. To the intelligent, nature converts itself into a vast promise, and will not be rashly explained. Her secret is untold.... We are escorted on every hand through life by spiritual agents, and a beneficent purpose lies in wait for us. We cannot bandy words with nature....If we measure our individual forces against hers, we may easily feel as if we were the sport of an insuperable destiny. But if, instead of identifying ourselves with the work, we feel that the soul of the workman streams through us, we shall find the peace of the morning dwelling first in our hearts, and the fathomless powers of gravity and chemistry, and, over them, of life, preexisting within us in their highest form....

"[W]e bring with us to every experiment the innate universal laws. These, while they exist in the mind as ideas, stand around us in nature forever embodied, a present sanity to expose and cure the insanity of men....Nature is the incarnation of a thought, and turns to a thought again....The world is mind precipitated....That power which does not respect quantity, which makes the whole and the particle its equal channel, delegates its smile to the morning, and distils its essence into every drop of rain. Every moment instructs, and every object: for wisdom is infused into every form." The innate values of nature are revealed in the small equally with the large, just as in the world of physics the unimaginably small, at the subatomic level, is as complex and mysterious as the unimaginably large at the cosmic level.

How can we separate this transcendent language from the language of mysticism? How can we penetrate the mystery? I think there are two avenues. One is to study science, which in detail has revealed to us a world that makes the wildest mysticism seem tame by comparison. Another way is by listening to the poet. From "The Poet," Second Series:

"The poet is the sayer, the namer, and represents beauty. He is a sovereign, and stands on the center. For the world is not painted, or adorned, but is from the beginning beautiful; and God has not made some beautiful things, but Beauty is the creator of the universe....Why should not the symmetry and truth that modulate these [natural events], glide into our spirits, and we participate in the invention of nature?

"This insight, which expresses itself by what is called Imagination, is a very high sort of seeing, which does not come by study, but by *the intellect being where and **what** it sees*, [emphasis added] by sharing the path, or circuit of things through forms, and so making them translucid to others....What a little of all we know is said!....when so many secrets sleep in nature! Hence the necessity of speech and song....that thought may be ejaculated as Logos, or Word."

I MIGHT QUIBBLE with Emerson about the specific definition of a poet. I would extend the definition to include all important communications, including the profoundest science and the most inspiring and insightful prose.

Again, how do I know that Emerson's words are true? I know for a certainty, not because I have written as a poet, but because I have read them (according to my expanded definition), and they do exactly as Emerson says. I know because I have been the recipient of the wisdom and beauty of more writers than I can name, all of whom channeled some aspect of nature to my mind and my heart. You know it when you see it. (And, in this context, " 'Beauty is truth, truth beauty' – that is all/Ye know on earth, and all ye need to know." John Keats.)

Another interesting point from the above passage is Emerson's apt Biblical connection. Of course he was entirely familiar with John, Chapter 1, verse 1: "In the beginning was the Word, and the Word was with God, and the Word was God." This is not the place to parse this suggestive and enigmatic passage; suffice it to say that the word and the creation are not merely causally connected, they are identical. This helps make sense of his assertion that "Beauty is the creator of the universe," for the Divine must indeed be beautiful, and the idea of Beauty must exist before it takes embodied form.

IN THE ACADEMIC world Romanticism is both an antiquated philosophy with loose empirical underpinnings, and a literary movement that produced some great art but has long faded into irrelevancy. The western world moved to realism. The closest thing to it in the contemporary literary world is, I suppose, Magical Realism, (which movement may have relevance to the subject but which I am reluctant to pursue, my knowledge being restricted to Borges and Marquez.)

The Romantic method is well known. The artist, a Wordsworth, say, places himself within a more or less natural environment, pastoral or in some situations more wild. The artist lays himself open to nature. This requires that he be emotionally aware of where he is. He must be sensitive to the world outside himself. This is important: too many people are emotionally deadened, made so by their own dullness, or by the wretchedness of their work or lives.

The artist also monitors his internal life, gauging his responses to his experience. His soul is affected. His feelings are primary, but his intellect is also engaged. After being influenced by the natural world, he carries that transcendent experience back to the easel or the pen and brings the intellect into play, to record and to communicate what he has discovered. Nature speaks to a receptive listener, the artist absorbs, then transcribes or creates.

This approach to discovery may not be as antiquated as it sounds. In fact, it may dovetail perfectly with Dworkin's assertion that value is intrinsic in The Creation and not dependent upon a deity. For isn't it true that this is really what we all do, at least in part, and at least occasionally in our lives?

The tourist bus pulls up to the Grand Canyon's south rim. Forty people emerge, toddle to the lookout platforms, read some of the signage, take their photos, and in twenty minutes are back on the bus.

It is easy to satirize this behavior. Yet the core of a genuine emotional and intellectual experience may be present. Some kind of connection may be there. And the experience, however brief, however superficial, may reverberate, however faintly, for years, enhanced by those photos. One day, one hour, one moment may lodge permanently within one's mind and produce salutary, and intense, feelings for many decades.

Most of us are a long way from Thoreau's passionate cry of *"Contact! Contact!"* (Thoreau's emphasis) as he gropes his way around Mount Ktaadn. Most of us experience less intensely and take away less. Yet the Romantic model is a way into the heart of the mystery.

A section of William Wordsworth's poem "Home at Grasmere" not only illustrates the Romantic method; it also expresses precisely the sentiments of both Emerson and Dworkin.

> I….would proclaim—
> Speaking of nothing more than what we are—
> How exquisitely the individual Mind

VALUE IS INHERENT IN NATURE

(And the progressive powers perhaps no less
Of the whole species) to the external world
Is fitted: and how exquisitely too—
Theme this but little heard of among men—
The external world is fitted to the mind;
And the creation (by no lower name
Can it be called) which they with blended might
Accomplish: this is my great argument.

Indeed. And Emerson's, and Dworkin's, and mine.

We don't need a belief in a deity to sense that nature is sublime, that nature is intrinsically beautiful, that nature can fill us with dread and joy. But what we do need is the will to establish contact. And when we do that we find that our lives are filled with value. And then we find that we have a moral obligation to protect the source of that value. This felt moral obligation may be one root of ethics.

One accusation that contemporaries may level at modern romantics—the terms tree hugger, greenie, etc. communicate this mild contempt—is that they have elevated their love of nature into a quasi-religion, and that this form of religion is inferior to the "real" thing, similar to when we say that he "worships" the dollar, or that he seeks "salvation" in physical conditioning; that these are ways of injecting meaning into life, just somewhat better than a hobby; superficial and comforting. Whether or not these criticisms are occasionally fair, it is true that there is a religious impulse behind Romanticism. Except that the religious content may be as real as any other religion, not quasi. For it is possible to be genuinely religious without a Jewish or Christian or Islamic God; that in fact it is far preferable, since, as I discussed in the previous chapter, these religions have not and will not foster, care for, or preserve the real source of our being, the natural world.

DWORKIN'S CONCERN IS not with a conservation ethic, but with recognizing the validity of a religion without God. Yet his key idea—that value is intrinsic and independent—reaches far beyond his thesis.

Aldo Leopold's great essay "The Land Ethic" presented two arguments for conservation: the pragmatic and the ethical. The pragmatic argument is simple: we should care for the land because it takes care of us. The ethical argument is that we should care for the land because we should find it within ourselves to love the land and the biological community it supports. This argument is profoundly important because it challenges the self: it requires us to grow intellectually and emotionally. It requires us to think beyond our narrow self-interests. It requires us to discipline our egotism. Above all, it provides the missing link between ourselves and value. Our connection to beauty is that we love beauty. Our connection to goodness is that we love goodness. Dworkin's argument, by extension, is that this is religious.

I DISCUSSED IN a previous chapter the problem in Alaska of maintaining a subsistence life within the Native cultures. Obtaining and ingesting food from the land and waters was and is an essentially religious experience for Alaska natives, and for the westerners among us, I offered the Christian communion as an analog: the ingestion of God Himself.

How can value be intrinsic in nature? The ingestion of nature as a religious experience may provide us with part of the answer. For the Alaska native who still lives on the land, nothing—nothing—is more important than absorbing a bit of The Creation into oneself. The practical necessity is obvious, the religious significance less so, especially for us westerners who are almost entirely severed from the sources of our food.

How would we see this situation if nature, The Creation, was itself the object of our religious veneration? Is there any evidence that humans have in fact found objective uncreated value, particularly ethical value, in the natural world of their experience? Do we have evidence that a non-traditional religious attitude can infuse an individuals' life with meaning, and with ethical value? In short, can Dworkin's (and Emerson's) claims be validated?

YES.

Let us first consider the thinkers who pre-date the three great established western religions, or who lived outside of the religious traditions of their time. This obviously includes the ancient Greeks and Romans who were untouched by the ancient Hebrews, and perhaps includes Gautama Buddha, who sidestepped Hinduism and established another path.

Socrates, of course, jumps to the forefront of my mind. His religious context, polytheism, violates most modern definitions of religion; and though he claimed to honor to some extent local religious conventions, he also added his own, such as his personal moral guide, as he explains in "The Apology." But it is obvious that he is keyed into something additional. His moral guide is interior and personal, and, paradoxically perhaps, universal. He does not draw inspiration from nature as moderns or Romantics think of nature, but this thoroughly urban thinker was connected to nature in the larger sense.

One reason why Socrates is admired as one of our greatest thinkers is because of his steady and true moral compass. His moral compass was governed by the rigorous use of reason. He was convinced that the universe was inherently, thoroughly rational (and therefore good), and adhering to the good therefore invariably produces the best outcome, even if it results in one's death, as it did with Socrates (and with Jesus, and with many less obvious examples.) "The good" here is notoriously difficult to define, but we can all agree that it nevertheless exists.

What justifies Socrates' reliance on reason as his infallible guide? Superficially, it appears to be founded on little but faith. Socrates may appear to be at heart simply an optimist. But do we have any empirical evidence that his optimistic view that the universe is both rational and good was founded on anything but his faith?

Yes, we do have such evidence, because we have the historical record. We can examine and judge Socrates' life and death, we can judge the quality of his thought, and we can judge his place in history, particularly his impact on subsequent generations. And we shall judge that he was right. Were he merely a deluded martyr who threw his life away for nothing, his life would be less worthy of study, and his death, which was largely a matter of choice, inspiring but meaningless. In short, he saw that ethical value is intrinsic in nature, and he demonstrated that truth through his actions.

Let us recall that Socrates was utterly untouched by the religions that have come to dominate the world, yet he is one of our very few greatest ethical teachers. Dear reader, I can think of no stronger argument that ethical value comes to us as a force of nature; intrinsic in The Creation, and unattached to an organization. Plato, Aristotle, the other great ones I mentioned above, and later the Romantics, Emerson, Thoreau, are all his descendants in this particular. He was religious in the larger, Dworkian sense.

The details of ethical behavior are important but secondary; that we *are* ethical is primary. To be ethical is our nature, and we are so because we are children of nature. One may argue, then why aren't all thinking organisms ethical, since they too are children of nature? Because it is our particular nature to be conscious and therefore self-reflective, which provides us with the choice of behaving rationally. For Socrates, it was the use of reason that enables us to tap our ethical choices, and the use of reason is a result of being self-reflective, though certainly not all self-reflection yields rationality.

The objections to my assertions are obvious. The first is that we are the result of an evolutionary process which in itself could account for ethical behavior. Altruism, so I read, can be explained in evolutionary terms. Likewise, ethics can be seen as one subset of social behavior. Humans are intensely social and we can readily explain ethical behavior as a result of this aspect of our evolution. And finally, there is the fact that people are not necessarily ethical, and that many, perhaps most, do not connect much with nature.

I find no contradiction here. Evolution is a natural process, and if it accounts for ethical behavior, or some part of it, so be it. We could say the same thing for our sense of beauty, that if it is a result of preferences that we developed as we evolved, then value is indeed innate; natural, as it were. And finally, there is the knotty fact that, with the development of our big brains, and the evolution of consciousness, we have the choice of leaving the evolutionary path. Which means that we may have the unpleasant choice of developing a different ethical path, one not connected to nature.

WE MODERNS HAVE slowly come to the conclusion that other organisms may indeed be self-reflective. (Did ancient humans honor the thinking ability of animals? If so, is this an indication that they were more closely attuned to the natural world than we are?) Two points are of interest here.

One has to do with our developing recognition of other conscious intelligences, such as cetaceans, elephants, and our old friends the canines. And how have we come to this recognition? By observing their social behavior primarily. We have recognized their intelligence through their behavior towards each other, and in some cases their connection to other species (dolphins and humans, canines and humans; there are records of wolves and bears at play with each other). In other words, their intelligence is most manifest in what could well be ethical behavior. (And it is worth noting that much of this social behavior is play.)

The second point follows closely upon this observation. Ethical behavior among humans is also largely social. Ethical behavior occurs for the most part between intelligent interacting organisms (though much ethical behavior involves decisions about how to treat oneself). Intelligence, ethical behavior, and social behavior are inextricably linked. This is true even in the cases of the very highest ethical acts, which seem at first glance to be anomalies. In the final, simplest analysis, both Socrates and Jesus acted in ways that required some authority to kill them. A soft way to say this is that they could have avoided their deaths but did not. Instead they acted in such a way that they forced their killers to act, to show themselves. This is closely akin to civil disobedience as practiced by Thoreau, Gandhi, and Martin Luther King: forcing the hands of those holding power, insisting upon incarceration (or death) as a way to illustrate the immoral behavior of their powerful enemies—*so that those holding power are forced to see the truth of their own bad behavior.* This is a most powerful tool. These five were teachers, using their very lives as instruments of instruction. We recognize this as an aspect of altruism, the highest ethical ideal: to instruct those who hate you, even at the cost of your life. This may be the highest manifestation of love. Their acts went far beyond the narrow social aspects of ethics, which reinforce cooperation while preserving one's self-interest. Our greatest moral guides act this way not because it is irrational and unnatural, but because it is rational and natural; i.e., ethical behavior is an integral part of their characters. As Thoreau observed, the least of our actions are "startlingly moral."

DEAR READER, YOU have probably noted that this discussion has circled around to a version of good old pantheism.

It is well known that Einstein, after his early period of intense creativity, devoted most of the rest of his life to developing a unified field theory. I am not up to a discussion of this topic, except to point out that he was convinced that the various contradictory, and plausible, explanations within physics of certain forces demand to be reconciled. He was convinced that nature must be all of one piece. In short, philosophically he was a rationalist, and his philosopher was Spinoza.

Baruch (Benedict) de Spinoza (1632-1677) was Einstein's philosopher, and he has traditionally been thought of as the philosopher's philosopher, not only for the rigor of his thought but for the quality of his life. This is not the place to develop an explication of Spinoza's philosophy. But some outline is necessary.

Following Descartes, Spinoza was convinced that logic was the key to understanding, which conviction must assert that logic as practiced by humans must coincide precisely with the cause and effect relationships to be found in nature. Nature must be thoroughly rational and could not be otherwise. As with Descartes, a concept of "substance" lies at the center of his philosophy. (I have used this term above.) "Substance" is that which requires nothing else for its existence, and our limited experience tells us that substance has two attributes that humans can know, extension through space, and thought; matter and mind. Nevertheless, since substance is by definition without limitation, we must recognize that it may have an infinite number of attributes. However, the human mind can only experience and identify two: extension and thought, matter and mind. Attributes exist everywhere in parallel; wherever there is substance, there is extension; wherever there is substance, there is mind. However, these attributes cannot interact, being of entirely different modes. Extension is utterly unlike mind; mind is utterly unlike matter; we cannot think about extension without thinking about something concrete, such as motion and rest; we cannot think about mind without experiencing an activity of the intellect or the will.

These necessary forms of thought have objective reality. They are not subjective human creations. Substance—God—must be material; it must be mental; indeed, it must be everything. The universe, in short, must be pantheistic. Matter (physics, chemistry, etc.) is one expression of substance; mind (aesthetics, ethics, etc.) is one expression of substance. *They are both expressions of the same thing.*

In the realm of mind, there is truth and falsity. Unanalyzed experience and uninformed opinion do not yield knowledge. "Clear and distinct" ideas do yield knowledge. "The criterion of truth is its intrinsic clarity.... Whoever has a true idea knows that he has it." And this true idea is the outcome of faultless logic. Muddled thinking cannot yield true ideas. There is a right and a wrong.

I find it interesting that this most comprehensive and rigorous of philosophers, Einstein's philosopher, the philosopher's philosopher, titled his major book the *Ethics*. Why not the *Physics* or the *Logic*? I think it is because every human action is as tied to value as it is tied to the physical world, and since we humans see the world as humans and only as humans, we must see it as ethical beings.

VALUE IS INHERENT IN NATURE

"Our whole life is startlingly moral." Here lies meaning. Here is the connection Einstein saw between the study of mathematics and physics and the meaning of his life.

Spinoza's conclusion was that "our highest good consists in the intellectual love of God." We must love this "substance," God, the universe, The Creation. One must be utterly benighted not to do so! When I feel delight in my physical being, my thought, my sense of beauty, I am experiencing what is *already present* in this pantheistic God. It is not merely *my* delight; it is not merely subjective. Though Spinoza's "intellectual love is God" is utterly dispassionate, I think my more emotional love is akin to it, as is I think Aldo Leopold's insistent love of The Creation.

(I owe much of the above to Frank Thilly and Ledger Wood, *A History of Philosophy*, Holt, Rinehart and Winston, 1962; pulled off my shelf where it has been a guest since my college days. Quoted material from Thilly and Wood. Ronald Dworkin also discusses Spinoza in *Religion Without God*, but with a different emphasis.)

IN A DIFFERENT section above I alluded to Frederick Turner's *Beyond Geography*, in which he points out that one of the results of the development of monotheism by the Hebrews was that religion entered history. The timeless world of myth came to an end, and time became strictly linear and directional. Judaism, then Christianity, then Islam, placed religion within time: there was a Before, then a Creation, then a foundation story; the story has a long middle section, which includes the now; and there will be an end, when the story is concluded, with varying but necessary outcomes depending upon the religion and the individual. For the world's many millions of Jews, Christians, and Moslems, time moves towards a certain end. "Infinity" and "eternity" are in this context simply words without referents. The world is small, the universe is finite; and, consistent with these limitations, the conception of God is petty, for I suspect that for most believers God is male, occupies a place which is directional (up), and functions in a way not entirely unlike Zeus, as an exaggerated human. I know that the more sophisticated of the theologians abandoned this view long ago, but I suspect that their views have not prevailed.

This viewpoint is entirely unsatisfactory. The metaphysics of the three religions from the near and middle east cannot describe reality.

History has shown that the three desert religions together have created a condition of perpetual war, regardless of the teachings of their founders. The Hebrews were subject to slavery, but upon their escape grew into a people of warriors, as the Old Testament abundantly shows; and a group capable of great cruelty. The seemingly endless religious wars of the Christians are thoroughly documented in European history, the most infamous being the roughly two centuries spanning the eight Crusades, centuries of barbarism inflicted upon the peoples they invaded (and upon the unfortunate people along their line of march). Islam holds the distinction in my mind of being the only major religion to establish itself primarily through warfare, which eventually extended its holdings into most of Spain. To these overtly religious wars we can add the secular wars that were buttressed by religion, most notably to my mind the incursions of the Conquistadors into the western hemisphere, always accompanied by a priesthood ever willing to back conquest with religion. And of course the effects of these wars continue in different forms today and are a plague upon the earth. Only the worst of our secular dictators have created more suffering.

The Spinozan and pantheistic view is far more plausible, and I think far more compatible with empirical science, and far more conducive to ethical behavior.

VALUE IS INHERENT IN NATURE

WHY MENTION THIS at all in a discussion of conservation? Because a discussion of Spinoza inevitably requires that he be contrasted to the dominant ethical and metaphysical forces in history. This contrast forces us to the conclusion that the desert religions cannot be of any help, and may be a considerable hindrance, as they are currently established. We can develop a conservation ethic only by sidestepping them.

Spinoza was expelled from the synagogue, threatened with death, and forced to leave Amsterdam. History has judged that he led an exemplary ethical life.

ON ANOTHER HEADING, dear reader: You have probably assumed that I have chosen to ignore nature's dark side. From where I sit, free of disease and well fed, I can easily and painlessly appreciate nature's beauty. But I am fully aware that nature is not necessarily the benevolent mother. I know that nature is plenty red in tooth and claw. She can be insidious and diabolical, when seen in human terms; a superficial study of parasitism and its many repellent forms is one excellent example. Creatures die horrible deaths; creatures suffer; life for most creatures is difficult most of the time.

But that does not obviate the fact that, nevertheless, beauty and ethics do indeed exist, and that they are intrinsic in nature, and are therefore just as true and sound and durable as nature, and that humans are a part of that natural continuum; and it is easier for me to understand evolutionary forces that place pressure on individuals and species than it is for me to understand a benevolent God who nevertheless created the tapeworm and the cancer cell. Spinoza's "intellectual love of God" must indeed be a dispassionate love; understanding must precede but not displace sentiment.

Whatever nature is, it is rational. Now, with Socrates, we must understand that it is therefore good.

FOUNDATIONS

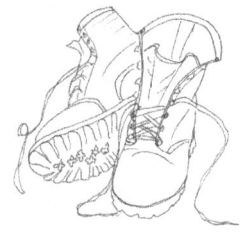

EXPLANATORY NOTE

I include these three essays here because I am convinced that large purposes must be behind travel in the wilderness—travel through space must have a larger purpose than amusement—travel through space is also emotional and intellectual travel—personal narratives without purpose are pointless, bordering on the nihilistic. These essays explore the thirst for knowledge that underlies human behavior; the need for the Quest; the tragedy of the Original Sin; and the recognition that fate and pride have profound effects on human behavior, including our relationships with the natural world.

Life's journey is larger than just going backpacking. Wilderness travel is more than a diversion. The loss of the Old People is a global tragedy. The Quest is a noble adventure at the core of human existence. Hence their inclusion here.

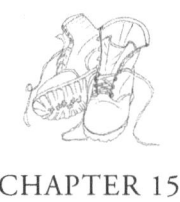

CHAPTER 15

Reading

"To read well, that is, to read true books in a true spirit, is a noble exercise, and one that will task the reader more than any exercise which the customs of the day esteem. It requires a training such as the athletes underwent, the steady intention almost of the whole life to this object. Books must be read as deliberately and reservedly as they were written."

H. D. Thoreau

I was long ago struck by the notion, unoriginal but fundamentally valuable, that only a few things in life are important. When I examined my life, having intuitively and almost unconsciously followed this principle, I concluded that they numbered but five: Beauty, Love, Human Development (including oneself and those one touched), the physical environment one connects with (call it Nature), and Reading. I think this list is inclusive. Every item in the list connects with every other item; they all together form a unity. Each item underpins all the others; all are necessary to the full development of the others.

Of the five, Reading appeals most strongly to the intellect, but also strengthens the other four emotionally. Few things, perhaps nothing, completes the human being more.

I think that the single greatest human artifact of our nation is the First Amendment, and our national response to it, in the form of a truly free press. To my knowledge, the only truly free market in the United States is the market of ideas, as represented in the various forms of speech, including and especially print.

However, to our discredit, too few Americans participate in this market. One of the big lies that too many Americans accept, and repeat, is that there exists a monolithic and monopolistic "media." "The media" is said to hide or control information, "the media" is said to control events by controlling the viewpoint. In truth, "the media" is simply an euphemism for television, and people feel controlled by television simply because they have chosen to place themselves under the control of television. If television controls people's minds and opinions, it is because people have chosen to make themselves slaves out of laziness and habit. People have chosen "the media" as their one source of knowledge, of all the splendid sources readily available to them, and then complain about hearing the single viewpoint they themselves have selected.

My grocery store magazine rack offers more solid information, week by week and month by month, than most people can absorb. Toss out the junk, which constitutes most of the choices, and you are still left with a half dozen or so worthwhile publications that, for most television watchers, would open up fascinating new worlds and viewpoints. On the supply side the goods are there, freely available and cheap, but few are buying. People instead complain about "media control," evading their own responsibility for obtaining the information that enters their minds. We are infants who haven't learned to exercise our intellectual freedom.

This is why the Internet is popular: it is easy.

To what is on the newsstands, add the scholarly press, the little publications, and the specialty publications, and we are rolling in intellectual wealth.

READING

And the books!

Let's leave aside for a time what Thoreau's "true books" might be, and look at reading "in a true spirit" as a "noble exercise."

As with all great writers, almost every individual word of Thoreau's, when he is at his best, is worthy of close examination. That reading is "an exercise," comparable to athletic training, is a shrewd comparison. Exercise requires regular, frequent repetition. Exercise, to be fruitful, must be selective; the training must be calculated as to kind and duration and quality; it cannot be casual and random. Exercise must continue over long periods of time—years, decades, for life—if it is to have a beneficial effect. A program of exercise that proceeds by fits and starts is a failure.

The only way to adhere to these requirements is to bring a sense of discipline into play. When I think of discipline here, either in athletic or intellectual training, I reject the notion of a clench-jawed, ironclad, rigid activity that depends upon the force of will for its execution. Rather, I think of an affectionate discipline that is equivalent to self-mastery, so that the exercise, though perhaps demanding, even painful, is embraced in joy and love. We don't bend something to our will; rather, we embrace something because it is a fundamental part of the good life; its difficulty or painfulness is subsumed under this larger heading.

This rational dedication is what makes the pursuit noble. It appeals to our higher self, and when engaged in it raises that higher self to yet greater heights: the whole person, intellectually and emotionally, is continually raised. We call this "character." Reading in a "true spirit" always trends this way. It carries us forward on our quest.

But what is it that forms the content of our exercise? What are those "true books?"

On the one hand, think of "the canon," the Great Books, the standard works enshrined in our culture. The program is laid out for us.

On the other hand, imagine a dedicated seeker who reads in a true spirit to ennoble his character. He follows his genius through the years. He begins by taking a bite out of the nearly infinite choices available; he begins almost at random, something off a library shelf, something from school, something he heard about; maybe a book he picked up off the floor in a school. (I found a remarkable and little known gem this way; someone was kicking the battered paperback down the hallway.) Time passes, one thing leads to another. Fiction, science, philosophy, history, travel writing, personal essays. Criticism, book reviews, textual references, bibliographies. One's reading grows outward like a globular web. Everything connects, and one day we discover that we have read "the canon" after all; we scan a Great Books list, and discover that we're among old friends. Following your genius may mean following the genius of your culture as well. Though we follow different paths, at different rates of speed, we trend in the same direction. Wisdom doesn't come wholesale or in too many flavors; though found in more than one place, it nevertheless isn't found at every port of call; all of us who seek will find ourselves together in the same few harbors at the end.

READING IS informed by love.

Plato taught that Eros motivates our desire for knowledge.

I have trouble writing the previous sentence in a form that is not a tautology. What is "desire" in this context if it is not Eros? Is the statement "I love knowledge" in truth identical to "My knowledge is love?" No, not quite, but separating Eros from knowledge by making it a predicate is to create too large a gap between the concepts. I would prefer a closer identity; they are nearly one.

READING

I learned to love Plato—not so much my idea of the corporeal man, but everything around him, including Socrates, and the beauty and content of the written works—on my third reading of *The Republic*, in the beautiful Cornford translation. By that time I had already concluded that I could not be a Platonist, that Platonic Idealism is a beautiful and comforting illusion, an elaborate, comprehensive, and well-unified fiction. (I never, here or elsewhere, use the word "fiction" in a pejorative sense.) Yet where could my love come from, and the beauty that radiated from the book, if not from truth? From the beauty of Cornford's English? From the wholeness of Plato's metaphysics, or the grace of Plato's presentation? Yes, yes, and yes. But those reasons don't satisfy in the end. There must be a bedrock of truth. The final ingredient was the presence of truth, not a grand comprehensive truth, but small discreet truths imbedded within the larger fiction. The beauty of the whole work is completed by the fact that, as a pragmatist, I could extract truths, and wisdom, from the larger work; I could mine it for beauty, wisdom, and utility regardless of the metaphysics. Call me uncritical, call me a dilettante, call me an eclectic; but I was able to find a significant quantity of beauty and truth that I could carry forward into the modern world, and marry to my other, apparently disparate, reading. I made Plato my friend and companion, or so he made me. His great vessel is docked beside Buddha's and Confucius', Spinoza's and Kant's, Kierkegaard's and Nietzsche's, Darwin's and Freud's and Einstein's, and I can board them all from my little skiff, rummage around in their holds at will, pirate away what I choose. The whole fleet, commanded by people I imagine to be my good friends, is mine, I want the cargo of every one of those great navigators, and I find no contradiction in that.

SUNLIGHT NORTH

As I wrote in Chapter 9, 1977 was an important year in my life. I took a major trip to the eastern Brooks Range, three weeks by foot in the mountains and ten days by kayak down the east fork of the Chandalar River and part of the Yukon. On the Chandalar I met Sarah and Johnny Frank, then aged ninety-five and ninety-seven. They were true aboriginals, having attained young adulthood before white men came to their country. I only visited with them for a few days, but they changed me permanently.

My books on that trip were two of Loren Eiseley's. His personal essays explore the nature of man and the universe, man in the universe, man as a recently evolving creature emerging from his animal past into self-consciousness. He too is my friend.

That fall my father died. That December Johnny Frank died. That year Loren Eiseley and Vladimir Nabokov died.

Nabokov's best work was and is my ideal of the art of the modern novel. He occupies an important place in my life, a place shared with Faulkner, Marques, Borges, and Grass. Unlike Eiseley's, his art keeps you at arm's length while you watch him work his magic, except for *Speak, Memory*, in which you share his past, his life, in the most passionate way. He transforms nostalgia, that killer of life, into the bearer of fine fruit.

I lost four fathers that year, my biological father; my adoptive spiritual father; Eiseley, my guide through the darkness and mystery of my biological past; Nabokov, the master of the imagination.

You say, how presumptuous of me to appropriate three of these men unto myself. Johnny I briefly knew. He, and Sarah, embodied a mysterious past that, with the death of their generation, will be—or is—gone forever, everywhere on the globe, ground up and indiscriminately destroyed by the irresistible machinery of European expansion into every cranny of the earth. Their passing—the passing of all the ancient aboriginal cultures—may be history's greatest tragedy and our greatest sin.

Eiseley knew this. He knew that the world-eaters are never sated. He knew the darkness of our hearts and the ruthless forces of change. He knew that *Homo sapiens*, in its self-consciousness, had managed to become the first organism to divorce itself from nature. We are following an unknown path—running, with little direction, blindly and headlong—into a future that was never before imagined, never before possible. We are living the story of our exile from the garden, probably the greatest myth ever recorded, certainly the most prophetic and comprehensive.

Hence the linkage in my mind, and heart, between Johnny and Sarah, two of the last aboriginals, and Loren Eiseley, their gloomy and prescient eulogist. Two fathers, one representing what is lost, the other striving to understand the significance of that loss.

LOREN EISELEY GRASPED the profoundly important fact that the glory and tragedy of *Homo sapiens* is our self-consciousness, our ability to project ourselves forward in time to view our own corpses. We know anxiety and dread because we know time. Because we are self-conscious, we are subject to egotism, and that most destructive of all human traits, pride. We insist on our own inflated importance regardless of the facts; our prideful insistence can be monstrous. This was Adam's real sin. As Ernest Becker well said, "*Hubris* means forgetting where the real source of power lies and imagining that it is in oneself." The tentacles of European culture have been maintained and extended in this same obsessive-compulsive manner; we are the culture of total control; precisely the opposite of the aboriginals such as Sarah and Johnny, who gave themselves to the vicissitudes of an uncertain and tenuous world that they knew they could not control. Paradoxically, they had the freedom to give themselves to fate.

The tragedy of the expulsion from the Garden is the tragedy of self-consciousness and ego, and Sarah and Johnny and all aboriginal cultures paid the price of death because of that. The Fall is the tragedy I have lived with all my life, and I can't anesthetize it or hide from it; sometimes I can achieve a momentary amnesia. We have infected the earth, we have poisoned it and exploited it, stripped it and gouged it, treated it with supreme and arrogant indifference, even hostility. The irony here is that those who are most destructive are the rich, the very people who can afford to conduct their affairs carefully.

It is a mystery to me why certain types of human behavior change quickly, others hardly at all. Scientific knowledge is usually grasped and implemented almost immediately after discovery. Technological change occurs quickly and people adopt it effortlessly. But in the area of ethics, change for the better is almost non-existent. The most outrageous acts of human cruelty, in terms of the most people killed in the most hideous ways, occurred within living memory. (If you want to trump this claim by narrating the cruelties of Atilla or the Conquistadors or certain Chinese emperors, I won't object. It will only strengthen my claim, because one would need to cite the very worst from the past to approach what we moderns have done.) The fact is, the teachings of the great ones, Jesus and Buddha and Socrates and Confucius, have not altered our collective behavior in any appreciable way.

I have a bias towards optimism, however, and I do suspect that we have ratcheted our behavior upward in some areas of environmental concern. We have achieved some success in improving water and air quality. We have managed to establish parks and wilderness areas. Public figures who are fundamentally unsympathetic to environmental protection at least have to mutter pro-environmental noises from time to time to keep their jobs. True, we move backwards in other areas: land use, farming practices, flood "control," water allocation in the West, energy consumption. But I nevertheless believe that if we are to make any advances in our ethical behavior, it will be, perhaps has been, in the area of environmental protection. And that is no small thing. If we can establish a right relationship between ourselves and our land, we might be able to correct other ethical problems as well, beginning with the establishment of a just economic system, including the development of a less narrowly materialistic society. I always keep in mind that the first chapter of *Walden* is titled "Economy." Ghandi, too, recognized that a right relationship between man and the environment, and man and man, has an important economic component. Contemporary citizens must consider the apparent paradox that we must strive for an economic viewpoint that is not strictly or narrowly materialistic. Perhaps the study of ecology can yield some important economic knowledge, one that includes ethics as well as money.

I LOVE THE ERA of the Big Book. I read and reread Dickens for love and pleasure, and I read and reread Tolstoy for his weight and density. I value Dostoyevsky for the same reason, though he perhaps seems less weighty because he is more volatile. These authors, I think, were less concerned with the artistry that so delights me in Nabokov, and more concerned with the world. I am humbled when I think of the breadth, the scope, of *Anna Karenina*, *War and Peace*, *The Brothers Karamazov*. And they are as deep as they are broad. Those authors, and Dickens, had the courage and audacity to actually map the world in its physical, social, psychological, and even philosophical dimensions. Breathtaking. They raised the art of the novel from the level of diversionary entertainment, manners, or social comment, to the level of *meaning*, rising to the level of history and almost to the level of philosophy. When I reopen *Anna* or *Karamazov*, I am not leaving my world for a while; I am entering a larger world that not only includes and subsumes mine, and the specific world of that time and place, but also the full human world of religious mystery, psychological complexity, and human meaning. A miraculous event: there the book sits: I have only to open it.

Other, lesser epics are close to my heart also: Hamsun's *The Growth of the Soil*, Rolvaag's *Giants in the Earth*, are two. Less comprehensive, less probing and philosophical, these works nevertheless also convey a sense of human significance as people live out their lives during a long span of time. Size matters; duration matters; it takes a Big Book to remind us of life's true scope.

THE GREAT NOVEL is, as we know, also history; the best history is a fine story.

In schools in America, the most difficult subject to teach, and to learn as it is now taught, is history.

This is so for several reasons. Young people are real Americans— they have early on adopted the famous anti-historical bias of their culture. Our culture has taught them to discard the past, retaining only a few selected myths, and this irresponsible attitude is very appealing to the young mind. It is too much to expect history teachers to correct this overwhelming cultural pressure.

Second, history teachers feel compelled to "cover" all the most "important" material, and so history is still studied as politics, war, and dates which have no meaningful context. Textbooks try to "cover" "everything," and can only do so very superficially. There is just too much to "cover."

Third, history is suited to the mature mind. To understand history as a *meaningful whole* and not a bewildering jumble of disconnected events requires a developed mind: some knowledge of human nature, politics, the history of ideas, literature, the historical development of science, religion, ethics. Young people should be taught a broad *conceptual* outline; they should fill in the gaps as they mature.

History is a story, the best there is, and should be taught and studied as such. It is vitally interesting, not dry as dust. I read my Gibbon in small bits over the years, but I also read my DeVoto, Parkman, Burkhardt, Huizinga, Keegan almost as novels. They tell compelling and important stories.

Accompanying the story, and the story's facts, is the need for analysis and a larger understanding.

Johan Huizinga was such a highly cultured analyst. His domain was art, literature, religion, theology, philosophy, and all the other more common areas of historical knowledge. His vast breadth of knowledge allowed him to understand his period, the Middle Ages primarily, and find *meaning* in it. This is a rare and grand outcome: to find meaning in the large movements of human society. But he did not presume to declare grand conclusions, such as "mankind is the pinnacle of historical development" or "modern man is the fruition of the past." Rather, he saw, for example, that *play* permeates human institutions (*Homo Ludens, A Study of the Play Element in Culture*), or that most human (or at least Western) behavior follows a fixed number of ideal forms ("Historical Ideals of Life"). To walk with Huizinga is to walk with a wise and cultured friend. I always feel immensely privileged to have access to his mind.

I HAVE NEVER known a wise person in the flesh. But of the thinkers who live or lived in the modern world, the wisest man I know from reading is Ernest Becker. I have found in him a passionate and courageous intellect. As with all intellects of value, his intelligence and courage were accompanied by hard work. (People often assume that the output of genius comes easy, a gift. We often don't recognize that one of the hallmarks of their achievement, be it Aristotle, Plato, Spinoza, Newton, Nietzsche, Darwin, Freud, is sustained and passionate work.) He is the perfect example of the eclectic thinker who was able to attain wisdom by selecting important information from a number of disciplines and integrating that wisdom into a meaningful whole. He was driven by a thirst for meaning, and had the courage to find it in the darkest and most forbidding places, staring at death most intimately as he did so. His work shows us that the integration of knowledge is a form of creativity, and that wisdom is the result of character and effort working with intelligence and not the result of intelligence alone. Pure intelligence, unformed by character, is empty and useless, even perhaps dangerous, since it is prone to contemplate its own magnificence and thus can be the main ingredient in hubris.

THE POET GALWAY Kinnell calls his readers his "unmet friends." This heartens me.

WE ALL KNOW about the isolation of the writer. The act is performed in solitude, and the writer must wonder, For whom am I doing this? Will someone hear my voice? How will I find my readers, or my readers find me? Will we connect?

So I don't feel presumptuous claiming friends, even fathers, among the writers of books. They want and need me, too.

What a marvelous artifact, the book. It sits passively on the shelf, infinitely patient, for years or centuries. Someone picks it up, has the good sense to attend to it, and two minds meet, bridging the barriers of time and space.

Beauty, Love, Human Development, Nature, Reading.

I watch my wife pocket bits of this and that as she walks the shore near our coastal cabin. I notice later that she has categorized and labeled these fragments of life and incorporated them into our cabin, along with the cuttings now leafing out and blossoming in a vase, the books, the photos, the kitchen arrangement—our raw little cabin is in its small way a beautiful place. Across the fjord a wall of mountains rise up from the sea; a gull's reflection follows it across the still water, Barrow's goldeneyes feed along the lowering tide line. A kayak sits on the top of the beach. Beauty here, large and small, produces harmony.

One is led thereby to love what one sees and experiences, and I am led to recall our children, students, colleagues, friends: the people we have loved and grown with. We have all developed along the way; we are all better than we were; we are all going somewhere; our lines of movement are good.

One cannot, however, live confined to immediate knowledge, immediate sensations, or one's recollection of a personal past. The human past, its history, wisdom, and literary art, lie available to hand; when I read, the beauty of the world is enhanced, deepened; my emotional range is extended, my capacity for love expanded; my knowledge allows me to make more and better connections between me and all of my surroundings; I am larger; I am more alive. More than anything, I understand that there is a fundamental unity within those few things that really matter.

"To read well, that is, to read books in a true spirit, is a noble exercise, and one that will task the reader more than any exercise which the customs of the day esteem. It requires a training such as the athletes underwent, the steady intention almost of the whole life to this object. Books must be read as deliberately and reservedly as they were written."

H. D. Thoreau

CHAPTER 16

Homo quaestus: The Search for Identity

Perhaps the oldest question, not in content but in form, is the question "Why?" Whether or not this is so, I do know that this is the first question that is persistently asked by every child I have known; perhaps it has always been so. Though I can't remember doing this myself, both of my children, when they were about two years of age, began to sound like tape loops with one word on them: why, why, why, why, why? Was this done to annoy? Did the child expect an answer? *Did he really want to know?* Was the question little more than a reflex, or was it asked in sincerity? What value do we place on the question?

In any case, I do know that the question is (perhaps universally) asked, and asked at an early age, and asked persistently. All three of the preceding points are interesting. Why is the question "why?" common to everyone? Why do we ask it when we are quite young? Why are we so persistent in the asking?

If questioning is such an essential part of being human, perhaps, instead of being primarily Homo ludens, Homo faber, or Homo sapiens, we are Homo quaestus.

NOBODY KNOWS what stories the old people of the planet told each other as they sat around ancient fires. The spoken word vanished as soon as it was heard. The only stories we know of the old people are those that are told by the few remaining aboriginal peoples, and the earliest stories that were miraculously captured in writing, such as the Old Testament and the chronicles of Homer. It is striking to me that these stories usually involve physical movement through space: Adam and Eve *ejected* from the garden and beginning their lives as outcasts; Moses *leading* the people on their long journey out of Egypt on their search for happiness; Odysseus *voyaging* from adventure to adventure, likewise finding his uncertain way home. The Yupik, Inupiat, and Athabaskan stories that I have heard often involve some journey that tests one's endurance and mental powers. The Medieval romances still appeal to us today, either in their original form or in some commercial disguise. The American myth of the Open Road: Horace Greely's advice to "Go West, young man," Huckleberry Finn's determination to "light out for the Territory ahead of the rest," and Jack Kerouac's wandering characters, to give but a few examples of many, communicates the idea that life is a story which moves through space. To what end?

The Latin verb *quaerere* is the common root of the English words "quest" ("to seek, ask") and "question" ("to ask, seek"). (This interesting word order is exactly as printed in my unabridged *American Heritage* dictionary.) This is a most provocative linguistic conjunction indeed.

IS IT POSSIBLE that *my entire life* is a question? That is to say, can it be that all the actions in which I engage themselves pose a question or series of questions, and that my primary *quest* in life is to attempt to resolve satisfactorily the *questions* which my life has posed? If this is so, several consequences must follow.

One is that the end of the quest results in death. Not that my body must necessarily cease functioning. But if I am indeed Homo quaestus, the conclusion of the quest would signal the extinction of what is most essential to me, my defining trait. Like a two-year-old, I must keep posing the question. The alternative is spiritual or intellectual death. As Socrates so well and famously said, "The unexamined life is not worth living." These are the most frightening words I have ever read. How many lives *are* worth living, by this standard? How many people have buried their *quest*-ions and might as well be dead?

Another consequence is that I must define myself by my *actions*. If my life—my very existence—is the *question*, and the trajectory of my life is the *quest*, then the only way I can understand *who I am* is to understand *what I do* and *why I do it*. If I understand *what* I do, then I can be fully engaged in my quest. If I understand *why* I do it, then my quest has both a motivating force and a direction. (I am leaving aside for the moment the likelihood that the "what" and the "why" may be dimly understood or even unconscious.) If I take Socrates' advice and examine my life, which I take to be the specific *activities* in which I engage, then I can determine if my life has value. I am what I do. If I want to know me, I look at my actions. If I want to judge me, then I judge those actions. My enemies are self-delusions, lies, rationalizations, intentions without actions. I must observe myself with ruthless honesty.

Yet another consequence is that I must learn to live with uncertainty. A quest, by definition, is a process, and according to my reasoning its cessation must be accompanied by a kind of death. Therefore my life must be forever open-ended. True, I love to accomplish goals and I love to have stopping places—points of rest—in my life. But those moments are not ends, merely times when I am gathering my forces. My periods of dormancy are times when my psyche is deciding where to go next. Much is unconscious. Sometimes I stride forward; sometimes I blunder in an uncertain direction; my way is often dark. These are the most frightening and memorable times.

How Can a Life be a Question?

I can remember taking a long hike with my son when he was six years old. It was late August, frequently a rainy time where I live. We hiked about eight miles into the mountains; made a camp; hiked farther the next day and returned to camp; and hiked to the car on the third day. We spent the entire time in a hard, unrelenting rain which turned out to be a record-setting storm.

What would this little fellow do while carrying a pack in a hard cold rain? Weep? Complain? Beg for comfort? No; he engaged me in conversation. He wondered how the universe began, and he wanted to express his skepticism about the creationist viewpoint. He couldn't accept the something-came-from-nothing theory and he didn't like the idea of God as a craftsman working from a cosmic blueprint; he also didn't like the idea that the creation, if it occurred, was compressed into a short period of time. I did not prime him on the subject. We had never discussed the Biblical creation before and he didn't know my thinking on the subject. He wasn't parroting Dad. I just listened, asked an occasional question, and marveled. I was reminded of Montaigne's conviction that philosophy should *not* be reserved for the mature. Indeed, he claimed that it was for the young. I think he was correct. In fact, I think most philosophical questions are asked by the child-like mind. The form is "Why?" or some variant. The content varies.

The child will ask, "Why is the sky blue?" The child will also ask, "What is beyond the sky?"

HOMO QUAESTUS: THE SEARCH FOR IDENTITY

The content, in other words, might invite scientific investigation; however, it might also invite metaphysical speculation. Those with an empirical bent are prone to ridicule the second type of question because metaphysical speculation cannot be verified. For the empiricist, there is a clear distinction between speculation and knowledge. The former is the nonsense generated by sophomoric discussions in dorm rooms; many hardheaded empiricists (or laymen who favor "common sense" over every other kind of knowledge) like to characterize all philosophy as being this undisciplined and careless. Philosophy for them is a bull session where everyone argues and no one is right.

Yet we have to admit that the latter question opens up many possibilities. How does one define "sky"? Once you have defined "sky", then what does "beyond" mean? Must one discuss the concept of infinity when one tries to talk about "beyond"? Does a discussion of physical limits imply that there are (or are not) limits in time? If there is a starting point in space, does that imply that there is a starting point in time? Are space and time somehow connected? How can we convert these speculations into something we can call knowledge?

"Daddy, what is beyond the sky?" can therefore be a very fruitful question indeed. However, when attempting an answer, we must stop using declarative sentences at that point where our knowledge ends. It is acceptable to say, "There are nine planets in the solar system, son," but it is not acceptable to say, "In my opinion, the universe began as a cosmic egg." At the point where my knowledge ends, my declarative sentences must be converted into questions. Like a child, I must recognize that humility must accompany my ignorance. The interrogative sentence is the proper expression of my humility; it admits my ignorance.

One large, albeit egotistical, question lurks behind the metaphysical questions asked by children, and that of course is

"Why me?" This question is a natural extension of the question, "Why is there something rather than nothing?" All questions of origin ultimately resolve themselves into this latter question, and since we are inevitably egoistic to some extent in our thinking, we must all eventually ask the question of the origin of our own existence. To wonder about the origins of the universe is to wonder about our own origins. If the universe is a mystery, then so am I. Apparently, the only way I can solve the mystery of my own existence is to understand the origin of the universe. This is why a story of creation is so important to all religions. According to this view, I only know who and what I am if I first know how *everything* began.

However, what if I come to the admission that I don't know the origin of the universe and most likely never will? Now I am at sea. I have a consciousness of myself, but I don't understand the context in which I am placed. I am convinced that I am real, but what kind of *relationship* do I have with the rest of the world? I am afraid that, in response to this dilemma, many people become solipsistic in varying degree, and "invent" the world they want. They make it up as they go. I once had a very intelligent high school student tell me that Hobbits were real. Not just real *to her*, or in the context of a story, but *objectively* real. She needed to make this claim because they were such an important part of her life. Another student once insisted that I had no right to argue against the existence of unicorns. Could I positively *disprove* their existence? As with Bigfoot, maybe they just haven't been *located* yet. These students were disgusted at my doltishness, my *arrogance* in making the dogmatic claim that there was an objective, verifiable reality! For these people, intensity of desire is a substitute for understanding. The need to believe creates the belief. These people may be gentle and well-meaning, however deluded, but they have no idea of their monstrous egotism.

They believe that they can create the universe. They are willing to stand in for God.

The reader can easily supply instances of people, in a variety of contexts, from drug induced hallucinations at one end of the scale to religious experiences at the other end, who presume to have answered the question of their origins by having a cosmic insight of one kind or another. I propose an alternate position. Instead of posing the question, and thereby *separating the question from myself*, I suggest that the question resides *in my very identity*. The fact that I am alive at all is the question—the *mystery*—and the only way I can deal with this mystery is to live it out through my actions.

I am convinced that I cannot come to an answer to ultimate origins in any other way. If I pursue the methods of religion, I will eventually come up against the ultimate fact that the nature of God and the Creation is an ineffable mystery. If I follow the methods of science and come up against, say, the Big Bang theory, I am still exactly where I would be if I followed the methods of religion. I would still be face to face with an unsolvable mystery. Every time I place the question outside of myself, hoping for an objective answer of some kind, I will defeat my purposes. Instead, I need to place the question where I can deal with it: within my life; that is, embodied in my actions. If *my life* is the question, then the answer lies where the question is, within my *actions*.

I do not think that this method is solipsistic, because I have no intention of inventing a bogus "objective" world to explain things. However, what I *am* willing to do is engage in a quest which, via action, makes my *quest*-ion live.

I suppose one could call this the pragmatic approach to metaphysics. What is it in my power to know? I can know what I do (including what I read, hear, and think). How can I know myself? By knowing what I do. What am I? I am what I do.

Does this place severe limitations on my knowledge? Yes. Does it tempt me to fantasize about Hobbits and unicorns, astrology, loose spirits, cosmic visitors from outer space? No. (This point is not trivial in an anti-scientific era, when people may actually and enthusiastically believe that George Lucas, Stephen Spielberg, and *Star Trek* are guides to truth.) Must I strive for humility? Yes. Why? Because I must freely admit the limitations that are placed on my knowledge; because I must always limit the scope of the known; because I must always put myself to the test. If the puzzle of my life is the question, then the actions in which I engage lead me towards, but never precisely to, an answer. To paraphrase Spinoza, joy is the passage from a lesser to a greater state of perfection. The key word here is *passage*: movement, voyage, the quest. In the transition am I happy. Or as Nietzsche suggested, I am human, all too human—and *only* human, nothing but human.

It takes considerably more courage to assert limitations than it does to claim answers. It takes more courage to say, "I don't know" (why I exist, why I have to die) than it does to say, "I know exactly" (what God's plan is, what happens to me after death). It also takes considerably more humility. Maybe that's why pride is nearly universally recognized as the greatest of all human failings. The person who is prideful enough to claim to know God's mind, to be able to answer cosmic questions off the cuff, is really a coward, because he hasn't really faced life. He has looked away from life's challenges, denied the quest, claimed to know the unknowable; put himself in the place of God, who never needs to strive. How much more courageous to say, "I don't know; I may be wrong; I may be on the verge of an awful mistake, but I will step forward in spite of my misgivings and fears."

The person who sets out on the quest is setting himself up for pain and joy. He has first recognized that his life is an enigma; he then has the audacity to respond to this enigma by living it rather than expecting to resolve it. Like a traveler in the wilderness, he is bound to bear hardship; but also like the wilderness traveler, he is bound to feel the joy of growth.

The Paradox of the Quest

I have suggested or implied that the person who engages in the quest has in some way seized his fate. This means that: 1) He has made a decision to act; and 2) The direction of the quest is somehow under his control. But these statements tell only part of the story.

I suspect that much of the "decision" to move ahead is either dimly understood or wholly unconscious. In fact, it may be that this uncertainty is actually a necessary condition of beginning the quest.

Contrast the quest with simple goal-making. The goal-oriented person decides what the goal is ("to be a doctor") and makes an explicit plan (take honors courses, obey the teachers, do well on the SATs, etc.) and at the end of the process they are not at all surprised to be where they expected to be. They ended where they expected to end. It is not certain that they engaged in a process of discovery.

By contrast, the quester may have a less explicit goal ("I want to see what life has to offer") but may not know precisely how to discover the answer. (Or the impulse to engage in the quest may be entirely unconscious, buried and working alongside the explicit goals). Should I attend a small liberal arts college? Take a year to travel? Live in a remote cabin for a year? Pursue a difficult or unusual profession? The quester may make a "wrong" choice, or get sidetracked altogether, but really, none of the "wrong" choices are wrong; no sidetrack leads away from the quest. *We simply don't know* where we will end up, or by what route, if we give ourselves to the quest, but that doesn't matter, because what we will have done was discover something.

Thoreau wrote, "I went to the woods because I wished to live *deliberately*, to front only the *essential facts of life*, and see if I could not learn *what it had to teach*, and not, when I came to die, *discover that I had not lived*" (emphasis added). I know of no better statement of the quest. Thoreau doesn't say, "I want to escape the rat race," or "I hate working nine to five," or "I want to write a great book." The fact is, he doesn't know *what* he will discover. He only knows that he wants to *live*—which I have defined as *acting*—because "living is so dear." He wants to "live deep and suck out all the marrow of life." What will he find? How will he do it? That remains to be discovered.

So it seems that we may suspect what the outcome of the quest might be, but we don't know for certain, and we have to be prepared for surprises, (a paradox in itself). And so, unlike the goal-oriented person, there must be a tension within the quester. He wants to move towards something, but what it is and how it is to be accomplished is only dimly understood. Two things we know for sure: it takes courage, and it takes action.

That is the paradox implicit in the quest: we move toward something, but we don't know what we're moving toward. The only way I can respond to this paradox is to put the statement "my life is the question" into the picture. I must pursue the quest not only by coping with the world, and discovering what the world offers, but I must couple the exploration of what lies outside of me with an equally thorough exploration of what lies within. I cannot strictly separate the objective from the subjective. While recognizing that they are distinct, I also recognize that they interact. It is not enough to discover the world ("the sky appears to be blue because of the refraction of light"). I need to put myself in a relationship with that world, and understand myself at the same time that I understand it. This might be the essential quality of the quester.

The paradox is simple: I am responsible for the decision to move forward, but I don't know exactly what I want; I am responsible for the direction of my forward movement, but I am not entirely certain of where I want to go. Of course, I am always making goals, short-, mid-, and long-range, but those goals are only attained within the context of the larger quest, which remains to be discovered. True, one must not simply let life slide by, passively give oneself to fate; yet I must also admit that I must yield to what fate has in store for me. I must move through life by establishing a productive tension between these two facts. I must act; I must yield.

IT MAY BE that to yield to the quest is to yield to larger forces at work in nature. This is a possibility that most people strenuously deny, because to accept that statement means that we accept the likelihood that we are not free.

Belief in our freedom is one of our greatest illusions. Americans may be particularly susceptible to that illusion because the conviction that we are free, in some vague, inclusive, generalized way, is preached to us from the cradle, especially in our classrooms, in our political dogmas, and in our economic theories. The doctrine of freedom is confidently used by advertisers to attempt to get people to relinquish their freedom and do what the advertiser wants. This seems to be effective in our very conformist society that is devoted to materialism. (Thoreau is used periodically by advertisers to sell this or that: "Step to a different drummer" and buy our product; behave slavishly while being convinced of your own freedom. This self-imposed slavishness is implicit in almost all television watching.)

The argument against freedom is simple and compelling. If the universe is a logical whole, then all events have a causal relationship to what precedes and follows them. Everything that happens now is a product of the past, everything that will happen is a product of the present. Human beings are a part of the natural world, which conforms precisely to physical laws that occur always and everywhere with mathematical precision. Were those laws to break down (of course they cannot), the entire universe would lose its integrity and dissolve into chaos. Physics and history have this much in common. I can insist that I am somehow different, that the laws of the universe somehow don't apply to me, but that is merely a quirk of psychology and an expression of my egotism, not a description of reality. There is a direct correlation between our insistence on our freedom and our ability to lie to ourselves. Examine any life and observe the habits, the conformity, the uniformity of action which people exhibit; then listen to them talk about freedom. We would rather embrace the comfort of hypocrisy than endure the pain of truthfulness.

A preferable approach would be to read Spinoza and the other great ones, who consistently observe that our insistence on freedom is our greatest illusion. As for me, I strive for what I call "an intelligent conformity to reality." (I must make clear that my discussion excludes what we call "political freedom." I am all for political freedom, which is simply responsible behavior in the absence of coercion.) I know very well that my freedom is restricted in literally innumerable ways, most of which can be subsumed under the headings of my historical context, my genetic inheritance, and the physical laws of nature. I have freed myself of the psychological need to deny this (though I enjoy acting as if I were free; and even as I do so, recognizing the paradox). I have instead, following Spinoza's advice, attempted to understand my place in nature rather than deny my place in nature.

I think that the quester does this on the unconscious level. He knows that a significant part of his life is out of his control, but he nevertheless finds the courage to relinquish himself to fate, uncertain of the outcome of his life; you might say that *he manages to control his life by yielding to his fate.* This may be the supreme act of courage and optimism. This is the courage of Socrates, who retained his faith in the goodness of the universe even as he stepped into the grave. This is the courage of Odysseus, who moved forward into the unknown, which was also the known. His wonderful paradox is that he was always the man of action who took charge of his fate—he was the person who acted as if he had the freedom to control events, and did so resourcefully and courageously—but who was nevertheless the tool of fate, and always protected by the goddess. At one level he was a human hero; but at another level he was simply the child of Fate. In the confusion and uncertainty of life, he gave himself to that fate. Perhaps this is what the quest really involves, right unto the lip of the grave. As Ernest Becker said, "*Hubris* means forgetting where the real source of power lies and imagining that it is in oneself."

AT THE CONCLUSION of one segment of his lifelong quest, at the end of his experiment at Walden Pond, Thoreau wrote words that are always haunting me. "I learned this, at least, by my experiment: that if one advances confidently in the direction of his dreams, and endeavors to live the life which he has imagined, he will meet with a success unexpected in common hours." And later: "Only that day dawns to which we are awake. There is more day to dawn. The sun is but a morning star." This man, who was dead at forty-two, possessed a realistic optimism that I think is most admirable. His dreams were not the softheaded kind: dare-to-be-different, be-all-you-can-be, and such common slogans. Like all true heroes, his dreams were of the real world and its limitations, rooted in his belief that the world is a good place if we can just bring ourselves to trust it. I think his trust was well founded. How do I know that? I don't. But I'll take the risk of believing that anyway. It's worth a venture.

CHAPTER 17

Three Foundational Myths:
The Lost Paradise; The Pride of Oedipus;
Odysseus and the Quest

The Lost Paradise

As with so many of the stories we hold in common, I thought that I knew the Eden myth, Genesis 2 and 3, quite well. Luckily, I re-read it one day, on a random impulse, and realized that I had been missing the meat of it for most of my life. The story is so common, so typed, that its substance was obscured from me by cultural assumptions and simple thoughtlessness. I found that it is in fact worth repeated readings and re-readings and careful study. It is endlessly suggestive. It is indeed one of the three greatest myths of our culture.

I don't use the word "myth" here in any slighting or derogatory sense. To use the word "myth" to mean a casual fancy—a falsehood or deception—is to misuse the word. Myths are profoundly true. Jewish and Christian believers may object to their creation story being appropriated to general use, but I make no apologies. The story of the loss of innocence is universal and profoundly important to the species. It transcends religions and cultures. It is a story, especially, for all moderns, and those who have been crushed by us moderns.

The idea that once-upon-a-time there was a Paradise, a Dream Time, an Age of Happy Innocence, is common, perhaps archetypal.

I doubt that the Romantics invented the concept with their idea of the noble savage; I think they simply gave form to a common, perhaps semi-conscious, archetypal idea.

The two common, and most important, characteristics of the Age of Innocence, is that our ancestors did not have to work, and that they were innocent (i.e., ignorant).

When Adam and Eve were expelled from Paradise, one of their several punishments was that they were condemned to a life of labor. "Cursed is the ground for thy sake; in sorrow shalt thou eat of it all the days of thy life; Thorns also and thistles shall it bring forth to thee; and thou shalt eat of the herb of the field; In the sweat of thy face shalt thou eat bread...." (Chapter 3, verses 17-19). In prosaic terms, it is easy to read this as an account of the transition from hunter-gatherer, for whom all the world is a garden, to settled farmer, condemned to a fixed routine in one place, certainly for generations, and probably for the benefit of someone else. Before the Fall, life may or may not have been easy, but the daily tasks were certainly less regular, less dictatorial, less rigidly controlled than we commonly experience. We sacrifice our freedom for security. It is a short step from the Gates of Paradise to the hollow men of "The Wasteland." When I worked in a foundry, I was a hollow man, surrounded by thousands of others, punching in and punching out in mobs, behaving robotically. The only spontaneous joy I observed—I felt none myself, at any time—was in the bars at quitting time on Friday night; and there was a meanness and anger there when the burden of work was momentarily lifted. These men's lives were appropriated to serve someone else's larger purpose. Job security and good wages were the tradeoff; but the price was nevertheless very high. They might just as well have been recruited in gangs to build pyramids.

Culturally, however, the second point, Adam's and Eve's innocence, is even more important. Adam's and Eve's happiness depended upon their ignorance. Something within us equates innocence and happiness, and innocence, we assume, is destroyed by knowledge. Knowledge is the enemy; knowledge is the serpent. Ignorant children are innocent; worldly-wise adults are corrupt.

What indicates our coming reliance on our great brains more than Chapter 3, verse 16? "Unto the woman [God] said, I will greatly multiply thy sorrow and thy conception; in sorrow thou shalt bring forth children…." "Sorrow," I suppose, can be read in a large sense, but the traditional view that it refers to pain in childbirth seems entirely plausible. And of course childbirth is complicated almost entirely by the infant *Homo sapiens'* enormous head, encasing an enormous brain. Our intelligence causes problems from the very beginning.

It is significant that, upon eating the fruit, their first thought was to be ashamed of themselves: not of their act, but of their bodies. Their first piece of knowledge was recognition of their nakedness, and their first response was to hide themselves, from themselves (with clothing) and from God. And of course their nakedness is connected to their sexuality; and the first punishment inflicted upon the woman is difficulty dealing with the consequences of sexual behavior. The suggestion here is that, for *Homo sapiens*, sexual knowledge is primary, and sexual knowledge is dangerous knowledge. True, all knowledge is forbidden, because it is dangerously explosive, but sexual knowledge is what we fear most. It remains to this day the most tightly circumscribed realm of human experience. It is also, paradoxically, what we most want. (I am reminded of a Booth cartoon in a *New Yorker*. Dad gazes with consternation and anger through the window as daughter kisses a boy in a car; Mom says to him, "You weren't so hung up on *my* chastity.") The linkage of "knowledge" with the Biblical "to know" as copulation can be no coincidence. In Chapter 4, verse 1, the word "know" in the specific Biblical sense is used for the first time: "And Adam knew Eve his wife; and she conceived...." The first murder occurs shortly thereafter.

The one kind of fruit forbidden to Adam and Eve was the fruit of knowledge. It is the great paradox of the myth, and of human nature, that the one thing forbidden to us is the one thing we most want. We nosy primates are into everything. There is no form of knowledge that we reject, though specific institutions have over the years promoted ignorance; but Galileo will use his brain despite the Inquisition.

TRADITION HAS IT that Eve was beguiled by the serpent; the serpent is to blame. (I think it very interesting that in many cultures, including the ancient Greek, the serpent is the symbol of wisdom.) But notice the sequence of events in Chapter 3, verse 6, after the serpent has spoken: "And when the woman saw that the tree was good for food, and that it was pleasant to the eyes, and a tree to be desired to make one wise, she took of the fruit thereof and did eat...." Eve didn't simply do the serpent's bidding, a dupe. She carefully appraised the tree, evaluated it, and came to a conscious decision. Gaining knowledge was one consideration of several. She weighed the situation, made a judgment, and acted on it. Nor did she secretly deliver the fruit to Adam so that he ate it in ignorance, for verse 6 also says that she "gave also unto her husband with her; and he did eat." By choice. He stood by her as she made her evaluation: "with her." And he concurred. Primates couldn't do otherwise.

I WROTE ABOVE that Adam's and Eve's happiness depended upon their ignorance. True; yet *Homo sapiens'* happiness is dependent upon its knowledge. We are divided creatures; as this myth shows, we are divided against ourselves. The conservative forces look back to the safety of the status quo; the liberal forces nudge us towards risk and change. We want both.

It is significant to me that the serpent was right. Eve repeats to the serpent God's dictum: "...for in the day that thou eatest thereof thou shalt surely die" (Chapter 2, verse 17). The serpent responds *truthfully,* "Ye shall not surely die [in the day thou eatest thereof]; for God doth know that in the day ye eat thereof, then your eyes shall be opened, and ye shall be as gods, knowing good and evil" (Chapter 3, verses 4, 5). And sure enough, God confirms this in verse 22, "Behold, the man is become as one of us, to know good and evil," and then introduces a shocking revelation, heretofore unconsidered, "and now, lest he put forth his hand, and take also the tree of life, and eat, and live forever....", they are cast out. Considerations of human immortality don't enter the myth until this point. In other words, when they gained knowledge, Adam and Eve became aware for the first time of their own inevitable deaths. The timid and skulking children of Chapter 3, verses 10-13, are suddenly adults. Not only will their knowledge of good and evil force responsibility upon them; their knowledge also forces them into the world of time. Their lives now have an end point. From now on and forever, the pressure of time will haunt humans as nothing else, bringing the shadow of death into life.

Prior to this episode, the only previous mention of the tree of life is in Chapter 2, verse 9, "...the tree of life also in the midst of the garden, and the tree of knowledge of good and evil." As we saw above, now that they possess knowledge, they are cast out in order that they have no chance at obtaining immortality.

Though Adam and Eve hadn't yet blundered on to the tree of life, its fruit was not denied to them. This raises interesting questions. Would their continued innocence and ignorance have resulted in their immortality? Would their corporal and temporal immortality deny them access to heaven? Would they never be god-like? Would they have escaped death by escaping responsibility? Would you rather be immortal and irresponsible or mortal and responsible?

Adam and Eve weren't driven from the garden because they ate of the fruit, but to deny them access to the tree of life. Does this fulfill God's promise that eating the fruit of knowledge will cause death? This is unclear to me, since Chapter 2, verse 17 reads, "...for *in the day* that thou eatest thereof thou shalt surely die."

It is also unclear to me that the tree of knowledge yields only knowledge of good and evil, or access to all knowledge, since Eve, in Chapter 3, verse 6, recognizes that it would "make one wise," and we learn elsewhere that this knowledge would make them god-like.

Why would knowledge be the one thing of all things, including immortality, denied to our ancestors by divine fiat? Of all things, why would access to knowledge result in our ongoing suffering; the one thing to bring down divine wrath?

Is there anything human that is not knowledge? Does all knowledge grow from, or is all knowledge based on, moral knowledge?

How do we account for the fact that, when Adam was given the task of naming the world's life, he was already in possession of our most powerful tool for recognizing and transmitting knowledge: language, and its fundamental power of using nouns to create intellectual categories? Happiness may be based on innocence, but our ancient parents were already fated for ejection from paradise from the beginning.

Disobedience is one requirement for human growth. To be fully human is to disobey: to go where it is forbidden to go.

THREE FOUNDATIONAL MYTHS

LIKE ALL GREAT myths, the story will yield a number of additional readings. No doubt the theologians have pondered the question of whether God could, or did, lie to his children (Chapter 2, verse 17), or how human responsibility, and hence dignity and meaning, could have occurred had God not been disobeyed.

To my mind, one element of this myth is very like the Greek viewpoint: Adam and Eve were fated to do what they did. Humans could only become human, responsibility could only have meaning, after the Fall. The Truth had to come out. Remaining in the garden would be completely contradictory to all human development both in the Aristotelian sense and in the observed biological sense. It was not consistent with human nature, especially with our insatiable curiosity and big brain, to remain ignorant. And it is inconsistent to suppose that our human nature is something to be methodically and consistently denied. It is right and just to be human. The Fall was necessary.

Or was it? History has shown that we have massively, unspeakably, failed in our responsibilities. We have come to recognize evil…and we have enthusiastically embraced it. The European descendants of Adam and Eve have, since the Fall, inflicted themselves time and again, in immeasurably cruel ways, upon each other and upon the less sophisticated peoples of the globe. (Note the assumption that "sophistication," supposedly a good, assumes "knowingness," something a bit sly and worldly.) Maybe innocence would have been preferable, however impossible. Something in mankind yearns for that. And another point that contradicts the Jewish and Christian myth of the Fall: the models of "innocence" that we have been able to observe before their forced disappearance, the aboriginals, were certainly not ignorant; nor are their few survivors.

The arrival of self-awareness is the central paradox of human life. This is our glory; this is our tragedy. It had to happen; we regret that it happened. We want to go back; there is no going back.

The Pride of Oedipus

The one major theological question that I did not discuss in the Creation myth is that of disobedience. From one standpoint, that is the crux of the question: Adam and Eve are guilty because of their disobedience, and no matter whom they try to blame it on, they remain guilty nevertheless, and all other considerations are secondary. Deconstructing the myth does not explain this existential human problem. The underlying question is: *why* did they disobey? And the most plausible answer is also the traditional answer: pride. Very likely pride is the fundamental human fault, the most ancient of flaws, the most universal of all human defects, and the hardest to correct. Their disobedience was therefore essential and inevitable.

All roots of the European tradition recognize this. For the ancient Jews, God is a mysterious, unexplainable force, one that cannot be penetrated or understood. By contrast, humans amount to little, and the appropriate human posture relative to God is prone: we must submit to the mystery; humility is the only truly rational response to God. Pride is foolishness at its worst.

Christians recognize that, of the seven deadly sins, pride is the worst, and the origin of the others. Pride not only makes it difficult to establish a right relationship with God and with the authority of the Church, it also interferes with the development of one's own character, and interferes with the destinies of individuals and nations. " Pride comes before a fall;" the prideful are ultimately humbled; pride is the source of arrogance towards other people; pride is the root cause of spite, anger, and other common forms of human nastiness; pride blinds you to yourself and to your circumstances; and above all, pride causes a severe sense of disproportion. Pride tempts one to assume an inflated and disproportionate sense of one's place in the universe.

THREE FOUNDATIONAL MYTHS

The third important root of European thought, the ancient Greek, was acutely aware of these characteristics of pride, particularly the last two. They did not tremble before an omniscient, monotheistic God, but before Fate. They knew that the fabric of the universe itself established the fate of all people; we may act as if we were free, we will be punished as if we were responsible, but in the end we are controlled by Fate. Our challenge is to see this truth, rather than to be blind to it. This profound paradox is at the heart of Greek tragedy, and elevates it to one of the highest of all arts. The paradox—that we are not free but we are nevertheless responsible—is every bit as important to us moderns as it was to the ancients.

As is well known, Oedipus' path in life was established before he was born. He knew the prophesies, took them into account, and acted upon them; and, of course, thus brought about their fulfillment.

(A refresher: Laius, King of Thebes, learns through an oracle that his son shall kill him and marry his wife, Jocasta. To forestall this he arranges to have his son killed, but Oedipus is rescued by a shepherd; he is then reared, as their own son, by the childless king and queen of Corinth. Oedipus too gains oracular news of his fate, and so to escape it he flees Corinth and travels toward Thebes. On this journey he indeed kills, in a fit of anger, a traveler on the road, and also solves the riddle of the Sphinx, thereby sparing Thebes from her tyranny. He is rewarded with the Theban throne, and with it the queen. Decades pass before he is revealed, by the seer Tiresias, to be the slayer of Laius. Thus does Oedipus embrace his fate by fleeing from it; and thus slowly does he learn the truth of himself.)

What kind of man are we examining? An essentially good man who began life as a victim, of the gods of course, but more immediately as one whose death was willed by his own parents. A man who early in life sought the truth, was horrified by what he found, and who acted to avoid the evil that he was condemned, by overpowering forces beyond his control, to commit. A man of wit an honor who ruled well, though in self-willed ignorance. A man who knew, in his most secret heart, the truth; but who avoided the truth during the years of his reign until his subconscious knowledge was forced into consciousness. Ultimately, a man who, in the end, had the courage to recognize the fate he had been avoiding, and with his own hand made manifest in the flesh of his body the reality of his intellectual and spiritual blindness.

The keys to this piece, pride and blindness, operate in tandem and feed each other.

A<small>NGER, BIOLOGISTS TELL</small> us, has a useful evolutionary function. It makes things happen *right now*, a useful survival tool in physically threatening situations. In most situations, however, anger is among our most destructive emotions, often appearing as a pathology rather than as a survival tool.

Anger is the parent of spite. Unlike five of the other deadly sins—sloth, avarice, envy, incontinence, gluttony—whose first and primary victim is the perpetrator himself, anger, and its various permutations, directly impinges on someone else, as well as having a corrosive effect on the character of the perpetrator. Its evil casts a wide net, and undermines character as nothing else.

Oedipus, by yielding to anger and killing his father, made the assumption, unconscious and reflexive, that he had the right to control another person's body. Murder is the extreme form of such arrogant control. The angry man who strikes out physically, the angry man who strikes out verbally, assumes the right to control someone's body and emotional equilibrium: someone's life. This is the ultimate pridefulness, the complete and most selfish form of arrogance, a comprehensive form of selfishness.

The prideful man is blinded by his anger, and is angry because he is blind. Oedipus moved blindly towards his fate by fleeing towards Thebes. This was the blindness of ignorance. He knew his prophesied fate, but he did not know the secret workings by which that fate would be fulfilled. He was powerless in the hands of the gods, innocent as far as his own will was concerned. But the act of murder, following prideful anger, was his, an expression of character. It is an unsolvable enigma if his character, like his fate, was beyond his control; what is certain is that he is nevertheless responsible, and that the harm he did reverberated far beyond himself, beyond the death of Laius, beyond the shame of Jocasta and her children, into the life of the city and every individual therein. We all say, "If I had only known…." "Know" here means "to see." If we could only have "seen," the harm we did could have been mitigated.

Of course, not all the harm of pride is expressed as the physical and emotional effects of anger. But the effects of spiritual or intellectual blindness persist nonetheless in the most common forms of pridefulness, usually expressed as egotism, narcissism, lack of empathy: a disproportionate sense of one's self in relation to other people, indeed to the creation itself.

We must, nevertheless, recognize the truth, on the ethical and philosophical level, as expressed by, say, Spinoza, that each human organism has an obligation to assert itself as a valuable creature, to take its rightful place in the world, to "persist in its own being," and to develop its powers. We must also accept, at a different level, the assertion of Freudian psychology that every human organism is driven, by instincts rooted in our biological heritage, to establish its value, its worth, in the face of a hostile world. This kind of personal power is both an ethical good and a biological and psychological necessity not to be confused with destructive pride.

I feel uneasy when confronted with the assertion that humility is a cardinal virtue. How is one to assert one's real power as a healthy organism if one is also tempted to undervalue one's place in the universe? As Nietzsche correctly pointed out, Christian hypocrisy is based on the assumption of a "humility" which is often a cover for resentment, particularly resentment of the strong; humility can be a cover for weakness and cowardice; and the weak, though told to turn the other cheek and learn forbearance, may cherish the belief that their enemies will roast in hell while they gloat from heaven. Scores will be settled, but not by them, and not in this world. This is one unpleasant face of humility.

Another kind of humility teaches debasement. This kind of humility, asserting that man is a worm in the face of the cosmic mystery, would be alien to any ancient Greek, and to my modern viewpoint as well. It misplaces man in the cosmos as certainly as does pride.

Yet, what would Oedipus feel as he drove the sharp metal shafts into his eyes? That he was, after all, absolutely nothing to the gods? And little to men? That his "sight," his "eyes," had failed him, and should be destroyed? What unimaginable anger and will it would take to place the pointed shaft against one's eyeball and force it in; and to do it twice. Did Oedipus sense a kinship with Tiresias, the blind seer (I invite you to relish this semantic conjunction), realizing that real sight was *in*sight and had its seat elsewhere within his organism? The obvious irony that he lost his sight when he gained true insight indicates that this is so. Did he learn that, though guilt is a normal and inevitable part of human experience, blind and destructive pride leads to unbearably crushing guilt, guilt so severe that one yearns for annihilation? Oedipus came hard to the realization that his true place in the world was far lower than he imagined, and his suffering was proportional to his error.

The challenge is to learn how to see, to know.

This kind of knowledge—an understanding of self in relation to the world—is a matter of character as well as intellect. Indeed, we know that intellectual pride can be virulent and vicious, aggravating and magnifying, rather than correcting, one's flaws. The ability to rationalize cleverly may create rather than prevent blindness. The intellect, to accomplish its necessary task of understanding one's proportionate place in the universe, must be linked to something else—call it temperament—before it can shape and correct character. This is a great conundrum. Have we been able to civilize ourselves over the centuries? Can we civilize ourselves? If an answer were to hand, the story of Oedipus would long since have lost its relevance, being reduced to a story of primitive and long-abandoned human behavior rather than the living myth that it is.

One must conclude that humans have changed not at all since this myth was conceived, and one is left with a deep pessimism. Perhaps the story of Odysseus will serve as a refreshing corrective.

Odysseus and the Quest

Odysseus asserts time and time again that he is an "unhappy man," that "the heavenly gods have given me an almost boundless supply of woeful experiences." Despite his pain and suffering, however, I imagine Odysseus happy.

This most complex of stories has many facets, many profoundly important themes. I am primarily interested in three: Odysseus' character, the contrast between Odysseus and Penelope, and the archetypal power of the idea of the quest.

Since Odysseus is No One—or Everyman—his qualities are almost beyond number. He is endlessly curious, shrewd, wily, deceptive. He is courageous, strong, athletic, competitive, prideful. Circe calls him "versatile, resourceful," his men call him in dismay "unpredictable man." He makes monumental errors of judgment, and then taps his own resources to make things right. He goes where men should not go. In the end, the most memorable aspects of his character are endless curiosity, backed by steadfastness and fortitude.

Though pride underlies all his other qualities, his is not the destructive pride that deforms character, but the healthy kind that generates the power for him to make a space for himself in the world, to affect events, to persist and to endure: he does not invariably prevail.

Above all, Odysseus is a divided man. He is driven to abandon the hearth and engage the world, and he is driven to circle back to the hearth. These two impulses are both irresistible, and work in tandem so that, though they are exact contraries, they form a unity. They completely define and form his life.

This is why Penelope is not a mere adjunct to the life of Odysseus. She is his equal.

If we see the myth as a clear division between the human urge to venture forth, and the equally human urge to cherish a home, then Penelope is fully half the story. This division can be seen as active versus passive. We westerners are accustomed to view the active as the entire picture. Our stories are usually driven by an active agent: without conflict there is no story, and passivity is a mere null. This may be nothing more than a cultural prejudice that ignores a large part of the real world.

Without Odysseus, there is no Penelope; and without Penelope, there is no Odysseus. Without Penelope, and the hearth and home that she represents, Odysseus' wanderings are pointless and empty, just a series of events, and Odysseus is a mere vagrant, bouncing around the world violently and

THREE FOUNDATIONAL MYTHS

meaninglessly, as uninteresting as raiding Vikings or the vacant lives of American mountain men.

Penelope does not affect events, as does Odysseus, as an intruder, using the intellect as a weapon. She does not affect events by inserting herself into other people's lives as a weapon-bearing warrior or a suppliant beggar. Odysseus is the manipulator, the primate whose curiosity gets him into trouble, the disturber of the peace who brings trouble and death to enemies and friends alike. After twenty years of war and wandering, he returns home with nothing but his most recently acquired prizes. The destruction of Troy was a complete waste.

Penelope's power runs deep and constant. She is the center around which all else revolves. Odysseus' strength is of the active intellect, muscle, and weaponry. Penelope's power is that of a magnet, invisible, constant, irresistible, and, in the end, dominant. To use Aristotelian language, she is the final cause, Odysseus the material cause. Odysseus blunders through life creating problems, whereas Penelope represents the resolution of all the problems. No matter how far away we circle, we arrive back home in the end. It is the nature of the western mind to overlook and undervalue her power.

THIS RAISES THE question: Is the quest, as symbolized by Odysseus, of any value at all? Does it have inherent value, or is it intrinsically meaningless? Does the quest give value to life, or is it a substitute for value? Is life's meaning to be found in active pursuit and seeking, or in centered, passive, and calm contemplation?

What was the object of Odysseus' quest? To conquer Troy, add to his wealth, enhance his reputation? To increase his understanding of himself and the world? To pursue action for its own sake? In the end, his great triumph was simply to return home and restore order.

I find it interesting that Nietzsche, that grand advocate of the intellectually and morally strenuous life, claimed that, if he must be religious, he would be a Buddhist. He also was fully aware that he was thinking in the Socratic tradition. Buddha and Socrates, though differing in technique, came to the same destination by different roads. Buddha, Socrates, Nietzsche, all saw the world clearly and found it good. Salvation, if such a condition exists, is to be found in this world and only in this world, and it is to be approached by human means.

The man of action is the existential man. He *is* what he *does*. Strip Odysseus of his actions, and there is no man left. Odysseus by the hearth is, I imagine, happy for a while, but his comfort in wine, food, possessions, and the bed, all material, is the comfort of negation: for a while he is relieved of strife. But I imagine this comfort to be short lived. For how long can he survey his demesne with content? How soon will he begin to remember the glorious past, and imagine another glorious future? How long will it be until the itch to be doing overcomes him? Hearth-bound Odysseus can only become a cranky and dissatisfied old man. Before long he must be up and gone again. Odysseus is as Odysseus does. Without action he does not exist.

I have been able to live my life only as a quest. During those periods when my quest is absent, I too am "absent," treading water, filling time, trending toward death: empty. My quests are of two kinds, usually conducted simultaneously: my journeys through space, in the wilderness; and my journeys of the intellect. Fortunately for me, journeys of the intellect are ready at hand, can be undertaken anywhere, and have no apparent end. Even so, to be fulfilled I also need my journeys through space. I am a material creature, I love the activities of the body, I love the material world, and I want to experience it with my feet on the ground. Yet, every time I venture forth, I circle back to the hearth. I don't know if this is a division in my character, or a sign of balance.

Perhaps I am mistaken in my love of the quest. Is the quest merely a cover for emptiness, a substitute for existence, an illusion that allows me temporarily to pull a veil over nothingness?

Am I better off to be at rest, Buddha-like? Or is my happiness identical with my activity? My culture and my temperament incline me to the latter. I may be wrong. I think I'll look around some more.

AND TWO MORE

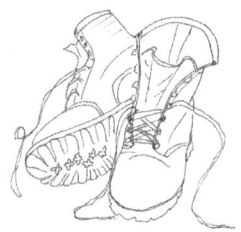

CHAPTER 18

Spring Canoe Trip

Where I live, in south central Alaska, April is not a time of gentle rain and early blossoms. It is usually a time of tedious and frustrating transition from our long winter to our short, intense summer. Snow has been on the ground since October, and is always slow to melt. Our March is a winter paradise, but when the snow goes rotten at the end of the month, and the human mind is prepared for spring, April is invariably a disappointment, even to the most seasoned northerner. The transition into spring is painfully slow, moving by infinitesimal degrees. We hear the first varied thrush, and it thrills us to the heart, but we know that the arrival of most songbirds is still six weeks away. The skeins of early geese excite us, but we know that nesting will be delayed until the marshes slowly thaw. The snow is uninviting for skiing and snow shoeing; after six months of snow sports, April slush doesn't appeal to me. What to do?

Plan for the future. When in the doldrums, make a plan.

I called my son in Fairbanks. Can you go on a canoe trip when the ice goes out? Yes. When? May 15; the lowland lakes are usually open by then. Good. Get your ticket.

I select a canoe, my old seventeen foot lightweight, the "Gavia," with stylized salmon painted by my daughter on the stern and the silhouette of the common loon painted by my wife on the bow. I select my paddle, a flexible light wood laminate with a comfortable oval shaft. I think about routes. We won't be exploring new country, some exotic, remote location. We will be revisiting places where I have canoed hundreds of times, according to my canoe log, and where Jeremy has traveled with our family since his infancy. We will revisit the canoe trails in the Kenai National Wildlife Refuge, a part of Alaska that remains dear to my heart in spite of its proximity and familiarity. I'll be visiting an old friend with an old friend.

I HAVEN'T SEEN Jeremy in several months. His school is out and he needs a break from his graduate studies. We have plenty to talk about, but the subjects tend to focus on two things: good books, and good trips together in the past. We establish this conversational theme in the car during our drive, and these topics dominate our discussions for the next week.

Near the end of our four hour drive we can see glimpses of bright water through the trees. The lakes are open, and the spring sun flashes off the water in a way we haven't seen in seven months. The spring sky is high and open; our sub-Arctic light is clear and almost palpable. Our days will, in fact, be filled with sunlight for months, because the northern sun dips just briefly beneath the horizon for most of the summer.

In mid-May the ground is bare and brown in the lowlands, and the birch and balsam poplar and cottonwood are just budding. The balsam poplars, in particular, excite me: their buds are filled with the richest sap imaginable. Squeeze one, and the tacky fluid fills my nostrils with the richest odor I have ever experienced, a concentrate of earth and vegetation that I call "essence of spring."

I keep one sprig in my pocket and one where I work to remind me of the promise that is latent in our slow spring. A whiff of balsam poplar invariably clears my head and focuses my mind; it serves to keep my metaphorical feet on the ground. On this trip, I smear my fingers with the resinous sap from a crushed bud so that the odor will be with me all day.

We perform our travel routines almost unconsciously. It takes only a few minutes to portage the canoe and backpack, paddles and fishing rods, to the lake. When Jeremy was an infant, he was cradled in the canoe in his mother's arms; later he occupied a little nest in the bow. Now he hauls the gear and packs the boat, and we shove off together, partners.

The past six weeks, and the past few days, and the past few hours, have been a prelude to what happens next. We align our canoe in the direction of the narrows on Paddle Lake. The canoe generates a small bow wave, silver on the black water; I can feel the pressure of the water as it is transferred through the paddle into my arms and shoulders; the air moves gently over my face; and a pair of loons appear from around the point, floating together, their necks and heads at first erect, then alternating between the horizontal and vertical as they probe the water or reach upward. One cries; its echo reverberates clear and loud from bank to bank; its mate joins the chorus; and all is well. This is why I am here.

When I was younger I often made the mistake, when traveling, of worrying about "getting there," making my miles, as if the purpose of the trip was to get to some goal. Somewhere along the way I came to realize that "being here" is far more important than "getting there," and I have learned to travel accordingly. Of course, one has to plan a wilderness trip to get to the pickup or takeout point according to plan, but I have also learned that one should, to a certain extent, let the progress of a trip unfold naturally, according to the dictates of whim and weather. Concerns about "getting there" can ruin a trip—thinking about an imagined future always casts a shadow over the actual present—and the "concerns" are usually psychological rather than objective. "Being here" is a state of mind that is much more conducive to enjoyment, of living in the present, a condition difficult to achieve. We call it "koviashuktok," a word we got from the writer Billie Wright, which names a concept inspired by the Nunamiut: "the condition of being fully and pleasantly in the present moment."

THE NEXT MORNING, Jeremy and I got out of our tents when we were rested, and traveled when we were ready to travel. No pressure to push on. During this second day, we effortlessly got into the rhythm of canoeing and portaging, loading and unloading. We learned long ago to pack a simple, tight load. We can easily transport our gear, including the canoe, across each portage in one trip. As we paddle, we take time to enjoy the country: a hillside of dark spruce backed by the lighter green of birch and poplar—the heartbreaking new green of spring leaves, so fresh against the sky, unlike the dark green of late summer; a cruising goshawk; a flock of widgeon braking into the edge of a lake; a feeding red-necked phalarope; a yellowlegs chiming from his perch overhanging a lake; loons, at least one pair on each lake.

We decided to camp on Swanson Lake. As we poked along the shore, we spotted a moose calf, only days old, in the water. Mom was in the forest at the top of the bank, shifting and turning nervously, her erect ears pointed not to us but to something back in the forest. The calf splashed strongly through the water, tried the bank, failed to climb it, splashed along the shore again. Mom continued her nervous movements, and I heard deep grunts in the forest, but I couldn't see their source. After several more failures the calf gained the top of the bank and mom immediately moved off at a fast pace, the calf hurrying to keep up.

We can't confirm what disturbed the cow moose, except that we know it wasn't us—she never looked our way—but we do know that bears, both brown and black, take a number of moose calves each spring. The bears are out of hibernation and on the move. Reliable food supplies like migratory fish, or berries, are not yet available. A healthy adult moose is not easy prey for a bear, but the calves are vulnerable.

We continued along the shoreline. We recalled past trips, and pieced together past adventures. I recalled a large trout I caught at the edge of this reed bed; we recalled camping at that site with friends; I remember on this lake wolves howling and northern lights in late August. Jeremy and I both eventually recognized a stand of birch that is our favorite camp on Swanson Lake, and pulled in.

Every wilderness traveler I know has a camp routine, and every wilderness traveler I know treats this routine as sacred: it is the one best and right way to go about living in the woods. In our case, we first unload and secure the canoe. We then decide where to cook. If a tarp is necessary, this is where it will be slung. We then pick our tent sites: they must be removed somewhat from the cook site, because of bears, and they must be sufficiently flat and level for comfort. Into our tents go our sleeping bags, sleeping pads, books, and journals. At the cook site we arrange our camp stove, cook pots, mugs, and food bags where they will be convenient. I gave up cooking on wood years ago for a combination of reasons. Gasoline and propane cook stoves are now very well designed, small, light, efficient, and convenient. They are also clean and fast. On the other hand, fire pits tend to become messy with the leftover bits of camping detritus left by other campers, because a fire pit, once established, tends to attract use. The scar is usually permanent. Also, Alaskan springs are generally dry and the forest is filled with highly combustible fuel in the form of dried leaves and last year's dead vegetation. It is a good time to avoid an open fire.

When we're settled in, we have a hot drink, perhaps read or write, perhaps nap. Dinner, talk, a turn on the lake in the canoe.

When I go to my tent, it is not to oblivion.

BETWEEN MID-MAY and late September I sleep in a tent most of the time. I enjoy tent living for many reasons, and all of them come home to me during the first night of the season. I open the door, always to a fine view of forest, lake, tundra, or ocean. Air moves through the tent, fragrant with the odor of forest or lake, tundra or rain, beach or ocean. And in the spring the air is rich with bird song. In the forest, the bird chorus is dominated by the ruby crowned kinglet and the thrushes: varied, Swainson's, gray cheeked, hermit, and the greatest singer of them all, to my taste, the robust American robin. The most common of the warblers, the yellow rumped, is also present; he sings a soft liquid song. The other warblers arrive later in the month: Wilson's, yellow, orange crowned, blackpoll. This chorus is particularly poignant at my latitude, because it doesn't begin until the second or third week of May and it ends by late June, meaning that we northerners must live for ten months without bird song. I listen to every song as if it were the last.

A different, complementary bird chorus comes from the lake, more dispersed and more individual than the forest chorus. Swans trumpet from the lake, sounding like rich French horns, ducks gabble from their nesting sites in the reeds, the grebes clamor in their heedless way, and the wail of the loon rises, singly and in pairs, to a crescendo which echoes time and time and time again across the lake before fading away. The songs of the forest, the songs of the lake, continue around the clock. I am in and out of sleep all night, and when I rise to the surface of sleep I note and absorb them.

And the swallows. They animate the horizon where lake surface and tree canopy meet the sky. My daughter, when quite young, declared them to be "happy and determined," and I know no better description of them.

One spring years ago I was camped with family and friends at a place I call Aviary Island. Aviary Island must be a natural sanctuary, because I have never seen terrestrial predators there, and many of the cavity nests are quite low. One clear evening, against the low light of the late sun, we observed a swarm of swallows circling and whirling above the reed bed in the bay of the island where we were camped. In the reed bed, grebes and ducks; on the lake, loons and swans; silhouetted against the red sky, a bald eagle where it perched on a birch limb.

But the whirling swallows, tree swallows and violet green swallows together, hundreds of them, were the center of activity. I assumed at first that a dense insect hatch had attracted them, but I eventually realized that there was an object at the center of their swirling activity, a piece of down or feather, white, about three inches long. A swallow would pick it out of the air, climb with it through a whirlpool of swallows, and then drop it, and another swallow would repeat the process. Or the fellow with the feather would be accompanied by two or three swallows who tried to pluck it from his beak. Sometimes the feather would be plucked from the air seconds after it was released; several times it was captured inches above the lake; but always it was the focal point of the gyrating mass of birds.

I at first thought that I was merely witnessing simple competition for a prime piece of nesting material. But five, ten, fifteen minutes went by and no bird escaped with the prize. For nearly three-quarters of an hour the swallows played this game in the dimming northern light. When I went in my tent, I could yet see the shapes of swarming birds.

JEREMY AND I decided to spend a long morning on Swanson Lake before breaking camp. We paddled slowly in a bay of the lake, trolling a Mickey Finn and watching birds. We released two cold hard rainbow trout, broke camp, and were on our way to the portage when we saw a lynx. It was, or seemed, large—I suppose that it retained much of its thick winter pelt. It looked heavy through the body, and it moved ponderously. Perhaps a large well fed old animal, or a gravid or nursing female. We sat quietly in the boat and let the breeze push us along the shore in the lynx's direction of travel. We drifted beside it for four or five hundred yards, and it never glanced at us that we could see, but moved in steady and stately fashion along the shore. It padded through our old camp without any show of interest in our recent presence. Eventually it angled away from shore, over the hill, gone.

LIFT A CUP OF lake water in the canoe trails, and it appears to be perfectly clear. Canoe a kettle lake, surrounded by dark spruce, on an overcast day, and the lake is black. Drift over shallows on a sunny day, and the water is transparent. But when I put my canoe on Gene Lake on a sunny, crisp day, with a brisk breeze creating a running chop, the phrase that seems most accurate to me is Homer's "wine dark sea." The lake surface is alive, the colors are rich and deep, like a good cabernet, and I feel in my heart and lungs that it is very, very good to be alive.

Jeremy and I paddled the length of the lake to its inlet stream, a stream snaking through the swamp that lies between Gene and Pepper Lakes. In some ways paddling these snaky little creeks requires more cooperation between bow and stern than paddling bigger water because of the timing of the turns and the switching of strokes. We got through without frustration, and we noticed as we approached Pepper Lake that the beavers had been busy damming the stream at that end; I expect significant changes on that lake in a few years.

Our favorite camp on Pepper Lake is redolent of memories for both of us. Aside from the fact that it has the requisites for an excellent camp: easy access to the lake, good tenting, lots of high ground, and excellent visual prospects, it is also part of our family history. When the youngsters were tiny, this place was often their home for a special while; they had made "forts" and created athletic contests here; and they had eventually made this a destination on their own trips.

THE NEXT MORNING we discussed our plans. We decided to make this a two or three night camp, and spend the day backtracking to Gene Lake, and from there to Eider, Osjold, Wonder, Wilderness, Nuthatch, Llerun, and Lynx Lakes, and their connecting waterways, the last of which completes a loop back to Pepper Lake. I had not done this route in twenty-three years, but I remembered well that it was difficult, sometimes tedious, with unmarked and uncut portages and difficult water passages. But Jeremy wanted a physical challenge and I was in the mood to explore.

As we prepared to leave after breakfast, we spotted a black bear making its way along the opposite shore. We also noted, perhaps four hundred yards from the bear, on the same shore, a cow moose and her calf feeding in a boggy part of the lake. The bear left the shore for the forest, and about ten minutes later, as we watched the moose, we realized that the bear had stalked the moose and was creeping towards them, using alders and brush as a screen. The bear charged, and the two moose plunged along the shore in the water, the bear following. But he gave it up and slipped back into the forest, and both moose returned to their original location. But the drama wasn't over. The bear again stalked the moose, using the thick vegetation as cover, and again the attack failed. But this time the moose did not flee. Instead, the female stood her ground and the bear retreated. Three or four more times the bear attempted to kill the moose calf, and each time the cow easily turned him back. This drama unfolded over the course of an hour, and when the bear had apparently lost interest and moved away, Jeremy and I launched our boat.

But I had to wonder: did the moose gain peace simply because the bear seemed to retreat? Wouldn't she really have to be alert virtually twenty-four hours each day to ensure the safety of her calf? Wasn't this bear likely to wear her down, if he was patient enough? How much of the drama was left to be played out beyond the reach of our human vision was an interesting and mysterious question.

OUR DAYLONG CIRCUIT of the surrounding lake country had numerous rewards. We saw lakes and waterways that are rarely traveled. The songbirds, shore birds, and waterfowl were abundant, and we saw, at the beaver dam which blocks the outlet of Lynx Lake, a fine bull moose. Eider Lake, in particular, attracted us because of its beauty and we decided to move our camp there the next day.

Our first thought was to camp on the island that is not far from the portage trail. We decided to circle the island before unloading the canoe, and we saw a remarkable thing. The island, a small one perhaps forty yards long and fifteen yards wide, was composed entirely of forest, mainly spruce and birch. The island was high ground, no swamp on the edge. As we circled the island we saw a loon on her nest. That in itself was not unusual; what was unusual was that she was nesting well above the water line on the forest floor. Common loons nest at water line, in bogs, and they cannot walk; they must drag themselves to their nest, and that is as far as they ever get from water during the course of their lives. What induced this loon to nest out of her normal habitat? How was she able to pull herself up from the water to the nesting site on the bank? And what would protect her nest from terrestrial predators, such as squirrels? Of course, we selected another campsite.

OUR SPRING CANOE trip was an experience marked by many deeply moving events, large and small. At the end of such an adventure the mind is filled with sharp visual images, such as the stately movement of a lynx, the stealthy movements of a black bear, and the wild expanse of sky swept by dark purple clouds, curving rain curtains, and light-filled blue. The ear is filled with the cry of the loon and the poignant liquid song of the Swainson's thrush. One remembers the moist smell of the air as it draws along the surface of a lake. The intellect has been fed by excellent conversation, and the emotions have been fed by immediate sensations as well as by memories. I make a date to go canoeing next May 15 with a good friend.

CHAPTER 19

The Arctic in Autumn

In the early days of my treks in the Arctic National Wildlife Refuge, I focused on July. Usually my treks included that entire month, which is mosquito season, and I took mosquitoes for granted. However, I eventually came to favor June as my Arctic time, and not just because it is free of insects. That preference resulted from my first June trip, in 1982; the advantages of June became readily apparent. The caribou were moving, the birds were arriving and nesting, wolves and foxes were raising litters, plant life was emerging. It was usually cold early in the month, but the season progressed rapidly. One could see leaf changes from day to day. The weather was generally dry. June remains my favorite month in the Arctic, though global warming has produced obvious changes, such as more rain, as a result of increased open water on the Beaufort Sea.

But we, wife Diane and I and friends, have discovered another beautiful face of the Arctic, the autumn. We had in the past done treks and river floats into mid-August—our time in the Arctic was not restricted to June—but nothing into late August and September except for one river trip on the Porcupine. Our experience was that August was wet, with a real threat of high water; and river crossings are the greatest of all hazards when trekking. But our pilot Kirk Sweetsir often told me that he likes fall the best—animals on the move, the country is alive—and in 2013 we decided to give it a try, trekking from August 17 to August 29. The trip was difficult in some ways: cold rain, snow, bog, and, ironically, lack of water in some valleys; but also rewarding: northern lights, wolves, leaf changes. Our time there did not extend deep into the fall, but it was a taste.

In 2014 we were invited by Heimo and Edna Korth to care for their property on the Colleen River during their absence at the beginning of freeze-up, September 27-October 11. This was a different kind of adventure. Rather than moving each day, we let the Arctic come to us, as it were. We felt completely at home; always something interesting to experience; and the season came to us fast, from bluebird days at first, then accumulating snow, and, each day, increased ice in the river.

Our fall trip in 2015 was August 25-September 8, and came to us as a surprise, because we had planned a trek in the north, close to the Continental Divide, but a storm had kept our pilot Kirk in Fairbanks. So we hiked out from and back to Arctic Village. Our farthest east was Old John Lake. We travelled at the height of the leaf changes. The trip was wonderful.

RECENTLY WE ACCOMPLISHED a long-standing goal, of canoeing the Colleen River in northeast Alaska, just west of the Yukon Border. (A word on the spelling of Colleen. The USGS map spells it "Coleen," and the *Dictionary of Alaska Place Names* states that the name was first reported as such in 1895. However, neither of my unabridged dictionaries list "Coleen" as thus spelled. I will therefore assume that the misspelling occurred carelessly in the past and will use the accepted spelling.) We deferred this trip several times, such as in 2014 when the Korth offer negated the float. This trip, in 2016, spanned August 23-September 7, and we again experienced the height of leaf changes, though that was enhanced for us because we drifted south into the leaf changes as the autumn advanced, from tundra to willow to poplar and aspen to birch. Like the 2015 trip, this trip was open-ended, with no fixed date and pickup point. That circumstance much improves a trip, creating a relaxing flexibility.

ONE DAY and night stand out particularly from the 2013 trip. We had circled Conglomerate Mountain from the west and north, and at the northeastern extension of the mountain base encountered the perfect camp, a toe of tundra bounded by a creek flowing around it, east and north. West of camp, a tundra ridge; east and north, tundra plains; south, a gentle slope leading to higher mountains.

As we approached this camp during the afternoon we took a break from walking and seated ourselves upon the mountain side looking north. This is a vast valley, the main river flowing west to east here, the north side of the valley rimmed with distant mountains. We rested, we looked, and we heard the howling of wolves in the big valley. This was not a single or a pair, but a full pack.

We moved on, made our camp, strolled across the tundra. I sat, wrote; Mary walked up the mountain spine (and was eventually accompanied by a black fox, who followed her back to camp); Joyce sketched. The sun was warm on an early fall day. All was well.

That night we heard wolves near our camp.

Though it was late August, the Arctic nights were still short. The twilight-dark was invigorating when I emerged from my tent after midnight. The night outdoors is always stimulating, mysterious, inviting. There is of course no ambient light, no human sound—no trucks in the distance, no airplane, no human rumble. As Josef Pieper writes, "Only the silent hear." And, consonant with my inward silence, I heard the silence of the night, which included the murmur of the creek. The orange half moon was bright, a few stars were visible in the dusky light, and to the north, along the horizon, the sky was crimson for miles along the mountain rim, though the time was mid-night, for the Arctic sun was not yet in abeyance.

In this setting did the wolves howl. They were near, one individual just across the creek, one group south of us, one group north of us. I heard wolves three or four other times during the night, scattered, though near, throughout the valley. What kept them so close to us for so long? Some people hate wolves, fear them, and long to kill them, but we can see from the wolves' behavior why they may be subject to domestication, paradoxically becoming "man's best friend" while simultaneously serving as both a symbol and an embodiment of man's worst enemy. For me, they both symbolize and embody the essence of wild.

The next night we were camped among large willows on the main stem of the river. Several days of clear weather had allowed the atmosphere to cool considerably at night, and when I got out during the night the air had that good cold sharp autumn feel. And above, along with our moon and a few stars, the northern lights were at play, forming long dense green ribbons.

In 2014 our friends Heimo and Edna Korth asked us to stay at their cabin on the Colleen River during freeze-up. The dates were September 27-October 11. Heimo had told me several times over the years that he "hated" that time in the Arctic. During the transition it is no longer fall, but it isn't winter: no winter trails, no safe river ice, no trapping. I feel the same about late October and November in southcentral Alaska—no good snow pack for skiing and winter travel—and I also dislike April there, another transition, that being break-up. The stability and activities of winter are gone, but spring is yet far away.

So the Korths used that time to travel for a bit before the work of trapping and winter life. They would use our air flight "in" as theirs "out" on September 27, and the reverse on October 11.

Why not just close up the cabin and leave? They could of course do that. But the grizzly bears are still out of hibernation, and September for the Korths is the time to hunt, and much of the winter meat was hanging in quarters from poles near the cabin, and would make for an abundance of food for bears before hibernation, and for wolves, marten, and birds, particularly gray jays. I was to be prepared to shoot a bear, if necessary (with a permit), but Heimo assured me that that was unlikely, since the wood stove would burn around the clock and a savvy bear would smell that and stay away. In the event, there were bear tracks (and wolf tracks) regularly around the area of the cabin, but they did not venture near, in spite of that large cache of valuable protein.

The meat cache consisted of one entire moose and several caribou. When I walked through the forest and on gravel bars, as I did daily, I was impressed at the self-control, if you will, of the bear. I followed his tracks, or crossed them as I walked. It circled at a fixed distance and I have no doubt whatsoever that its super-sensitive nose told it exactly the nourishment near the cabin. I have often marveled at the intelligence of bears, and in this case intelligence was linked to some sort of judgment which may or may not be simple fear. The odor of wood smoke also contributed to the information that the bear somehow processed.

SUNLIGHT NORTH

One is tempted to suppose that the creature has the power to draw inferences from its sensory data.

LATE SEPTEMBER IN FAIRBANKS, our starting point for our commercial flight to Fort Yukon, is near the end of the leaf changes, mainly birch, aspen, and cottonwood, my gauge of the progress of autumn. In Fairbanks, you know that the Big Dark is coming down. Fort Yukon, one hour of air time north, is of course deeper into fall. Here we met our pilot, Kirk Sweetsir, of Yukon Air, and began our flight north, to the upper Colleen River.

Here one becomes aware of the vast distances of the North. The Yukon Flats scroll beneath the airplane. Hills appear, and increase

Kirk Sweetsir, Yukon Air Service; Cessna 185, landing on a Colleen River gravel bar, early October

in size as we fly. True mountains become visible in the distance. Mile after mile of boreal forest unroll beneath the airplane. I trace waterways with my eye: Porcupine, Sheenjek, Boulder Creek, Pass Creek, Marten Creek, the Colleen. After about seventy-five minutes of flying, at 130 miles per hour, Kirk communicates briefly with Edna on the avionics radio, circles the cabin, lines up with the gravel bar; we seem to be travelling impossibly fast for the length of the air strip; and we are down. I am reminded that bush pilots actually fly their airplanes, continually adjusting to conditions and always prepared to make an instantaneous decision. No radar, no autopilot; no ground crew to prepare the "runway"; no mechanic nearby except himself. And we are strung out far beyond the far edges of civilization. This latter observation came home to me with increasing intensity as we settled into our temporary home.

IT IS EARLY WINTER. The leaves are all down. Patches of snow. This day was clear, the air crisp; calm; warm in direct sunlight, freezing in the shadows. Heimo and Edna were buoyant, active. To the cabin, a ten minute walk from the river. We were briefed quickly on the workings of the cabin: wood stove, cook stove, utility water hole (not quite pure enough for drinking), drinking water hole. Kirk visits, gets to stretch. Then we are off through the forest to the gravel bar.

One memorable characteristic of Arctic, indeed all, wilderness travel, is the disappearance of the airplane. Kirk loads the gear, Edna and Heimo strap in, Kirk settles into the pilot seat, left side. Pre-flight checks. Warm-up. Taxi into position, as far down the gravel bar as space allows, just off the river. Increased RPMs—this piece of industrial equipment dominates one's hearing and attention. Movement; gradual acceleration; the tail finally lifts; the strip seems hopelessly short; the wheels separate from the ground; up, just over the river, turn towards the south, climb, gone. The engine noise thins out to nothing in the distance. We are alone.

We settle in, walk around the area of the cabin. We locate the Korths' local trails, including Heimo's running track. (He is always fit.) We breath the air, absorb the sunlight, feel where we are; unpack, orient ourselves to the interior of the cabin. We establish our domestic lives.

During our first several days at the Korths I became aware of the central fact of our lives there—it slowly seeps in—that we are far, far away from everything, "everything" being a blanket word for human contact, human assistance, anything we associate with normalcy, safety, comfort. The isolation is spatial and emotional. You feel the vast distance separating you from the nearest human, in this case in Fort Yukon and Arctic Village. No rumble of traffic, no truck brakes, no power line in the distance. There is not so much as a distant contrail visible, nor any sound of a jet overhead. I am reminded how keyed in we are to the many sounds generated by humans, and also how we screen those sounds from our consciousnesses. To survive among humans, we generate a numbness to much of our surroundings. I love the absence of human noise and visual clutter, and I am reminded of their distance from us.

Now, I have spent a large part of the past fifty years in the remote wilderness, especially the Arctic, and I am intimately familiar with extreme isolation. But the difference here was the approach of winter, and it was approaching quickly. The nights were not yet long—we were just past the Equinox—but the plunge into the Big Dark would happen quickly. More immediately apparent were the plunge in temperatures, accumulating snow, and increased ice running in the river. (Daytime highs ranged from +15 to +25, nighttime lows from +5 to +15.) The emotional effect was an increased feeling of isolation. The country was empty of humans for hundreds of miles. I liked the excitement of that feeling.

There is a mystery and excitement during the onset of winter

I wrote in my journal that at the Korths I inhabited time, I did not pass through time. Outdoor life and cabin life contribute to that feeling, because you are not living in a box following regular routines. Time is diurnal, to be sure—this remote world is not timeless—but you are in much closer touch with your surroundings than when in civilization, and you are much more likely to do something on impulse, or not do something; to prolong an activity, take another trail, not be concerned about what comes next. There is plenty of work, plenty of activity, but not too much regularity. I see the water supply is getting low, I'll fetch some from the drinking water spring, drag the sled and two buckets through the forest to the spring and back. A marten ate into the moose, I set a trap. Cut some wood. Walk with the rifle looking for caribou, take this route, try that route, explore the country. Walk down river to see the ice run, walk to the gravel bar to see the sun rise. Spy a wolf track, follow it to see where it goes. Everything is interesting. Nothing is onerous. We're not on any clock, except watching the earth spin towards sunset and the next sunrise; or watching the snow drift before the wind.

On the hunt

THE ARCTIC IN AUTUMN

Our fall 2015 trip, August 25-September 8, happened by accident, and was excellent. Our intention was to fly into the mountains to the north, from Arctic Village, but a storm arrived the day we were to fly—a huge storm, covering much of our state, and due to last several days. Our pilot, Kirk, was trapped in Fairbanks by the weather and would be for several days, but he probably couldn't have flown from Arctic Village had he been there. (We made it into the village from Fairbanks because the commercial flight followed IFR, Instrument Flight Rules. Small planes like Kirk's follow VFR, Visual Flight Rules. In other words, he can only fly where he can see.) After a day of pondering and talking to villagers we decided to hike directly from the village, returning to the village, within the boreal forest.

Most hikers avoid the forest, fearing obstructions and bog—even some villagers told us that!—but I knew better because I had hiked in the forest on three occasions. The footing is generally good, there is little understory, and the forest is open enough to allow for easy navigation. In many places it appears that the trees are growing in alpine tundra. The forest is growing near the northern limit of the tree line in North America, and the trees themselves are small by southern standards, almost entirely white spruce—we located one stand of balsam poplar—interspersed with willows and dwarf birch. The limbs on the spruce are short, the height barely thirty feet at the tallest, the diameter at most about eighteen inches, usually much less. (As in any forest, there are a few trees that exceed these dimensions.) These are the trees that allow for the construction of log cabins, and which provide invaluable firewood. These trees are the reason that living within the tree line is considerably easier than living farther north, which fact points to the supreme ingenuity of the Eskimos. (The correctness of this term is evolving; in Alaska the "Eskimo" is grouped as Yupik and Inupiat.)

This was an unusual trip for the five of us, Lori, Joyce, Mary, Di, me. We were not transferring to a more remote location. The logistics were simple, the terrain was novel (to everyone but me), and, most important, perhaps, it was open-ended, in that we were not locked into a daily quota of miles to walk and did not need to attain an end point. An added advantage, which we discovered later, was the beauty of the leaf changes, which would have been much diminished on the tundra farther north.

Another advantage for me was nostalgic. My first big trek was from Kaktovik on the Arctic coast, over the mountains, to Arctic Village. This took twenty-eight days, was strenuous, and was chancy at the time, because in 1974 there were few visitors to the Arctic Wildlife Range, hence very little air traffic (we saw no airplanes except for perhaps two contrails per week, from Europe I suppose), and electronic communications for ground travelers did not exist. We had no lifeline, no backup.

We saw the glitter of metal roofs when we were in the mountains two days northeast of the village. The fact that our goal was in sight, after weeks of uncertainty, was immensely exciting. Walking into the village two days later was intensely emotional. But I remembered best the walk itself: a land of lakes, including Old John Lake, open forest, good footing; a place that felt like home. I had for decades wanted to revisit the area, but had not. After forty-one years, this was the opportunity.

Our weather was various. We hiked in two rain storms and camped in three snow storms, but after the first big storm moved off we had mostly clear or at least dry weather.

This trip was also unusual because, for me, it was intensely internal. Of course my emotional connection to my wilderness environment is always primary, and the daily narrative is the skeleton upon which the emotional flesh is draped. But on this trip I was unusually sensitive to the ambience of autumn in the Arctic. In particular, the leaf changes were intense and absorbing. The willows were yellow and gold, the blueberry bushes purple, and, most striking, the dwarf birch were a broad range of orange-to-red. (These dwarf birch were, paradoxically, unusually large, some four feet tall.) Every day, all day, we were walking in beauty. Also, we had a long streak of fair weather and cold nights, and the northern lights were active. During the nights I got out at least once; the mystery of the dark and the activity of the lights stimulated me. In order to enjoy the cold mornings more fully, each evening I assembled a pile of dry dead wood of various sizes, and my morning routine was to kindle the fire and enjoy the warmth and the frost. I was intensely alive.

East of Arctic Village

SUNLIGHT NORTH

Looking northwest from Old John Lake

From my journal:

"August 29. This day condensed the fleeting essence of the fall: yellow willows, red dwarf birch, the varying reds and purples of bearberry and blueberry. The occasional distinctive odor of fall, very faint. The warmth of the sun, quickly banished by a cloud or cold breeze. The feeling that everything was just right, exactly as it should be. All of this was enhanced by the ease of walking, a great pleasure."

"September 5. A clear cold night and a brilliant clear day. At about 1:00 AM I got out, and the northern lights were rampant! The bright moon is down to half and the lights had no competition. They spanned the entire sky, and extended well to the west. Behind the northern mountains, a scarlet band.

"This is a sensuous, aesthetic trip and the experience is internal."

"September 8. On the flight south to Fairbanks I tracked the East Fork Chandalar River from the airplane, and observed the increasing color below. On the approach to Fairbanks we were back into the height of fall, flying south from early winter. The gold of the birches, aspens, and poplars was intense, as if powered by some inner glow.

"This journal [and this essay] does not contain my true emotional response to our changing environment on this trip. I could name facts and describe events, but I could not find words for the emotional connections I felt. I was continually stimulated and delighted, as much by snow storms as by sun. I felt comfortable, at home, centered. I must return, to a base camp or a river float."

2016. After years of anticipation we finally launched canoes on the Colleen River. (The canoes are Allys, a fine portable canoe that fits into a duffel and is easily packed into a Cessna 185.) Joyce, Chuck, Di, me. Our start date on the upper river was August 23, which was the height of leaf changes on the tundra. We ended September 7, a bit earlier than our preferred date, in the boreal forest downstream. (We adapted to our pilot's restricted schedule.) We ended at the height of the leaf changes down river—as we floated south we left the tundra for larger willows, then willows and poplars, and on September 5 we saw our first birch tree.

This trip too was open-ended. We had plenty of food, and held open the option of floating to Fort Yukon, on the one hand, or being picked up somewhere on the Porcupine or lower Colleen. In the event we dallied upriver and at the Korths and were eventually picked up on the lower Colleen. Technology makes this possible: reliable satellite phone communication with Kirk.

It is both pleasant and prudent to dally upriver. One great pleasure of an Alaskan river float is observing the changes from headwaters to take-out. Timberline is low in most of Alaska and so there is usually a great contrast between start and finish. Such was the case here. We were at the start of our trip camped on tundra in a big magnificent valley. We were happy to be exactly where we were, and were pleased to both prepare for the float and to hike.

Preparing for the float meant carrying gear to the river, at least a quarter mile away, and assembling the canoes. This work can be pleasurable if there is no pressure to go go go, get on the river, and is even more pleasurable in fair weather. Do some work, look up and enjoy your surroundings. Smell the air. Scan the horizon. Resume at your leisure.

During our second full day, August 25, Joyce, Di and I ferried to the east bank to climb into the high country. The Brooks Range here tails off to foothills to the south. Our mountain was modest in height and extent but put us high enough to see far up four vast valleys, all Colleen water, all with grey limestone, russet tundra, fringes of spruce. This was a delightful excursion: the vast landscape, the variety and scale and scope of it, the dynamic sky, the radiant heat of the sun, the pleasure of walking.

To the north a cluster of poplars were bright *orange*.

Part of the upper Colleen River valley

Finally, after years of anticipation, launch day.

The river came at us quickly, the quiet upper river becoming steep only a few hundred yards from where we launched. A mile of continuous fast Class II, then a section of tight corners where the river was cutting a new channel, then a bigger river below the confluence and we're already beyond the alpine tundra, into bigger willows. Root gobs, some steep runs. Then a heavily braided section, probably the most difficult part in which to make decisions, because the river is spread out and it is hard to detect shallows. The Colleen is considered to be an easy river, but it has power and requires attention and judgment. It also offers variety. The river changes, as I have indicated, as it flows south, and those changes are of interest as they reflect gradient and geology, and create conditions for a variety of streamside plant growth. Floating a river from the headwaters is a bit like seeing the world in cross section.

Here, two days down, was my favorite camp of the trip, the night of August 27. Now we are within the northern fringe of the boreal forest. On the approach the gravel bank on the inside curve did not appear to be a good landing, but it was. A small beach, a low bank, open understory in the spruce forest. The camp faced west and on this clear afternoon it was even hot at times, always comfortable. A trail through the flat forest to the east was a temptation. Moose? Heimo? An old grown-over camp fire, on the forest floor rather than on gravel, and aged cut wood, suggested a winter fire. Willows across the river are gold—the height of fall at this latitude.

One invaluable routine I adhere to on fall trips is the morning fire. I lay it the evening before. I gather my wood, spruce if we're in the forest, willows if on a gravel bar. I sort the wood into three sizes, kindling, build-up, large for sustained burning. I carry a ration of one candle stub per day, and I place this beside my kindling, on gravel or bare ground, in the open (though perhaps behind a windbreak), near water (a necessity for any camping). The first action I perform on a cold morning is light the candle and carefully place the kindling on and around it, then build up the flame with slightly larger pieces. Once this is established I go about the rest of my morning routine: light stove, boil water, mugs of coffee, oats.

We paddled into the Korth gravel bar on August 29, the seventh day of the trip and the fourth of floating.

THE TRANSITION FROM WILDERNESS solitude to social engagement was sudden but not jarring. Edna and Heimo Korth spend much of their year in a solitude that would confound and distress most moderns, but they are intensely social people when the appropriate occasion presents itself. This was one such. They are careful to limit access to their lives and property, but they welcomed us enthusiastically—we were invited and expected—and conversation commenced immediately we approached the cabin. Edna is communicative and reserved, Heimo is ebullient.

The Korths use one of several cabins from year to year to reduce their pressure on the country; this was the same cabin that Di and I tended in 2014. We feel extraordinarily comfortable here, in the open flat forest. I don't know exactly why some spaces and areas seem comfortable, others emotionally alien. Of course it has to do with quiet, proportions, visual harmony, and much else; so it is at the Korths. The outdoor space is comfortable; it feels like home. It is home.

THE ARCTIC IN AUTUMN

WE STAYED AT THE KORTHS for the better part of five days, from the afternoon of August 29 to the afternoon of September 3. We hunted upriver twice, Heimo and I, by canoe, the second time successfully. We hiked, cut wood, fetched a washing machine from an abandoned Korth cabin, dug a hole for a new outhouse, walked the gravel bar, watched for caribou on the mountain, cooked on the outdoor fire, sat by the outdoor fire, and talked talked talked.

Our time passed very comfortably and we were in danger of settling into our shore life and forgetting our river. Edna enjoyed having us, especially enjoying her two amiable and interested female companions; I think Heimo was equally glad to have some society, and someone to hunt with. Edna, Joyce, and Diane spent much time investigating the gravel bars for attractive rocks; Edna discussed and examined various plants that had medicinal and food value (willow bark for headache, "Eskimo potato") and also plants that had aesthetic value; she instructed her friends in moccasin-making. We all scanned the mountain for caribou every morning, and Heimo and I hunted on the two days they were numerous. The second hunt was successful.

Upstream to hunt

Launching a hunt meant taking a minimum of gear in Heimo's 17' plastic canoe pushed by a 6 hp Mercury four-stroke motor. He hunted upstream towards the mountain and Lois Creek, which took about an hour of skillful motoring. Heimo ran the motor in shallow water drive all the time. To properly balance the little boat, I sat as far forward as I could and Heimo kneeled in the middle, running the motor with a tiller extension. I came to admire his skill in difficult sections of river, where the river raced through the shallow sections, or where he negotiated sweepers, especially when running down stream. This is hard to do with a tiller extension while kneeling, and kneeling for an hour or more is itself very difficult. For Heimo this was all normal.

We each killed a caribou on the second afternoon and were motoring downstream by 6:50 PM into a glaring sun. Heimo did a masterful job without sunglasses or billed cap—I could barely see.

Here I learned of a hunting tradition that I like and intend to follow. I don't know if this is unique to Northern subsistence hunting or not—Heimo says he craves this—but within minutes of our successful return, while we hung the meat, Edna had the fire kindled and the caribou heart, liver, and kidneys were cooked in sequence in light oil. All were delicious. I thought the heart most flavorful, the kidneys most interesting.

WE WERE BACK on the river the next day. Edna wanted us to stay, and said so, with sadness. I too felt sad as I surveyed the familiar setting around the cabin. Our farewell from Heimo was quite warm.

WE FLOATED another forty-four miles before leaving the river. We experienced more fall in the boreal forest: blue skies, golden leaves; cold north wind and scud; the appearance of the first birch tree; western bluffs rich in birch gold and poplar yellow and orange. Our final night was clear and cold, and the northern lights were extremely active.

Such is my autumn in the Arctic.

Headed downstream to our pick-up

www.ingramcontent.com/pod-product-compliance
Lightning Source LLC
Chambersburg PA
CBHW050928240426
43671CB00019B/2952